You show me the path of life.
In your presence there is fullness of joy;
in your right hand are pleasures forevermore.
(Psalm 16:11, NRSV)

Path of Life

Finding the Joy You've Always Longed For

Rick Howe

Books by Rick Howe

Path of Life: Finding the Joy You've Always Longed For, 2012, University Ministries Press Revised Edition, 2017. 279 pages.

River of Delights: Quenching Your Thirst For Joy, Volume 1, 2015, University Ministries Press Revised Edition, 2017. 230 pages.

River of Delights: Quenching Your Thirst For Joy, Volume 2, 2015, University Ministries Press Revised Edition, 2017. 250 pages.

Living Waters: Daily Refreshment for Joyful Living, 2017, University Ministries Press. 393 pages.

Reasons of the Heart: Joy and the Rationality of Faith, 2017, University Ministries Press. 250 pages.

For Small Group Studies

Enjoying God: Discovering the Greatest of All Pleasures, University Ministries Press, 2017. 122 pages.

Love's Delights: The Joys of Marriage and Family, University Ministries Press, 2017. 104 pages.

Sacred Patterns: Work, Rest, and Play in a Joyful Vision of Life, University Ministries Press, 2017. 122 pages.

Kingdom Manifesto: A Call to Joyful Activism, University Ministries Press, 2017. 104 pages.

Joy and the Problem of Evil, University Ministries Press, Boulder, 2017. 122 pages.

For more information, visit www.rickhowe.org.

UNIVERSITY MINISTRIES PRESS
BOULDER, COLORADO

University Ministries Press Revised Edition, 2017.

ISBN: 978-0-9987859-1-2

To Sue
Faithful Life Partner
Bright and Shining Joy

Abbreviations

ESV	English Standard Version
JB	Jerusalem Bible
KJV	King James Version
NASB	New American Standard Bible
NEB	New English Bible
NIV	New International Version
NKJV	New King James
NRSV	New Revised Standard Version Bible

CONTENTS

AUTHOR'S NOTE

I didn't set out to write books about joy. Joy beckoned, I followed, and the quest has found literary expression in *Path of Life: Finding the Joy You've Always Longed For*, *River of Delights: Quenching Your Thirst for Joy, Volumes 1 & 2*, *Living Water: Daily Refreshment for Joyful Living*, and *Reasons of the Heart: Joy and the Rationality of Faith*.

The apostle Paul wrote to the church in Rome: "The gifts and the calling of God are irrevocable." I've done many other things over the years, but my work on joy has seemed very much like a gift and a calling. I've been wonderfully enriched by it, and at the same time have felt summoned to pursue it. I believe that God is behind both. My prayer is that this gift and this calling will bear fruit for his Kingdom.

As you will see, there are many endnotes in *Path of Life*. My suggestion is that you read first without interacting with the endnotes to trace the flow of thought without interruption, and then read it again with them.

The "Questions for Thought and Discussion" for each chapter reflect my hope that you will study this book with others, my belief that learning in community is the best way to learn, and my hope that God will use this book to create communities of joy for the advancement of his Kingdom.

PREFACE

For more than three centuries the Church in the West lived under the oppressive rule of the Enlightenment and its brood, demythologizing her Scriptures, demeaning her doctrine, and driving her from the public square of discourse and thought. That intellectual regime is in serious decline, however. It is being eclipsed by new ways of thinking, collectively known as *Postmodernism*. The most prominent feature of postmodern thought is a rejection of modernity's vaunted claims about reason and its imperious role in human affairs.[1] This has led some to abandon any quest for truth, others to look to the East, and others to seek wisdom that predates the modern Western tradition and its distortions.[2]

Whatever you think about Postmodernism as an intellectual trend or cultural phenomenon, it seems to me that followers of Jesus have been given a unique opportunity to speak to our generation about God and his design for life. Many are open in ways that previous generations were not. But what will we say? And how will we say it in a way that connects with a postmodern world? *Path of Life* (and other volumes to come) is my attempt to do this.

I am not a professional theologian, but this is a theological work. The Church desperately needs theology. Good theology. Fresh currents of thinking running over the riverbed of God's Word. As a Christian standing in the radical center of the evangelical world, my convictions lead me first and foremost to seek to be true to the Scriptures. But this includes a resolve to be completely open to those sacred writings, allowing God to speak in ways that the Church (I) may not have heard clearly before.

This is a theological work, but it is not a systematic theology. It is a theological exploration of joy and its significance for Christian living. Another way of viewing it would be to see joy as an integrating motif in theological ethics, and one that helps us to see truths from God's Word that we might miss by looking through another theological lens.[3] It takes readers through the terrain of a Christian worldview, using joy as a travel guide.

Path of Life is an example, I hope, of what Thomas Oden calls "paleo-orthodoxy" (old, seasoned orthodoxy).[4] It values and affirms the consensual theology of the Church over the centuries. It reaches beyond that, however, in its belief that the ancient people of faith, whose inspired testimony has been given to us in the Bible, have much to say to us today – even if we must translate their insights into the day in which we live.

In this work (and in *River of Delights*, to follow) I see myself with an opportunity to teach Christianity 101 to those who already profess faith in Christ, but may not have ventured far into its theological terrain, as well as those who might be exploring Christian faith and life for the first time. I believe that in the contemporary cultural context joy provides a platform for doing this in a way that is both biblical and relevant.

When the apostle Paul stood before a pagan audience in the village of Lystra, he pointed them to the ways in which God had already made himself known:

> We are bringing you good news, telling you to turn from these worthless things to the living God, who made heaven and earth and sea and everything in them. In the past, he let all nations go their own way. Yet he has not left himself without testimony: He has shown kindness by giving you rain from heaven and crops in their seasons; he provides you with plenty of food and *fills your hearts with joy*. (Acts 14:15-17, NIV)

Paul understood the significance of joy for people of faith and for those who are on the outside looking in. Joy connects with ancient and contemporary pagans alike, because both have been made for joy, but don't know it yet!

Our culture is religiously devoted to narcissistic hedonism: making an "idol of one's sensuality, body, and immediate pleasures."[5] We are grimly reaping the spiritual harvest. It is an addiction that has gone horribly bad on us, but makes us increasingly obsessed with its diminishing returns. In the process of writing I have kept this in mind, as well as Aquinas' observation that the person who is "deprived of spiritual joy goes over to carnal pleasures."[6] My most cherished aspiration is to play a part (even if it is very small) in leading our generation "back over" to joy, which, as you will see, embraces all the healthy pleasures of life in a robust relationship with God.

Finally, I believe with C.S. Lewis that theology must be practical. When he wrote about the doctrine of the Trinity he cautioned, "I warned you that Theology is practical. The whole purpose for which we exist is to be thus taken into the life of God."[7] If this is true, I believe that good theology will draw us into the joy of the Lord: into the life of the One in whose presence there is fullness of joy, and in whose right hand are pleasures for evermore.

INTRODUCTION

The night was dark, the sky turbulent. A spiritual storm swirled across the Holy City, powered by unseen currents, gathering into a tempest that would change the world forever. Much more hung in the balance this Passover week than mortal minds could fathom.

The hearts of the disciples had risen and fallen with the events of the week. They soared the day Jesus entered Jerusalem. The excitement that moved through the crowd like a wind, filling hearts with anticipation and cheer, was vivid in their minds. They could still see the living wall that had formed along the road, palm branches dancing in the hands of jubilant men and women, and garments laid on the path, creating a royal carpet for the joyous procession. The many-voiced cry still echoed in their ears: "Hosanna to the Son of David! Blessed is he who comes in the name of the Lord! Hosanna in the highest!"[1] Jesus had all but claimed the title of Messiah, entering Jerusalem on the foal of a donkey in fulfillment of an ancient oracle,[2] and dismissing the attempts of the Pharisees to stifle the messianic fervor of the multitudes.

Then from that lofty height they fell. Nothing from that point on made sense. They were bewildered. Numb with confusion. What did the cleansing of the temple mean? Why did Jesus spend his time sparring with religious leaders instead of challenging the Romans? Jerusalem was swollen with pilgrims who had come for the Passover: thousands upon thousands of potential troops. Why did Jesus make no attempt to rally them? There were legions who would have followed him and fought to take the Holy City from its Roman overlords. Instead he talked obliquely about its destruction. About the temple being reduced to rubble. Trampled underfoot by pagan boots. Surely none of this could be if Jesus was the long-awaited Messiah!

And then the situation worsened. A plot was formed. A thinly veiled machination of the scribes and elders to take the life of Jesus. He called his disciples to a carefully orchestrated, clandestine meeting: the Passover meal. As they made their way to the upper room of a house in Jerusalem, questions filled their hearts and a sense of foreboding grew. Oil lamps cast shadows from the twelve as they reclined about Jesus and darkness overtook the land. The shadows did not move. An explanation must be offered. Answers must be given.

Jesus didn't give his disciples the answers they expected, yet the sound of his voice filled the room with peace. In his presence, shoulders relaxed. Breathing deepened. An aura of assurance, nearly sensible, surrounded Jesus as he spoke the words, "Let not your hearts be troubled; believe in God, believe also in me."[3] They might have been confused, but he was not. They might harbor doubts, but he seemed not to have any. He knew who he was. Whence he had come. Why he was there. Where he was going.

The words of Jesus were luminous that night as he summed up the whole of his teaching: "These things I have spoken to you, that my joy may be in you, and that your joy may be full."[4] In these words the disciples saw faintly what they would see clearly in the full light of his resurrection – the unity and goal of all that he had said and done: a joy that triumphs over all that the world can hurl against the heart. A joy that can't be robbed, even by death. "Fullness of joy," he said. Overflowing and unending.

Before the night was over Jesus would promise a joy that would displace their sorrow, a joy that no one would be able to take from them. A triumphant cheer.[5] He would once again give the sum and aim of his teaching as he poured out his heart to the Father: "But now I am coming to you; and I speak these things in the world, so that they may have my joy made complete in themselves."[6] This is why he came. This was the gift he set his heart on giving. Not conquering the Romans, but imparting joy, was his great messianic task![7]

Shifting Paradigms

That was revolutionary for the earliest followers of Jesus. It required a paradigm shift: a radical re-orientation of their beliefs about God and what he was doing in history. It is exactly what happened, however. People who had invested their Messianic hope in the stock market of clashing swords and overthrown governments found themselves committed instead to a message of joy, rooted and grounded in the words and work of Jesus of Nazareth: the Messiah, to be sure, but not the one they had expected; offering deliverance, true, but a salvation far greater than anything they could have imagined. Greater than political freedom as the noonday sun is brighter than moonbeams veiled by a blanket of clouds.

Revolutionary joy turned the ancient world upside down! But what is revolutionary in one era may be taken for granted in another and forgotten in still another. If we are to learn anew in the twenty-first century what the early disciples discovered in the first, we will have to venture from our own world into theirs. We will have to let them guide us through the terrain of the Scriptures, show us what they saw, what they experienced, how it transformed their lives and their world, and teach us how to discover that same joy in our day.

If you are open to that quest, I welcome you to this book.

Part One

The Nature of Joy

CHAPTER 1

THE HIGHEST AND BEST OF ALL PLEASURES

In his preface to *The Everlasting Man* G.K. Chesterton described a story he always wanted to write but never did:

> I conceived it as a romance of those vast valleys with sloping sides, like those along which the ancient White Horses of Wessex are scrawled along the flanks of the hills. It concerned some boy whose farm or cottage stood on such a slope, and who went on his travels to find something, such as the effigy and grave of some giant; and when he was far enough from home he looked back and saw that his own farm and kitchen-garden, shining flat on the hillside like the colours and quarterings of a shield, were but parts of some such gigantic figure, on which he had always lived, but which was too large and too close to be seen.[1]

I can't think of a better way to begin this exploration of joy. We won't get very far in our quest until we see that joy is like that cottage, and we are very much like the boy. Say "supralapsarianism" and a definition is in order. Say "joy" and nothing more needs to be said. We feel very much at home with it

. . . like Chesterton's boy and his farm. We think we know it, but know it not at all.

Joy is "too large and too close" for us to see fully and clearly without stepping back, so to speak, and viewing it against the landscape of God's written Word to us. It is only then that we begin to see its true features, and it turns out to be something far greater than we could ever have guessed. Something more fascinating and alluring than the experience we thought we knew so well.

JOY AND THE PLEASURES OF LIFE

If you were to ask, "What is joy?" of the ancient Jewish Scriptures, the answer you would get is that joy is a kind of pleasure.[2] You would learn, perhaps to your surprise, that sacred prophets, poets, and historians esteemed it as the highest and best of life's pleasures, and the one Pleasure that embraces and enhances all other pleasures given by God.[3]

Let's start with the Psalm that inspired the title of this book. To appreciate its significance you should know that Hebrew poets did not rhyme words, but ideas: in this case with a second line echoing the thought of the first.[4] Addressing God, David wrote:

> You make known to me the path of life.
> in your presence there is *fullness of joy;*
> at your right hand are *pleasures for evermore.*[5] (Psalm 16:11, ESV)

"Fullness of joy" and "pleasures for evermore" are two ways of describing the same thing. When David thought of joy, images of exquisite and enduring pleasures came to mind. When he thought of such pleasures, the word "joy" best summed them up.

If you are not used to thinking about joy this way, you might knit your brow when I tell you that the writers of the Old Testament not only thought of joy as a kind of pleasure, they were not at all uncomfortable likening joy to earthy delights. The Psalmist, for instance, could say that God had put "more joy" in his heart than the unrighteous have "when their grain and wine abound." [6] Joy is like the pleasures of food and potent drink, but is distinguished by the fact that it is much greater.[7] Joy is likened elsewhere to the pleasure of a feast, [8] the pleasure of wealth, [9] and the delight of a bridegroom in his bride.[10] Joy surpasses these pleasures but is significantly like them.

"Well, that's what you would expect from the Old Testament," you say. "If you want a more *spiritual* view of things, you must look to the New." I can tell you, however, that you won't find anything different there. Like writers of Scripture before him, Jesus drew analogies between joy and other pleasures. He likened the joy of salvation to the excitement of discovering a priceless treasure,[11] and the future joy of the Kingdom to the gaiety of a wedding celebration.[12] He found common ground between the joy of God over a sinner's repentance and a shepherd's pleasure in finding a lost sheep, a woman's delight in finding a lost coin, and the elation of a father in the return of his lost son.[13] He invited people to a greater understanding of joy by likening it to other pleasures and delights in life.

The apostolic company responsible for the New Testament drew from the same well. You can see it in the words they chose to describe their joy. They borrowed a number of terms from the Greek vocabulary of pleasure, from sensual pleasure in general to the delights of food and drink, to a raucous, merrymaking celebration of life. [14] True, these words were transformed when they were put to use in describing Christian experience; nevertheless, they were considered the right place to begin thinking and talking about joy. As they were brought into the service of a fledgling Christian movement they came laden with nuances of pleasure that the pagan world sought and that found their true fulfillment in the overflowing, life-encompassing experience of joy.[15]

Not only did the ancient people of God view joy as a kind of pleasure, they saw clearly how it related to the yearning that lay beneath their world's quest for the good life. Pleasure is the best way to begin thinking about joy, and common pleasures begin to give us an idea of what we are talking about. Joy is like, and yet far surpasses, the many pleasures that enrich our lives and bring us delight.

THE SCOPE OF JOY

We tend to put a halo over joy, to restrict it to contexts we consider *sacred*, which we define very narrowly. Not so the Scriptures! There we discover that joy encompasses all of life's wholesome pleasures. It is not only the highest and best pleasure, it is the one Pleasure that embraces and ennobles other pleasures given by God. Take the Hebrew word, *sameach*, for instance. It is used to depict joy in God.[16] It is also used to describe romantic delight in one's betrothed,[17] the sexual pleasures of marriage,[18] pleasure in one's youth,[19] one's work,[20] one's wealth,[21] in all that one does under the blessing of God,[22] and in all the gifts God bestows in life.[23] Joy and these pleasures belong together.[24]

Does this surprise you? You may begin to sense that your old distinctions between what is *spiritual* and what is *not* break down before the biblical understanding of joy. Joy welcomes other pleasures. It receives them gladly, exalting them as the good gifts of a good God. Joy orders and unites all the healthy pleasures of life. By its very nature joy affirms every wholesome delight. It hallows our gladness in the good things of life by directing our hearts to God in thanksgiving and praise.[25]

JOY AND PLEASURES OF OUR SENSES

Let's get more specific. How is joy related to the pleasures of our senses? All joy is pleasurable, but not all pleasures are joyful.[26] It is possible to indulge yourself in every pleasure imaginable and remain a stranger to joy. It is possible, in the words of Pascal, to "lick the dust" in the pursuit of "earthly pleasures" and never taste heaven's joy.[27] There is no greater demonstration of this than the hedonistic quests of our own generation.[28]

We can experience physical pleasure without joy, and joy without physical pleasure. The claim I am asking you to consider is that joy can, and often does, include pleasures of our senses. We have already seen that the Bible draws analogies between joy and tangible pleasures, uses the vocabulary of pleasure to describe joy, and uses the vocabulary of joy as a palette for painting many pleasures in life. And yet, if my guess is right, you may still be reading with a gathered brow and skeptical look. Can our experience of joy really include sensory delight? If the answer is "Yes," it would be Copernican in the way many of us understand spirituality!

Many Christians envision a great chasm between joy, which, they think, is spiritual, and the pleasures of our senses, that are not. To change the metaphor, as they see it the oil of joy cannot be mixed with the water of sensual delight. But this is not what we find in the Scriptures:[29]

> And there you shall *eat* before the LORD your God, and you shall *rejoice*, you and your households. (Deuteronomy 12:7)

> And if the way is too long for you, so that you are not able to carry the tithe, when the LORD your God blesses you, because the place is too far from you, which the LORD your God chooses, to set his name there, then you shall turn it into money and bind up the money in your hand and go to the place that the LORD your God chooses and spend the money for whatever you desire—oxen or

> sheep or wine or strong drink, *whatever your appetite craves.* And *you shall eat* there before the LORD your God and *rejoice*, you and your household. (Deuteronomy 14:24-26)

> Then you shall keep the *feast* of weeks to the LORD your God . . . and you shall *rejoice* before the LORD your God. (Deuteronomy 16:10-11)

> You shall keep the feast of booths seven days . . . you shall *rejoice* in your *feast.* (Deuteronomy 16:13-14)

> All these, men of war, arrayed in battle order, came to Hebron with full intent to make David king over Israel; . . . And also their neighbors . . . came bringing food on asses and on camels and on mules and on oxen, *abundant provisions of meal, cakes of figs, clusters of raisins, and wine and oil, oxen and sheep*, for there was *joy* in Israel. (1 Chronicles 12:38-40)

> And all the assembly blessed the LORD, the God of their fathers, and bowed their heads, and worshiped the LORD, and did obeisance to the king. And they performed sacrifices to the LORD, and on the next day offered burnt offerings to the LORD, a thousand bulls, a thousand rams, and a thousand lambs, with their drink offerings, and sacrifices in abundance for all Israel; and they *ate and drank* before the LORD on that day *with great gladness.* (1 Chronicles 29:20-22)

> Go, *eat* your bread with *enjoyment*, and *drink* your wine with a *merry heart.* (Ecclesiastes 9:7)

The link between joy and pleasures of the palate in these texts provides us with a paradigm for joy's relationship to other pleasures, as well. If they are framed by the goodness and wisdom of God, and they are received as his blessing, they are not only compatible with joy, they are enriched by the touch of that higher pleasure. Joy is honored by the retinue of other pleasures. They become nobler in its royal presence.

We can indulge our senses without giving a thought to God. We can even pursue sensual pleasure as a surrogate for God. Aquinas explains, "No one can live without delight and that is why a man deprived of spiritual joy goes over to carnal pleasures."[30] They are "carnal" pleasures because they are pursued apart from the God who created them. They become a substitute for joy (pleasure enjoyed in relation to God). Our senses can even be indulged in defiance of God. This is what Paul was thinking of when he described people who are "lovers of pleasure rather than lovers of God."[31] This is what he had in mind when he said that, apart from Christ, people become "slaves to various passions and pleasures."[32]

This observation has led some Christians to conclude that our sensory life is irrelevant to, if not incompatible with, our spiritual life. But this is a false conclusion. It means only that a good thing can be used badly. Something wholesome can be spoiled.

The place to begin thinking about the relationship between spirituality and our sensory life is the inspired narrative of creation.[33] There we see the original goodness of our sentient existence. The God who created our souls also created our bodies and the ways in which they interact with the world. Body and soul, senses and spirit, are woven together into a single fabric (which is what we mean when we say that we are *psychosomatic* beings). God created us this way and declared his creation good.[34]

It is true that the entrance of sin into our world brought desecration and devastation where once there was none. We must reckon with sin; however, we are wrong in our reckoning if we think that good has been overthrown by evil. Evil does not have that power. Not in God's world. According to the apostle Paul, even in our fallen state everything created by God is good and is to be received with thanksgiving.[35]

If *creation* is the first word about the goodness of our sensory life and its place in true spirituality, *resurrection* is the last.[36] The final state of believers will not be an ethereal existence, floating on clouds with harp in hand and halo overhead (Shame on us for ever thinking such things!) but life in glorified bodies[37] in "new heavens and a new earth in which righteousness dwells."[38] In the day when the new heavens and the new earth are the habitat of those who share in the resurrection of Christ, sensual pleasures will also be spiritual pleasures: experiences of sensory delight, given and governed by God, and offered back to the Creator in joyful adoration, thanksgiving, and praise.

We are not now what we were created to be, nor yet what we will one day become. Still, what we will one day know in its fullness we may know in part today. The beauty of a sunset over the Rocky Mountains. The white-water laughter of a mountain stream flowing downward over its rocky bed. The shimmering golden leaves of aspen stirred by an alpine breeze. The song of a meadowlark. The quenching of a thirst. Our favorite foods. The smell of the earth after a summertime rain. We could spend a lifetime counting the pleasures that God intends for our joy!

JOY AND THE TRANSPOSITION OF PLEASURE

In *The Imitation of Christ*, Thomas á Kempis gave us the principle that in spiritual things the highest does not stand without the lowest.[39] C.S. Lewis used this with great insight in his study of love.[40] The highest love, *agape*, he said, ascends to its height on the steps of the lower loves: *storge*, *philia,* and *eros*. It also transforms and perfects the lower loves so that they more fully realize the unique role that God has ordained for them. They are transposed, given a new and higher place, by the touch of *agape*.

The same principle illumines the relationship between joy and other pleasures. What *agape* is to other loves, joy is to other pleasures in life. It is the highest of all pleasures,[41] reaching its throne upon the stairway of life's many delights, transforming them into something greater than they could ever have been without its touch, enabling them to be more fully what the Creator meant them to be. Joy does not negate lower pleasures; it fulfills them. It does not drive a wedge between the good gifts of God; it unites and orders them, and lifts them to the highest plane possible in God's good and wise design.

Joy embraces, enriches, and ennobles other pleasures given by God. It does more than this, however. It transposes them.[42] Lower pleasures are drawn into the higher pleasure and become part of it.[43] Drawing on this principle of transposition, C.S. Lewis wrote, "The sensation which accompanies joy becomes itself joy: we can hardly choose but say 'incarnates' joy."[44] This is an astonishing claim! If Lewis is right, the transposition of pleasure in the experience of joy is a window through which we faintly glimpse the Incarnation itself. In the Incarnation deity was not converted into flesh (the higher transformed into the lower). Our humanity was taken up into God (the lower transposed into the higher).[45] To experience sensual, aesthetic, and intellectual pleasures *joyfully* is to put our feet into the surf of a very great ocean. We are given a tiny hint of the life of God incarnate in Christ.

NEED-PLEASURES AND PLEASURES OF APPRECIATION

In *The Four Loves*, C.S. Lewis distinguished between "Need-pleasures" and "Pleasures of Appreciation."[46] Need-pleasures follow a sense of deficit. The pleasure of a cool drink on a hot summer day follows the sensation of thirst.

The pleasing warmth of a fire follows the sensation of being cold. Pleasures of Appreciation, on the other hand, don't command our attention because we are needy. We are drawn by the pleasure itself. In the appreciation of beauty or an alluring fragrance, our pleasure does not lie in the satisfaction of a need, but in the gift to our senses and our appreciation of the gift. As Lewis put it, "We do not merely like the things; we pronounce them, in a momentarily God-like sense, 'very good.'"[47]

Joy unites both of these pleasures. We see this most importantly in our relationship with God. The enjoyment of God begins as a Need-pleasure. We have been made by God and for God. This is the defining feature of our creaturehood. We need God and find our fulfillment in him. In this fulfillment we find joy. Many have experienced what C.S. Lewis called *Sehnsucht*: an intense longing that is not satisfied by anything in this world. It is a yearning in which "the sense of want is acute and even painful, yet the mere wanting is felt to be somehow a delight."[48] When this heart-rending desire is satisfied in an encounter with God, we experience joy as a Need-pleasure.

Psalm 63 captures this experience in poetry. In the first verse we see the Psalmist's yearning for God:

> O God, you are my God; earnestly I seek you;
> my soul thirsts for you;
> my flesh faints for you,
> as in a dry and weary land where there is no water. (ESV)

In verses 5-7 we see that longing fulfilled in the experience of joy:

> My soul will be satisfied as with fat and rich food,
> and my mouth will praise you with joyful lips,
> when I remember you upon my bed,
> and meditate on you in the watches of the night;

for you have been my help,
and in the shadow of your wings I will sing for joy. (ESV)

The enjoyment of God begins as a Need-pleasure, but becomes a Pleasure of Appreciation in a robust experience of worship. Worship begins with a need that cries out for fulfillment: "As a deer longs for flowing streams, so longs my soul for you, O God. My soul thirsts for God, for the living God."[49] In our heart's encounter with God, however, our poverty and need are eclipsed by something infinitely bigger and brighter. Emptiness gives way to adoration and awe. We become spellbound, captivated by the majesty, holiness, goodness, and power of God, and his worthiness to receive praise. When this happens, joy is transformed from the pleasure of a satisfied need to a Pleasure of Appreciation.[50]

When joy embraces the pleasures of God's world, it lifts them to a higher plane. Need-pleasures begin with a deficit keenly felt, but in the satisfaction of a need, joy leads us to appreciate the humble pleasure as a gift of the Creator, to pronounce it "good" and to respond with thanksgiving and praise. If I enjoy the pleasure of food with a thankful heart, the experience is more than a Need-Pleasure. It becomes a reflective delight. The same is true of Pleasures of Appreciation. If I enjoy a beautiful sunset with a worshipful heart, my experience is both aesthetic delight and enchantment with the artistry of God. Joy weds an appreciation of the Giver and his gift, like a woman receiving a bouquet of flowers at her doorstep and discovering that it is from her beloved. She delights in the giver and the gift, her delight in one enlarging and enriching her pleasure in the other.[51]

GROWING IN JOY

Some Christians think of joy as an all-or-nothing kind of experience. It is always pristine and full, or we are mistaking it for something else, like happiness (more about that in the next chapter). Luther knew better: "Not even the more perfect saints have a full and constant joy in God."[52] This is what we find in the Scriptures. Our joy may fall anywhere along a great continuum. The Bible speaks of joy without any superlatives, rejoicing greatly,[53] an exceeding joy,[54] an exceeding great joy,[55] the fullness of joy,[56] overflowing with joy,[57] one's highest joy,[58] and an "unutterable and exalted joy."[59] What we now enjoy in part we can experience more fully. What we experience in this life, even at its highest and best, is but a glimpse or a foretaste of the "pleasures forevermore" held for us in the loving hand of our God.[60]

I don't know about you, but this encourages me to pursue joy. Because it is not all or nothing, I can begin where I am, take small steps toward joy, venture further into joy's terrain, and look forward to something higher and better every step along the way. I can look forward to a richer experience the more I give myself to the quest.

Questions for Thought and Discussion

1. In *Little Gidding*, T.S. Eliot wrote, "We must not cease from exploration and the end of all our exploring will be to arrive where we started and know the place for the first time." Before you read this chapter, what came to mind when you thought about joy? What new light has this chapter brought to your understanding of joy?

2. If you have never put joy into the context of pleasure in your thinking, can you identify beliefs that have kept you from that?

3. As you survey the pleasures that enrich your life, what steps can you take to make them part of your response to the exhortation to rejoice in the Lord?

4. Are there pleasures that attract you that seem to be incompatible with joy? If so, why? What makes them problematic for joy?

5. How does pursuing joy as the crowning pleasure of life change the way you look at pleasure?

CHAPTER 2

JOY AND THE PURSUIT OF HAPPINESS

If popular piety is right, happiness and joy are two different things. Joy is heavenly, happiness, mundane. Joy is exquisite; happiness, quite plain. Joy is spiritual; happiness, an ordinary experience that even the most benighted pagan can have. This has become cliché in sermons and popular Christian literature:

> Happiness depends on happenings, but joy depends on Jesus!
> Be joyful! It beats being happy.[1]

Theologians make the same distinctions, only in more sophisticated language.[2] At the risk of challenging the party line, it seems to me that this is worth exploring. The adventure may lead us to a clearer understanding, and a greater appreciation, of joy.

Is joy like or unlike happiness? We should first be clear about what we mean by happiness. Unfortunately, there are as many opinions about what happiness is as there are people in pursuit of it. Aristotle observed this long ago:

> When it comes to saying in what happiness consists, opinions differ, and the account given by the generality of mankind is not at all like that of the wise. The former take it to be something obvious and familiar, like pleasure or money or eminence, and there are various other views; and often the same person actually changes his opinion: when he falls ill he says that it is health, and when he is hard up that it is money.[3]

Centuries later, Augustine saw the same diversity of opinion in his day: "The desire for happiness is certainly universal, though the great variety of beliefs as to what constitutes happiness proves that the knowledge of it is by no means equally so."[4]

There is at least that much confusion in our day. For the purposes of our exploration, a simple distinction will make the task a little easier. It is the distinction between what happiness is, and what people think will make them happy. Some people think that money will make them happy, but wealth isn't the same thing as happiness. Others think that pleasure will make them happy, but pleasure isn't the same thing as happiness.[5] Money and pleasure don't answer the question, "What is happiness?" but "What do some people think will make them happy?" Here I am more interested in the former. I want to know what kind of thing happiness is so that we can compare it with joy.

Because philosophers in antiquity gave serious thought to the nature of happiness, this would be a good place for us to start. Two views presented themselves to the ancient Greek mind. One envisioned happiness as an *activity* of the soul; the other saw it as a desirable *state* of being. Aristotle taught the first[6] and the Stoics the second.[7]

ARISTOTLE ON HAPPINESS

Let's begin with Aristotle's version of happiness-as-an-activity and see how joy compares with it. To understand Aristotle, we must begin with his notion of the "function of man."[8] We know the functions of musicians and artists. They are to perform music and to create art. But is there a function that belongs to humans-as-such? There is, according to Aristotle. It is to live a life of reason and virtue. Happiness is *doing* this. It is a flourishing in life that coincides entirely with this enterprise. Happiness is living well, and living well is pursuing reason and virtue.

Is this what Christians mean by joy? Joy has much to do with functioning well and flourishing in life. It is a sign that our hearts are working the way God intends them to. Joy results from a harmony between our desires, decisions, and deeds, and the congeniality of our hearts with God's. When it is ours, we live robustly in God's world. We flourish in life beneath his good hand.

There is a rational dimension to joy.[9] As a Pleasure of Appreciation joy involves our minds. It engages our thoughts in reflective delight. When Aristotle thought of the rational life, he had in mind the cultivation of intellectual virtues,[10] and a life informed by the disciplines of physics, metaphysics, ethics, and the like. We, too, can experience joy in these rational endeavors. (Augustine reminds us: "All good and true Christians should understand that truth, wherever they may find it, belongs to their Lord."[11]) We are closer to the target, however, if we see joy emerging in the more focused project of loving God with our minds, seeking to honor him in all of our thinking (which will involve intellectual virtues and may include academic disciplines).

For Aristotle, happiness coincides with the pursuit of virtue. Joy has ethical dimensions, too.[12] Again, however, there are significant differences between Aristotelian and Christian views. Aristotle's understanding of virtue – a human enterprise from first to last – includes such dispositions as courage, temperance, liberality, and so forth, defined by the rational calculation of a mean between two extremes.[13] For followers of Jesus, joy's focus is the imitation of God's character and obedience to his commands. It is a harmony of wills. A heartsong whose meter is the beat of God's own heart. It is the beatitude of love for God. Pleasure in his purposes. Delight in his designs.[14] These facets of joy make a world of difference, because, in fact, joy hails from another world – one whose terrain Aristotle seems not to have known.[15]

Let's get to the more fundamental point: Is joy an activity? Yes and no. Joy is a dance of the heart: a dynamic movement of thought, will, and affection in harmony with the music of Heaven. In this sense joy is active rather than static. It is more like play than sleep. More like a flowing fountain than a motionless pond. It is an effervescence of spirit that spills out in songs of thanksgiving and praise.[16]

Joy is active, but it isn't an activity as Aristotle thought of it. It isn't something we do, like swinging a baseball bat, riding a bike, or singing a song. These things are largely up to us: our decisions, our actions. Aristotle thought of happiness this way.[17] Here we come to a fork in the road: Aristotle's version of happiness takes us in one direction, and the joy God offers us will take us down a very different path. Joy is a "fruit of the Spirit."[18] It occurs only as God gives himself to us. If we were to choose between *active* and *static*, we would say that joy is active. If we distinguish between *active* and *passive*, we would have to say that joy is passive. It is the gift of God. We are its recipients.[19] Aristotle would have said that we are not talking about the same thing.

THE STOICS ON HAPPINESS

If Aristotle emphasized the active dimension of happiness, the Stoics stressed its character as a desirable inner state. Stoicism viewed the ideal inner life as a state of tranquility undisturbed by, and utterly indifferent to, the events and circumstance of life.[20] Many Christians have been influenced by this view in their understanding of joy. Commenting on the Beatitudes in the Sermon on the Mount, one scholar describes this ideal state as "serene and untouchable, and self-contained" and "completely independent of all chances and changes of life."[21]

My reading of that Sermon sees Jesus' understanding of joy moving in a very different direction. He says, "Blessed are those who mourn, for they shall be comforted."[22] Joy (or *beatitude* to use the more technical term in this context) belongs to those who mourn. It is difficult for me see how one who mourns and is in need of comfort is someone whose experience is "serene and untouchable, and self-contained." No, joy is much more than inner tranquility. It is an experience granted in and through life's realities, harsh as they sometimes are. It transforms our experience of them, but is not untouched by them.

HAPPINESS AND THE FULFILLMENT OF DESIRE

Very well, joy is not the same as Stoic imperturbability. The Stoics weren't the only ones to think of happiness as a desirable inner state, however. In contemporary culture, many think of happiness as a pleasurable state that results from a *gratification of desires*. Is this the same as joy? Let's start with some qualifications. You may think that I am quibbling over words, but the *fulfillment* of desire seems to me to be a better candidate for talking about joy than *gratification* or *satisfaction*. You can be satisfied but not fulfilled. It depends on how easily you allow yourself to be satisfied! It is possible to be satisfied with mediocrity, but mediocrity is not fulfilling. Pornography might gratify your sexual desire, but it cannot fulfill your sexuality. If happiness is linked to mere satisfaction or gratification of desire, we are very far from joy.

We are also far from joy if we are only talking about superficial interests in life. If the desires we have in mind are for a style of clothing, the make of a car, the size of a house, or a vacation destination, we are not within shouting distance of joy. If joy is an alpine summit, these desires are marshes in the vale. Happiness must be more than this if we are to compare it with joy. In the best sense of the word, if someone asks, "Are you happy?" she wants to know whether the more significant desires in your life are being fulfilled, and if that in turn has made you glad to be alive, to be who you are, doing what you are doing. Is this the same thing as joy? Yes and no. Let's take the latter first.

For many Christians this can't be joy because it involves the contingencies of life. Whether your desires are fulfilled depends upon the shifting sands of circumstance. For them, this is what distinguishes happiness from joy. I disagree. The real problem with equating joy with this version of happiness is not that the fulfillment of desire is contingent upon circumstances and joy never is, but that our desires are often skewed. Even if they are good, often the way we seek their fulfillment is not.

If happiness is based upon unhealthy desires, or healthy things pursued wrongly, it cannot be what Christians mean by joy. Augustine put it this way: "In so far as all men seek the happy life they do not err. But in so far as anyone does not keep to the way that leads to the happy life, even though he professes to desire only to reach happiness, he is in error."[23] This is an important observation. Once we make it, however, what should we say about a scenario in which our desires align with God's good and wise design, and we see their fulfillment as his gift to us? Is it fitting to speak of this as joy? *Yes!*

Joy can be ours in the worst of circumstances. The prophet Habakkuk gave words to this experience:

> Though the fig tree do not blossom,
> nor fruit be on the vines,
> the produce of the olive fail
> and the field yield no food,
> the flock be cut off from the fold
> and there be no herd in the stalls,
> yet I will rejoice in the LORD,
> I will joy in the God of my salvation. (Habakkuk 3:17-18)

But what should we say if the fig tree blossoms in our lives, there is fruit on the vines, the produce of the olive flourishes, and so forth, and we enjoy this as a gift from God? Some may insist that this is happiness, and not joy, but it is no longer meaningful to differentiate between the two. If, as Augustine saw it, happiness is "the satisfaction of all wants when nothing is wanted wrongly,"[24] and it is received thankfully, distinguishing between happiness and joy is a distinction without a difference.[25]

We are now in a position to answer the question that began this chapter. Is joy like or unlike happiness? How are the two related? When happiness is the fulfillment of significant and wholesome desires, and that fulfillment is received as a gift from God, happiness enters joy's domain.[26] Happiness and joy become nuances of the same experience: "Delight yourself in the LORD (the centerpiece of joy) and He will give you the desires of your heart" (the essence of happiness).[27] When it is experienced in relation to God, happiness becomes joy in one mode, just as pleasure becomes joy in another. Joy is more than happiness, but often includes it, just as joy is more than other pleasures in life, but can include them. *Joy is the consummation of both.*[28]

Happiness and pleasure point to joy (for it is greater than they), and find their true fulfillment in joy (for it gladly includes them in its court when they acknowledge its royal status). Joy transposes happiness-as-a-gift-from-God in the same way that it transposes pleasures-enjoyed-in-relation-to-God. The lower is caught up in the higher and becomes part of it. Happiness and joy are not meant to be competitors for our hearts, but partners in the dance of life, moving as one to the song God sings to us.

PAGAN HAPPINESS

Wherever it is found, happiness – the pleasurable experience we find in the fulfillment of healthy desires – is a gift from God: "You open your hand, satisfying the desire of every living thing."[29] It is granted in some measure to all, but it is robust and full when God grants us the desires of our hearts and we offer our hearts back to him in thanksgiving and praise. It is then an important dimension of joy:

> May he grant you your *heart's desire*,
> and fulfill all your plans!
> May we shout for *joy* over your victory. . . .
> May the LORD fulfill all your petitions! (Psalm 20:4-5)
>
> O LORD, in your strength the king *rejoices*,
> and in your salvation how greatly he exults!
> You have given him his *heart's desire*
> and have not withheld the request of his lips. (Psalm 21:1-2)

In a Godward life, happiness and joy are nuances of the same experience. But what about the happiness of those who live as if there were no God? C.S. Lewis wrote about a long-time acquaintance of his: "I have an elderly acquaintance of about eighty, who has lived a life of unbroken selfishness and self-admiration from the earliest years, and is, more or less, I regret to say, one of the happiest men I know. From a moral point of view it is very difficult."[30]

What are we to make of this? It won't do to discount the experience. It may be entirely contingent upon circumstances, which makes it fragile and unreliable. It may fall short of a full-bodied experience of joy. It seems to me, however, to be less than honest to demean pagan happiness. The challenge is to understand it from a Christian perspective.

The writer of Hebrews saw desires that are contrary to God's will as the "fleeting pleasures of sin."[31] They are the corruption of something that God intends for our good. He has given us the capacity for pleasure, whether we use it for good or for evil. But there are many wholesome desires. A desire for marriage connects us with God's design for our lives. Believers and unbelievers alike can find happiness here. Parents can find happiness in their children, even if they do not see them as good gifts from God. The desire for meaningful employment is good. Work can contribute to happiness in life, regardless of one's faith. How is this related to joy?

An understanding of grace can help us.[32] Theologians distinguish between special grace and common grace. The former is the exclusive blessing of the redeemed. The latter, as its name suggests, is given to all people, irrespective of their status in redemption. The purpose of common grace is to keep life from becoming as bad as it would otherwise be in a fallen world. It is also is a token of God's goodness, given to draw us to the fuller expression of his goodness in the grace of salvation.[33]

What common grace is to special grace, happiness is to joy. As an expression of God's goodness, happiness offsets the destructive power of sin in our world. It mitigates the misery that would otherwise be our lot. But it also foreshadows joy and is meant to draw us to it.[34] Happiness is an appetizer; joy, the feast.

Let me illustrate. On one of his missionary journeys, the apostle Paul stood before a pagan audience and told them that although God had allowed them to "walk in their own ways" in the past, he did not "leave himself without witness." He went on to say: "for he did good and gave you from heaven rains and fruitful seasons, satisfying your hearts with food and *gladness.*"[35] This was Paul's way of setting the table for the good news of what God has done for us in Christ. He saw these gifts – rain, fruitful seasons, and gladness of heart – as tokens of God's goodness foreshadowing the blessings of salvation. In fact, some did respond to his message and embraced the Giver of every good gift.[36]

Happiness is a gift from God. It is a "witness," to use Paul's words. It is a sign, pointing to something greater. Something higher. For those who never move beyond happiness to its fulfillment in joy, it is the best that life has to offer. As Jesus might have put it, those who are satisfied with happiness alone "have their reward."[37] They miss the true significance of their experience. C.S. Lewis wrote:

> The settled happiness and security which we all desire, God withholds from us by the very nature of the world: but joy, pleasure, and merriment He has scattered broadcast. We are never safe, but we have plenty of fun, and some ecstasy. It is not hard to see why. The security we crave would teach us to rest our hearts in this world and oppose an obstacle to our return to God: a few moments of happy love, a landscape, a symphony, a merry meeting with our friends, and bathe or a football match, have no such tendency. Our Father refreshes us on the journey with some pleasant inns, but will not encourage us to mistake them for home.[38]

Those who settle for happiness alone mistake inns along the way for their true home. For those who receive it from God as a refreshment on life's journey and follow its lead, happiness becomes a prelude to a great symphony, an aperitif before a splendid banquet; a faint but tantalizing fragrance that draws us into the rich, verdant garden of grace; a signpost on the path of life that points our hearts to their true habitation.

There are three ironies to pagan happiness. The first is the incongruity between this experience and the moral structure of the world. In another place Lewis supplied his own commentary on the happiness of his friend: "A bad man, happy, is a man without the least inkling that his actions do not 'answer,' that they are not in accord with the laws of the universe."[39] Those who pursue happiness in life apart from God live as spiritual strangers in his world.

A second irony is that happiness, misunderstood, keeps many from pursuing a relationship with God. They see no need to do so because they are "already happy." It is here that we must underscore how significant happiness truly is. It is meant to lead to the greater and richer dimensions of joy found only in a love relationship with God through Jesus Christ. If it does not, and here we meet the third and greatest irony of all, it will end in eternal misery. As Peter Kreeft has put it, the "opposite of true joy is far worse than anguish, as joy is far better than happiness. In fact, its opposite is hell."[40] Happiness that does not lead to joy will lead instead, and ultimately, to sorrow. Unending sorrow. Happiness is a great and serious gift from God, never to be spurned or belittled by those within the faith, and taken for granted by those outside only at their own great peril.

Questions for Thought and Discussion

1. If you have tended to separate happiness and joy in your thinking, can you identify the sources of influence that have shaped your understanding?

2. If you have put happiness and joy in different categories, what have the distinguishing characteristics been in your understanding of them?

3. How can the fulfillment of desires in your life become part of your response to the exhortation to rejoice in the Lord?

4. How do you assess your values in life in light of Augustine's claim that happiness is the satisfaction of all wants when nothing is wanted wrongly?

5. If you have friends or family members who are indifferent to the Gospel of Jesus Christ because they are "already happy," how can you use the understanding of happiness in this chapter to challenge them?

CHAPTER 3

JOY AND THE FULFILLMENT OF OUR EMOTIONS

So far we have seen that joy is a Godward pleasure. It includes the vast array of wholesome pleasures in life when they are shaped by thanksgiving and praise. Another dimension of joy is the experience that follows when God grants the significant desires of our hearts, which is what we call happiness. Joy is the consummation and crown of happiness and pleasure.

In this chapter we will see that joy engages and enhances our emotional life. Joy is to our emotions what truth is to our minds. Our emotions were made for joy as our minds were made for truth. As truth is the fulfillment of our minds, joy is the fulfillment of our emotions. As truth enlightens our minds, joy illumines and enriches our emotional life.[1]

THE TRANSFORMING TOUCH OF JOY

Joy spans a range of emotions, from cheerfulness to hilarity, from gladness to jubilation, from delight to ecstasy, from exuberance to rapture.[2] However it is experienced, joy leads us to say with Augustine, "You introduce me to a most rare affection, inwardly, to an inexplicable sweetness, which, if it should be perfected in me, I know not to what point . . . life might not arrive."[3]

Although we can think of joy in its own right, it is usually found in company with other emotions.[4] Joy caresses our emotions. They are enriched by its touch. When it takes them up in its dance it changes them. Joy transforms love from duty into delight. Courage becomes a cheerful confidence. Humility becomes the pleasure of honoring others. Joy makes peace a celebrative serenity. It transforms gratitude into a song of thanksgiving.

Joy can even share company with emotions with which it seems, at first glance, to be incompatible.[5] Sometimes joy banishes sorrow:

> They shall obtain joy and gladness,
> and sorrow and sighing shall flee away. (Isaiah 35:10)
>
> Weeping may tarry for the night,
> but joy comes with the morning. (Psalm 30:5)
>
> May those who sow in tears
> reap with shouts of joy!
> He that goes forth weeping,
> bearing the seed for sowing,
> shall come home with shouts of joy. (Psalm 126:5-6)
>
> You will be sorrowful, but your sorrow will turn into joy. (John 16:20)

Other times sorrow remains, but becomes a *bittersweet* experience when it is touched by joy:

> When the *cares* of my heart are many, your consolations *cheer* my soul. (Psalm 94:19)

> *Happy* are those who *mourn*: they shall be comforted. (Matthew 5:4, JB)

> We are treated as impostors, and yet are true; as unknown, and yet well known; as dying, and behold we live; as punished, and yet not killed; as *sorrowful, yet always rejoicing.* (2 Corinthians 6:9-10)

It is not that sorrow and joy come one after the other; they are facets of the same experience.[6] I have known this myself (as you may have) when, in grieving over the death of a loved one, joy comes quietly and gently, not removing sorrow, but transposing the lament into a calm and soothing key.[7] Joy in the midst of sorrow is like a soft light illumining the darkness, or the pleasure of a crying child in the comfort of her mother's loving arms.[8]

Joy and fear can be experienced together. After the resurrection of Jesus, the women who had come to his tomb "departed quickly from the tomb with fear and great joy."[9] The Psalmist exhorts us to serve the Lord "with fear, and rejoice with trembling."[10] Jonathan Edwards could say, "In the saints, joy and holy fear go together."[11] Nearer to the present, A.W. Tozer wrote knowingly of a "delighted trembling" in the presence of "the High and Lofty One that inhabits eternity."[12] Trembling joy? Joyful fear? If we find ourselves strangers to these emotional bedfellows, it only shows how impoverished our hearts have become, and how much we have to learn from our ancient sisters and brothers of faith.

Although joy is not incompatible with sorrow and holy fear, it is with other emotions. There is no such thing as joyful bitterness, joyful anxiety, or joyful envy. They are not contrary emotions. They are contradictory. Bitterness, anxiety, and envy are symptoms of heart sickness; joy epitomizes health and wholeness. They are emotions of fallenness; joy is an emotion of godliness. They are the downward pull of iniquity; joy is the upward call of

God. They are dimensions of darkness; the many facets of joy are "patches of Godlight."[13] When joy reigns, the others are cast out as the riffraff that they are. When they usurp the place of joy among the emotions, joy departs, and beckons from a distance. But they and joy cannot exist in the same heart at the same time.

VARIETIES OF JOY

I remember my surprise when I first read Psalm 16:11 in its original language and saw that the last two phrases aren't quite what they are in our English translations. This would be a more literal rendering:

> In Your presence there are *joys* in fullness;
> in Your right hand there are *pleasures* forever.

There are joys in the presence of God, and pleasures in his hand. As there are many pleasures in life, so there are many joys. Joy is not a single flower, but a garden with winding paths and many species bursting with fragrance and color.

Pleasant joys. Some pleasures command our attention, and though we gladly give it to them for a time, we could not endure their intensity for long. Others are amiable company with whom we would enjoy spending an entire day. This often describes joy. Like pleasant weather – warm with an occasional soft, cooling breeze, or cool with a splash of warm sunlight – it cheers and revives our hearts. Søren Kierkegaard knew this joy: "There is an indescribable joy which . . . cools and refreshes us like a breath of wind, a wave of air, from the trade wind which blows from the plains of Mamre to the everlasting habitations."[14]

The Psalmist likened joy to the dawning of a new day, with its soft hues of yellow, orange, and pink painting the morning sky:

> Light dawns upon the righteous,
> and joy on the upright in heart. (Psalm 97:11)

The prophet Isaiah could liken joy to the blossoming of a desert flower with its alluring fragrance and adornment of color:

> The wilderness and the dry land shall be glad,
> the desert shall rejoice and blossom;
> like the crocus it shall blossom abundantly,
> and rejoice with joy and singing. (Isaiah 35:1-2)[15]

For ancient people of faith, joy was like an anointing of oil that makes skin shine[16] and makes life more bearable under a searing sun:

> You have loved righteousness and hated wickedness.
> Therefore God, your God, has anointed you
> with the oil of gladness beyond your companions. (Psalm 45:7)

> The Spirit of the LORD GOD is upon me,
> because the LORD has anointed me
> to bring good tidings to the afflicted; . . .
> to give them a garland instead of ashes,
> the oil of gladness instead of mourning. (Isaiah 61:1, 3)

Peaceful joy. Joy has the power to calm the turbulent waters of life, and to bring with it a refreshing serenity. It is not surprising that when Paul thought of joy as a fruit of the Spirit, he thought next of peace.[17] One brings the other. We might even think of peace as the soothing, tranquil side of joy. It is the calm that comes with a harmony between our hearts and God's. It is what the Bible calls *shalom*: "a peace which at its highest is *enjoyment*. To dwell in shalom is to *enjoy* living before God, to *enjoy* living in nature, to *enjoy* living with one's fellows, to *enjoy* life with oneself."[18]

Contemplative joy. Another quiet kind of joy is the joy of contemplation: the delight that arises in our hearts when we direct our thoughts to God. We see this joy in Psalm 63:5-6:

> My soul will be satisfied as with fat and rich food,
> and my mouth will praise you with *joyful lips*,
> when I remember you upon my bed,
> and *meditate on you in the watches of the night.* (ESV)

Jonathan Edwards described this joy:

> It primarily consists in the sweet entertainment . . . (that believers) have in the view or contemplation of the divine and holy beauty of these things (of God), as they are in themselves.
>
> True saints have their minds, in the first place, inexpressibly pleased and delighted with the sweet ideas of the glorious and amiable nature of the things of God. And this is the spring of all their delights, and the cream of all their pleasures; 'tis the joy of their joy. This sweet and ravishing entertainment, they have in viewing the beautiful and delightful nature of divine things, is the foundation of the joy they have afterward in the consideration of their being theirs.
>
> The first foundation of the delight a true saint has in God, is his own perfection; and the first foundation of the delight he has in Christ, is his beauty; he appears in himself the chief among ten thousand, and altogether lovely.
>
> They first rejoice in God as glorious and excellent in himself, and then secondarily rejoice in it, that so glorious a God is theirs.[19]

Grateful joy. It is almost impossible to think of joy without also thinking of thanksgiving. They are experienced together. If there is a cycle of joy, it is this: We give thanks for the blessings we receive; joy follows as our heart's pleasure in the goodness of God; we are thankful again, this time for our joy. It is no coincidence that the apostle Paul exhorts us to rejoice and to give thanks in the very same breath, "Rejoice always, pray constantly, give thanks in all circumstances; for this is the will of God in Christ Jesus for you.'[20] The Psalmist knew this experience, as well:

> Make a joyful noise to the LORD, all the earth!
> Serve the LORD with gladness!
> Come into his presence with singing!
> Enter his gates with thanksgiving,
> and his courts with praise!
> Give thanks to him; bless his name! (Psalm 100:1, 2, 4, ESV)

Lewis Smedes saw this ancient and important truth: "In moments of joy, when we are glad to be alive, we experience life as a gift. Now and then we feel the reality of being held up in life by a power beyond our control and we feel gratitude, which is the essence of joy."[21]

Hopeful joy. Hope is an anticipation of the heart. A longing of the heart. A belief that heart-pangs do not occur without reason. They point to something beyond themselves. Hope is a confidence that our hearts will find what they long for. We may think we hope for many things: prosperity, power, or peace, but our hearts can rest in none of these because joy is the true object of hope. "The hope of the righteous ends in gladness."[22] What we truly long for is the joy that will be realized in the new heavens and the new earth, when we enter into the fullness and consummation of our life in God.

The relationship between hope and joy is captured in Paul's letter to the church at Rome, "May the God of hope fill you with all joy and peace in believing, so that by the power of the Spirit you may abound in hope."[23] The God of hope fills us with joy, and joy inspires hope in God. Whatever our present joy may be, a greater joy always beckons, and our hearts are drawn to it.[24] Paul wrote, "Be joyful in hope."[25] He could just as well have said, "Be hopeful in joy." Joy inspires hope and is hope's fulfillment.

Courageous joy. Like hopeful joy, this is a joy that faces the future, but with a different nuance. It is the virtue of a godly woman: "Strength and dignity are her clothing, and she laughs at the time to come."[26] It is a joy that defies any challenge the future may bring. This joy is found in the New Testament exhortation: "Be of good cheer!"[27] "Cheer up!"[28] "Take heart!"[29] "Take courage!"[30] And "Have courage!"[31] Unlike Aristotle's mean between the extremes of rashness and cowardice, the courage of the Christian in the face of an uncertain, and possibly hostile, future is a joyful confidence in the goodness, wisdom, and power of God: a cheerful assurance that in his goodness God is committed to our well-being, in his wisdom he knows how best to bring this about, and in his power he is fully able to secure it.

Invigorating joy. There are times when we are faint-hearted. We are overtaken by emotions that weaken our will and sap the strength of our soul. When joy meets us in this condition it invigorates. It imparts new strength and determination to go on. The Psalmist knew something of this when he wrote, "When the cares of my heart are many, your consolations cheer my soul."[32] It is found in the prescription that Nehemiah gave to a disheartened nation, "Do not be grieved, for the joy of the LORD is your strength."[33] When this joy fills our hearts it leads to the exclamation:

> For it is you who light my lamp;
> the LORD my God lightens my darkness.
> For by you I can run against a troop;
> and by my God I can leap over a wall. (Psalm 18:28-29, ESV)

It is a vigorous joy that inspires the exclamation, "I can do all things in him who strengthens me!"[34]

Healing joy. "A joyful heart is a good medicine."[35] Sometimes joy meets us not in our weakness, but in our pain and sickness of heart. We experience it as a balm, a fragrant, soothing remedy. Pain is eased. Brokenness is mended. Our spirits are lifted. Health returns. We all know the pleasure of quenching a thirst, or filling an empty stomach. Pain gives way to pleasure; in fact the assuaging of the pain is itself a pleasurable experience. Joy does the same thing to wounded hearts. It is the great medicine of the soul. It can also remedy physical disorders. Dallas Willard writes, "Full joy is our first line of defense against weakness, failure, and disease of mind and body."[36] Peter Kreeft makes the same point: "A joyful spirit inspires joyful feelings and even a more psychosomatically healthy body. (For example, we need less sleep when we have joy and have more resistance to all kinds of diseases from colds to cancers.)"[37] Joy connects us with God, and that is the healthiest place for us to be.

Musical joy. When God chose to share his joy with mortals he gave us the gift of music. Music was made for joy, and joy for music. In its highest form music is the overflow of joy. Joy uncontained. Spilling over. Music at its best is joy performing for the praise of God and the delight of others. When asked why his music always sounded so happy, Franz Joseph Haydn responded, "I cannot make it otherwise. I write according to the thoughts I feel. When I think upon God, my heart is so full of joy that my notes dance and leap, as it were, from my pen."[38]

There is a joy that is best expressed in singing:

> Let the nations be glad and sing for joy. (Psalm 67:4)
>
> My lips will shout for joy when I sing praises to you. (Psalm 71:23)

Serve the LORD with gladness!
Come into his presence with singing! (Psalm 100:2)

Sing for joy, O heavens, and exult, O earth;
break forth, O mountains, into singing! (Isaiah 49:13)

There is a joy that is expressed in the skillful use of musical instruments:

Praise the LORD with the lyre;
make melody to him with the harp of ten strings!
Sing to him a new song;
play skillfully on the strings, with loud shouts. (Psalm 33: 2-3)

Make a joyful noise to the LORD, all the earth;
break forth into joyous song and sing praises!
Sing praises to the LORD with the lyre,
with the lyre and the sound of melody!

With trumpets and the sound of the horn
make a joyful noise before the King, the LORD! (Psalm 98:4-6)

From ivory palaces stringed instruments make you glad. (Psalm 45:8)

It is not merely that this joy inspires music; music is part of the joy itself. The pleasures we find in voices and instruments are caught up in the pleasure of joy, with a resulting delight that is greater than the artist's original inspiration and our enjoyment of their musical creation.

Dancing joy. There is a joy that inspires a movement-in-harmony of body and soul in the celebration of life before God. In the sacred dance of joy, one's body becomes one's instrument, and one's movements become the lyrics of worship offered in joyful adoration of God. In the Bible the dance of joy is inspired by God.[39] It is the opposite of mourning.[40] It is akin to the carefree gaiety of children.[41] It is the joyful celebration of the mighty deeds of God,[42] a graceful and rhythmic praise to the Lord of life,[43] thanksgiving for the healing of relationships,[44] and an anticipation of the final restoration and harmony of all things in the new heavens and the new earth.[45]

Playful joy. There are times when joy expresses itself in playfulness. Children play when they feel safe, their hearts are unfettered by the burdens of life, and they see their lives as something to be enjoyed and celebrated. Joy can inspire this response to life in older souls, as well. It is a joy pictured in Malachi 4:2, "But for you who revere my name, the sun of righteousness will rise with healing in its wings. And you will go out and leap like calves released from the stall."[46]

In the New Testament, the Greek word *skirtáo* is used to describe this joy. It means literally to leap or spring about as a sign of joy.[47] It was used of the infant John the Baptist, who "leaped for joy" in his mother's womb at the arrival of Mary, the expectant mother of Jesus.[48] It occurs again in the words of Jesus to followers who encounter persecution for his sake: "Rejoice in that day, and *leap for joy*, for behold, your reward is great in heaven; for so their fathers did to the prophets."[49] (I suspect that what Jesus is doing is something like this: He takes an experience of joy that his followers know in ordinary situations in life, and then applies it to a situation in which it doesn't seem to fit. If we don't know what it is to jump for joy apart from persecution, we won't be able to respond that way if persecution comes!)

Laughing joy. Playful joy often includes laughter. I don't understand why some Christians belittle laughter when they talk about joy. C.H. Spurgeon wrote that a man of joy may not be a man of much laughter, and then added, "There is a joy that laughter would but mock, there is a sacred mirth within to which the merriment of fools is but as the crackling of thorns under a pot." [50] His Anglican contemporary, J.C. Ryle, wrote, "True happiness *does* *not consist of laughter and smiles.*"[51] Many would nod their head in somber agreement.

I am willing to grant, as the good bishop was quick to point out, that laughter and smiles are not a perfect index of a person's inner life, "There are thousands who laugh loud and are merry as a grasshopper in company, but are wretched and miserable in private, and almost afraid to be alone. "[52] Nevertheless, laughter and smiles are a fitting expression of joy.

There is a laughter of derision,[53] a laughter of disbelief,[54] a laughter of defiance,[55] and foolish laughter.[56] But there is also laughter that is the spontaneous overflow of joy. Sarah laughed once because she found God's promise that she would bear a child in her old age so unlikely.[57] But she laughed later in a joyful celebration of her child – a laughter that she shared with all who knew her and entered into her delight.[58]

When the people of Israel returned to Jerusalem from captivity they could say:

> Then our mouth was filled with laughter,
> and our tongue with shouts of joy;
> then they said among the nations,
> "The LORD has done great things for them."
> The LORD has done great things for us;
> we are glad. (Psalm 126:2-3)

There are times when joy cannot help but laugh. We should see holy mirth is a gift from our God.[59]

Soaring joy. There is a joy that for a time transcends the difficulties of life. A joy that defies the downward pull of heartache and grief, breaks free of anxiety's hold, towers above trials, soars above sorrow, and glides on the winds of heaven. There is a joy, in the words of Spurgeon, which seems to "play with the young lightnings that are at home with the sun," and to live, even briefly, "in the very presence of God."[60] It is the kind of experience described in the words, "You have seen what I did to the Egyptians, and how I bore you on eagles' wings and brought you to myself."[61] It is a joy that is lofted above the tumult and trials of life, and is taken to a place of safety in the presence of God. Even if we can't live there (yet), God knows that there are times when we must be taken there to gain strength to meet life's challenges.

Joy unspeakable. There is a joy so pure and so powerful that it is beyond words. It is a "joy unspeakable and full of glory,"[62] as Peter described it. We have no lexicon with which to approach it. It would be like trying to describe a field of wild flowers or a rainbow with the words "black" and "white." To approach this joy with words would profane it. To describe it would only demean it. It is too heavy for words; they cannot bear its weight. It is too lofty; they cannot reach its heights. It is too profound; they cannot plumb its depths. At best they convey the merest glimpse of a breathtaking beauty. They impart only the barest taste of a rapturous feast. The only response worthy of this joy is hushed wonder.

Raucous joy. As joy becomes more intense, its constraints weaken, and its decibel level sometimes rises. It becomes a "loud, exultant rejoicing,"[63] a "joyful noise"[64] or a "sounding joy" as we sing in the Christmas carol, *Joy to the World.*

Let those who delight in my righteousness
shout for joy and be glad. (Psalm 35:27)

Clap your hands, all peoples!
Shout to God with loud songs of joy! (Psalm 47:1)

Shout for joy to God, all the earth;
sing the glory of his name;
give to him glorious praise! (Psalm 66:1-2)

> There Zadok the priest took the horn of oil from the tent, and anointed Solomon. Then they blew the trumpet; and all the people said, "Long live King Solomon!" And all the people went up after him, playing on pipes, and rejoicing with great joy, so that the earth was split by their noise. (1 Kings 1:39-40)

> And they offered great sacrifices that day and rejoiced, for God had made them rejoice with great joy; the women and children also rejoiced. And the joy of Jerusalem was heard afar off. (Nehemiah 12:43)

Anyone who has been around children or avid sports fans knows that the greater the enthusiasm, the louder the voice. When joy becomes spiritual excitement, it becomes less inhibited and more animated. In the words of Jesus, it feels that if it "were silent, the very stones would cry out!"[65] Grasping the greatness of God, and in an almost overwhelming rush of elation, it seems that there is nothing to do but fill the lungs with air and propel it out again in a high-spirited shout of praise. A grand cheer for God! And, strange though it may seem to some, our God hears and is pleased.[66]

Ecstatic joy. When joy crowds and spills over the limits of our human frame, it becomes an experience of ecstasy. It is no longer merely pleasant; it is virtually unbearable. It is possible to be enthralled by joy, intoxicated with its elixir. The experience is disorienting, unsettling, and overwhelming. To be in this state is to be "overjoyed." Filled beyond the capacity of our human vessel. It is the joy experienced by Pascal on November 23, 1654, recorded, sewn into his coat, and not discovered until after his death:

> From about half past ten in the evening until about half past twelve,
>
> FIRE

> God of Abraham, God of Isaac, God of Jacob, not of the philosophers and scholars.
> Certitude. Certitude. Feeling. Joy. Peace.
> God of Jesus Christ.
> *Deum meum et Deum vestrum.*
> "Your God shall be my God."
> Forgetfulness of the world and of everything else, except GOD.
> He is to be found only by the ways taught in the Gospel.
> Greatness of the human soul.
> "Righteous Father, the world has not known You, but I have known You."
> Joy, joy, joy, tears of joy.[67]

There are two classic examples of this ecstatic joy in the Bible: David dancing before the Lord when the ark was returned to Jerusalem, and the disciples following the resurrection of Christ.

In David's case he was bringing the ark of the Lord back to Jerusalem after defeating the Philistines in battle. With the thrill of victory still throbbing in their hearts, David and his men were "celebrating with all their might before the LORD, with songs and with harps, lyres, tambourines, sistrums and cymbals."[68] As they entered the Holy City to the shouts of people and the sound of trumpets, David, clad only in a linen ephod, "danced before the LORD with all his might."[69] It is the picture of a man "outside himself" (the literal meaning of *ecstasy*) with joy, uninhibited, totally absorbed with the God of his rapture, oblivious to all else and utterly indifferent to what others might think of him in this state of near delirium.

His wife, Michal, didn't appreciate this wild display of joy and chided him for being a "vulgar fellow," to which David responded, "I will celebrate before the LORD. I will become even more undignified than this, and I will be humiliated in my own eyes."[70]

This unusual form of joy (It is rare in the Bible, and is never heard of again in David's life.) makes social protocol and decorum absolutely irrelevant, and perhaps even irreverent. One could not, even if one wanted to, defer to others who do not share the joy.

The disciples of Jesus experienced this joy after the Resurrection. The eleven were huddled in hiding in Jerusalem when Cleopas and an unnamed disciple came to them from Emmaus, where they had an eerie encounter with the risen Christ. As these two were telling their story to the apostles, the Risen One suddenly appeared among them. Their response was just what yours and mine would have been: "But they were startled and frightened, and supposed that they saw a spirit!" This is full-fledged terror. And then, while they were paralyzed with fear, the risen Christ spoke! "Why are you troubled, and why do questionings arise in your hearts? See my hands and my feet, that it is I myself; handle me, and see; for a spirit has not flesh and bones as you see that I have."[71]

The text then says that they "disbelieved for joy."[72] Their fright became the trembling and astonished joy the women had experienced earlier at the empty tomb.[73] Their joy was so stunning that they were unable to think calmly from the perspective of faith, recalling what Jesus had told them before his crucifixion. It was more than they could bear, their joy now greater in intensity than even their terror had been, to have their Lord returned to them from the grave.

Haunting joy. This is the opposite of the last joy. If ecstatic joy crowds the limits of our human frame, this joy dances just outside, elusive, beckoning, luring, and even haunting. It reveals something of itself in the pleasures of life, but only enough to let us know that it includes but transcends them. It is something more. Something better. It gives a taste of itself in happiness, but leaves even the happiest person feeling bereft, hungry for the greater reality to which happiness points, and in which happiness finds its true fulfillment.

This joy touches believers and unbelievers alike, but with a different purpose for each. For those who haven't yet come to faith in the true God, this joy is a *praeparatio evangelium*: a preparation for the Gospel. It is the tantalizing fragrance of the Spirit,[74] inviting, drawing, wooing, allowing us to explore the world's arcade of imitations and substitutes, but never letting us rest until our hearts find their repose in God's redemptive work in Christ.

It is this same joy in the life of the Christian that creates a sense of being a stranger in this world. It is a hand that beckons, and a finger that points beyond this world to the next. It is a voice "from far more distant regions," in the words of C.S. Lewis, inviting and even summoning.[75] It is a taste of the "powers of the age to come,"[76] a sample which, savored, creates a longing that nothing in this world can satisfy. It is both a filling and a void. Having and wanting. Joy and joy desired. Gift and promise. Already and not yet.[77]

Those who know this joy sense that they are not (as Jesus was not) of this world.[78] They "desire a better country, that is, a heavenly one."[79] They know and love the joy of the Lord, and yet are haunted by it – and will be – until at last they come to "the city of the living God, the heavenly Jerusalem, and to innumerable angels in festal gathering."[80] There, there will be no more hauntings. No more visitations of joy. For that place is joy's native land. All who are there know its regal splendor, sourced in the undimmed presence of God and bestowed without end by his beneficent hand.[81]

Dispositional joy. Lesslie Newbigen wrote, "Joy is a visitor who comes when she will, and who sometimes calls when we least expect her and sometimes fails to turn up when we were sure she was coming."[82] This is true of some joys. They may come once in a lifetime, and maybe not at all. Others are like old college friends, surprising us occasionally with a visit, and then passing on. But that isn't true of all joys. Some make the heart a home.

Joy can become a steady Godward disposition, orienting our hearts and inclining us toward him. It can be a foundational emotion. A shaping and empowering affection. It can be a current that flows steadily beneath the surface of all that we experience. This is not the joy of a spiritual novice, but of seasoned saints who, like Paul, have their spiritual senses trained, focused, and centered in God, and who can say, without hypocrisy, that they rejoice in the Lord always.[83]

Questions for Thought and Discussion

1. How do the varieties of joy discussed in this chapter help you to see your emotions as a response to the exhortation to rejoice in the Lord always?

2. Have you cultivated emotions in your life that are incompatible with joy? What will you begin to do about that?

3. Of the emotional dimensions of joy that were discussed in this chapter, which one/s do you have the hardest time relating to in your life? Why do you think this is so?

4. Of the emotional dimensions of joy that were discussed in this chapter, which one/s connect well with your experiences in the Christian life so far? Why do you think that is so?

5. How does this chapter's understanding of joy differ from the emotionalism that characterizes some Christians?

Part Two

The Triune God of Joy

CHAPTER 4

THE JOY OF THE LORD

A. W. Tozer wrote, "What comes into our minds when we think about God is the most important thing about us. . . . We tend by a secret law of the soul to move toward our mental image of God." What we think about God affects the way we relate to him and the way we live our lives before him.[1] If we think of God as a dour deity, scowling over his creation in an unchanging mood of displeasure, we might submit to his rule (if we also believe that he possesses great power and that we are vulnerable to its exercise), but we would not want to get too close. We would not expect to enjoy God, and it would never occur to us to relate creature-joys to him. We would think of our joy as something to which he is indifferent, and perhaps even hostile.

What we think about God not only affects the way we relate to him, it influences our understanding of ourselves.[2] If, as the Bible teaches, we are beings-in-the-image-of-God, and beings-in-relation-to-God, we can't know ourselves rightly unless we know God aright. We will never understand the true nature and dimensions of life if we do not know the One in whom we live and move and have our being.[3] If we get God wrong, we will get ourselves wrong as well. If our bearings are off in our theology, our self-understanding and grasp of the meaning of life will also be skewed.

If God were joyless, and we have been created to mirror him in the world, we could not pursue God and joy. The closer we moved to joy, the farther we would find ourselves from him; the closer to him, the greater our distance from joy. But that is not the living and true God: "Happy the people whose God is the LORD!"[4] If we take our cues from the Bible, and the ancient people of faith through whom it came to us, we will see that all creature-joy is grounded in the Creator's joy. His is the wellspring of joy in all places and all times. It is the Joy from which all joy in the universe flows.[5]

JOY IN THE PRESENCE OF GOD

Where God is, there is joy. Of those who contributed to our Bible, King David saw this most clearly. We find it three times in the poetic legacy that bears his name:

> For all the gods of the peoples are idols;
> but the LORD made the heavens.
> Honor and majesty are before him;
> *strength and joy are in his place.* (1 Chronicles 16:26-27)

> *In your presence there is fullness of joy,*
> in your right hand are pleasures forevermore. (Psalm 16:11, NRSV)

> You bestow on him blessings forever;
> you make him glad with *the joy of your presence.* (Psalm 21:6, NRSV)

Joy in the presence of God is not something outside him, like an angelic attendant ever before his throne. It is something about God himself. It is his glory, the radiant splendor of his deity.[6] This is the way C.S. Lewis saw it:

> Good things as well as bad, you know, are caught by a kind of infection. If you want to get warm you must stand near the fire: if you want to be wet you must get into the water. If you want joy, power, peace, eternal life, you must get close to, or even into, the thing that has them. They are not a sort of prize which God could, if He chose, just hand out to anyone. They are a great fountain of energy and beauty spurting up at the very centre of reality. If you are close to it, the spray will wet you: if you are not, you will remain dry.[7]

If we knew the true nature and dimensions of joy, we would see that it is always, and never less than, our heart's encounter with the Joyful One. Joy is the touch of God. The fragrance of his presence. A taste of his goodness. A glimpse of his beauty. An echo of his voice. Joy is a quality of divine life, residing there in infinite fullness, warming like a fire, or spurting up as a great fountain, spraying all who draw near.

TRIUNE JOY

God enjoys being God.[8] Can you really imagine a God who didn't like himself? Who was bored or frustrated or disappointed with having to be the Supreme Being? Who secretly wished that he could be someone else? I can't. Even if I could, it wouldn't be the true God.

But there is more to God's joy than this, which brings us to the heart of the Christian understanding of God as a Trinity. To say that God is love[9] is shorthand for saying – before anything else – that the Father loves the Son and the Spirit, the Son loves the Father and the Spirit, and the Spirit loves the Father and the Son. God's love for his creation is an overflow of that love.[10] The joy of God, too, is Trinitarian: It is the Father's joy in the Son and the Spirit, the Son's joy in the Father and the Spirit, the Spirit's joy in the Father and the Son, and the shared joy of the Three-in-One.[11] All joy in the universe begins here.

Lewis Smedes wrote:

> What did God do before he had a world to tend? He was planning hell, it has been impishly suggested, for people who ask such impertinent questions. But the question is not at all improper. The fathers who gave us the doctrine of the Trinity were really responding to the same question. Their answer was that God the Father was eternally generating the Son and that both collaborated in the generation of the Spirit. *And the three of them were simply enjoying being with each other.* Three persons with nothing much to do, no time schedule to keep, no superior's orders to obey, no problem of survival, and no creatures to worry about. If in some impossible fantasy we could have looked on, we might have scolded the holy Trinity for wasting time. But we would have been outsiders, unable to understand the freedom of the Trinity to have their own rules to play by. And we would have been mystified, perhaps, by *the enormous pleasure that they seemed to have in what they were doing.*[12]

A glimpse of what would otherwise be an impossible fantasy has been given to us in God's self-disclosure. We see something of the Triune life of God before creation when Jesus spoke of sharing glory with the Father before the world began[13] and being loved by the Father before the foundation of the world.[14] We see it again in the prologue of John's Gospel. "In the beginning was the Word, and the Word was with God, and the Word was God. He was in the beginning with God; all things were made through him, and without him was not anything made that was made. In him was the light of men."[15] Christ, the Word of God, is the deeper fulfillment of the sage's celebration of wisdom:

> Before the mountains had been shaped,
> before the hills, I was brought forth;
> before he had made the earth with its fields,
> or the first of the dust of the world.
> When he established the heavens, I was there,
> when he drew a circle on the face of the deep,
> when he made firm the skies above,
> when he established the fountains of the deep,
> when he assigned to the sea its limit,
> so that the waters might not transgress his command,
> when he marked out the foundations of the earth,
> then I was beside him, like a master workman;
> and *I was daily his delight,*
> *rejoicing before him always.* (Proverbs 8: 25-30)

If this is a hint of the pre-Incarnate Word, we see the Son as the continual delight of the Father, and the Father rejoicing always in the Son. This is just what we find in the Gospels: The Father delights in the Son,[16] and the Son delights in the will of the Father.[17] To complete the theological picture, the Spirit is the beatitude of love between the Father and the Son.[18] He is the effervescence of joy shared by the Father and the Son, and overflowing into human hearts.[19]

GOD'S JOY IN WHAT HE DOES

God takes pleasure in all that he does:

> Whatever the LORD *pleases*, he does. (Psalm 135:6; cf. 115:3)

> *The LORD was pleased* for his righteousness' sake, to magnify his law and make it glorious. (Isaiah 42:21)

> I am the LORD who practices steadfast love, justice and righteousness in the earth; *for in these things I delight*, says the LORD. (Jeremiah 9:24)

> I will make with them an everlasting covenant, that I will not turn away from doing good to them; and I will put the fear of me in their hearts, that they may not turn from me. *I will rejoice in doing them good . . . with all my heart and all my soul.* (Jeremiah 32:40-41)

> Who is a God like you, pardoning iniquity
> and passing over the transgression
> for the remnant of his inheritance?
> He does not retain his anger forever
> because *he delights* in steadfast love. (Micah 7:18, ESV)

> I praise You, O Father, Lord of heaven and earth, that You have hidden these things from the wise and intelligent and have revealed them to babes. Yes, Father, for thus it was *well-pleasing in Your sight.* (Luke 10:21, NASB)

> Fear not, little flock, for it is your Father's *good pleasure* to give you the kingdom. (Luke 12:32)

Whether it is keeping a planet in its orbit, sustaining the life of a microbe, bringing salvation to a lost world, or simply admiring his handiwork in creation, God delights in all that he does.[20] (Among other things, this has tremendous significance for our prayer life. If we think of prayer as seeking to persuade God to do something that he is reluctant to do, we are out of touch with reality. There is no universe in which that is possible, simply because God is who he is and he delights in what he does. Prayer is never twisting God's arm to do something. Before it is anything else, it is learning what pleases him, and then aligning our lives and our requests with his good pleasure.)[21]

GOD'S JOY IN CREATION

Why did God create a universe? It was not a metaphysical necessity, as ancient Neoplatonists taught.[22] Nor is God dependent upon the world, as process theologians in our own day would have it.[23] To an audience of philosophers in the city of Athens, the apostle Paul said of God: "Nor is he served by human hands, as though he needed anything."[24] A God with no needs is not served by human hands or a cosmos. We must look in another direction for an answer to our question.

Creation was neither necessary nor inevitable. The best place to start thinking about this is the Creator's love. If the essence of love is giving, we see God's love first in creation and the gift of life itself. The words "In the beginning God created" are an expression of divine love. To say that God "gives to all men life and breath and everything"[25] is to say that he loves all people. To say that we "live and move and have our being" in God[26] is another way of saying that we live in and through God's creative love.[27] God created to express his love beyond the circle of his own Triune life.

If we think of joy as the beatitude of love, or love's delight, then joy, too, helps us understand the purpose of God's creative acts.[28] He created from the plenitude of his pleasure. Creation is an overflow of his joy. In the words of Peter Kreeft, "God created the world not out of reason or necessity or practicality, but out of sheer joy. It is all gloriously superfluous."[29] Creation does not remedy a deficit in the life of God; it is an expression of his love and the fullness of his joy. When you consider the vastness of the universe, from its tiniest elements to its billions of galaxies, that is an astonishing statement about divine delight!

At the end of the first century Clement of Rome wrote to the church at Corinth: "For the Creator and Master of the universe himself rejoices in His works." And "The Lord . . . adorned himself with good works and rejoiced."[30] This is exactly what we find when we turn to the creation account in Genesis. The creation story is punctuated throughout with the divine benediction, "It is good." God saw that it was pleasant, agreeable, good, and delightful – all nuances of the Hebrew original.[31]

The divine approval not only excludes a Platonic view of the physical world, which would make it evil, or less than real, it tells us a great deal about God's joy in creation. His exclamation is like that of an artist, who, after completing a series of brush strokes, stands back to admire her work and to revel in aesthetic pleasure. Or like that of a master chef, who, after adding the finishing touch to his *pièce de résistance,* allows his senses to be filled with its aroma and beauty, and then exclaims loudly his culinary delight. Our God rejoices in his works.

> May the glory of the LORD endure for ever,
> may the LORD rejoice in his works! (Psalm 104: 31)

GOD'S JOY IN HIS PEOPLE

The joy of God in his people shares a kinship with his joy in his workmanship, since that is what we are.[32] The context here, however, is not creation, but redemption. It is God's joy in the people whom he graciously draws near to himself, and upon whom he bestows the blessings of salvation. If you could hear God singing his joy in creation you would be utterly enthralled by the music. If you can imagine his voice in song, imagine the song of redemption as his favorite hymn of all.

Two of the most vivid pictures of God's joy in his people are found in the prophets (yes, those often-stern men, so full of grit). The first is from Isaiah 62:3-5, looking forward to the restoration of Israel following God's judgment of their sin. It expresses the beautiful, if surprising, truth that the joy of God in his people is like our own pleasure in romantic love. It is like the joy of a bridegroom in his bride:

> You shall be a crown of beauty in the hand of the LORD,
> and a royal diadem in the hand of your God.
> You shall no more be termed Forsaken,
> and your land shall no more be termed Desolate;
> but you shall be called My delight is in her,
> and your land Married;
> for the LORD delights in you,
> and your land shall be married.
> For as a young man marries a virgin,
> so shall your sons marry you,
> and as the bridegroom rejoices over the bride,
> so shall your God rejoice over you.

The second picture, from Zephaniah 3:17, is taken from the celebration of a holiday, with its festive spirit and sheer pleasure in the company of others, breaking out into an uncontained, boisterous song of joy:

> The LORD, your God, is in your midst,
> a warrior who gives victory;
> he will rejoice over you in gladness,
> he will renew you in his love;
> he will exult over you with loud singing
> as on a day of festival.

God not only delights in us, he delights in doing good things for us.[33] He delights in our welfare,[34] and in delivering us from danger.[35] He finds pleasure in the prayer of the upright,[36] and delights in their sincere thanksgiving and praise.[37] He takes special pleasure in those who fear him, and put their trust not in themselves, but in his steadfast love.[38] He delights in sacrificial gifts of love,[39] in obedience,[40] and in enabling his people to do his will.[41] It is his pleasure to give them the Kingdom and all of its blessings.[42] God takes joy in us. There is no greater affirmation of our worth than this.

THE HAPPINESS OF GOD

One of the loftiest descriptions of God in the Scriptures is found in 1 Timothy 6:15-16, where he is extolled as "the blessed and only Sovereign, the King of kings and Lord of lords, who alone has immortality and dwells in unapproachable light, whom no man has ever seen or can see." My interest is in the first word used to describe God: He is the "blessed" One. The word in the Greek is *makarios*.[43] The Greeks used it of their gods, who, they thought, enjoyed a transcendent happiness beyond the cares and struggles of mortals. When used of humans it became a "leading philosophical term for inner happiness."[44]

To say that God is "blessed" is to say that he is happy, and, since he possesses all properties supremely, that he is the happiest of all beings. What does this mean and why is it important? The heart of happiness, as we experience it, is the pleasure that follows the fulfillment of our desires and the success of our plans. As Aquinas put it, "to desire happiness is nothing else than to desire that one's will be satisfied"[45] This points us in the right direction for thinking about the happiness of God. It lies in the fulfillment of his desires and the success of his plans, and his pleasure in this. In other words, the happiness of God lies in his sovereignty.[46] He is the happiest of all beings because his plans cannot be frustrated. His counsel is never endangered:

> What he desires, that he does. (Job 23:13)

> I know that you can do all things,
> and that no purpose of yours can be thwarted. (Job 42:2, ESV)
>
> The LORD brings the counsel of the nations to naught;
> he frustrates the plans of the peoples.
> The counsel of the LORD stands forever,
> the thoughts of his heart to all generations. (Psalm 33:10-11)
>
> I am God, and there is no other;
> I am God, and there is none like me,
> declaring the end from the beginning
> and from ancient times things not yet done,
> saying, "My counsel shall stand,
> and I will accomplish all my purpose." (Isaiah 46:9-10)
>
> According to the purpose of him who accomplishes all things according to the counsel of his will. (Ephesians 1:11)[47]

Why is this important? If our happiness depends upon God fulfilling our desires and granting success to our plans, it follows that our happiness is grounded in the sovereign happiness of God, in the fulfillment of his desires and the success of his plans, which include us in their scope. Our happiness depends upon God's, and his happiness lies in his sovereignty. "The LORD reigns; let the earth rejoice!"[48]

THE SORROW OF GOD

If the happiness of God lies in the fulfillment of his desires and the success of his plans, how do we account for his sorrow?

> The LORD saw that the wickedness of man was great in the earth, and that every imagination of the thoughts of his heart was only

> evil continually. And the LORD was sorry that he had made man on the earth, and it grieved him to his heart. (Genesis 6:5-6)

> And when he drew near and saw the city he wept over it, saying, "Would that even today you knew the things that made for peace!" (Luke 19:41-42)

> And do not grieve the Holy Spirit of God, in whom you were sealed for the day of redemption. (Ephesians 4:30)

Some philosophers and theologians say that emotions aren't possible for God. They are incompatible with his status as the Supreme Being. Since emotions, as we know them, come and go, and God is eternally unchanging, he can't have them. Others argue that since emotions are passions linked to our finitude, and God is infinite and cannot suffer, he can't have emotions. Still others contend that emotions are tied to physical states. Since God doesn't have a body, he can't have emotions. I can only say that denying what is often attributed to God in our sacred Scriptures, and in fact lies at the heart of his personal relationships recorded there, may appease a philosophical society, but it is not bowing before the living and true God.[49]

Another way of rejecting divine sorrow is to deny it any occasion. This begins well by linking the happiness of God to his sovereignty, but goes wrong from there. In this view the sovereignty of God is simple: Everything that happens in God's universe is the perfect, ineluctable outworking of his plan, and the fulfillment of his desires. I can't believe this. (I can frame the thought and entertain the idea, but I cannot bring myself to affirm that it is true.) For one thing, it would require us, again, to deny or take less than seriously the sacred texts that describe his sorrow over human rebellion. It would seem further to entail making our sin the satisfaction of his will and his desire for creation. Such a God might be happy (though not in the highest sense of the word), but he would not be good.

There is a better way to approach this. Without flinching theologically, we must begin by saying that God is saddened by the rebellion of his creatures. He experiences sorrow. Truly. The sorrow of an infinite God is like, and yet far greater, than anything we know. But we also know what it is to have *bittersweet* experiences. Our pleasures are sometimes tinged with sadness, and our sorrows with joy. Why should we not think that this is possible for the God whose image we bear, and in whose likeness we have been made?[50] God's joy lies first in who he is and what he does; his sorrow is a response to who we are and what we do in our revolt against him. He is grieved by our sin, but he does not willingly grieve us.[51] He takes no pleasure in the death of sinners,[52] yet he reigns over our sinful world in righteousness and justice (including the wages of sin),[53] and in these things he delights.[54]

We sometimes think of happiness as a momentary feeling about life. The ancient world saw it as a way of summing up a whole, or judging the totality of life.[55] If we take this view, we can see an important way in which happiness differs from sorrow. Sorrow is situational: the death of a loved one, a wound from an angry word, or the loss of a valued opportunity. (If the experience is more diffuse, we call it *melancholy*, and if it is prolonged, we call it *depression*.) It is possible to be happy about life as a summary judgment, and yet know sorrow over something that happens in its course. If this is true of our experience, and we bear God's image, might it not also be true of his?

Whatever the magnitude of divine sorrow, it is not great enough to call the happiness of God into question. Paul did not call him a sorrowful God, but the blessed, or happy, God. The felicity of his reign far surpasses the impact of our sins. Our abuse of the freedom God has given us is contrary to his design and brings him sorrow. It has not, however, taken him by surprise![56] Even our misdeeds have been factored into his plan: a plan that is certain of success, and in which he finds great pleasure. The sins of humanity, from the dawn of our creation to this day, are a pebble thrown into a mighty current: They may create a ripple, but they do not, and cannot, alter the river's course or mute the laughter of its waves as they break upon its banks.[57]

THE SIGNIFICANCE OF GOD'S JOY

Joy is central to our *raison d'être*, our reason for being. It is the culmination and fulfillment of our existence. Joy is possible for us, however, only because we are the image-bearers of a joyful God. We were designed *for* joy, and find it in the God *of* joy. To seek this highest of all pleasures is to seek the God in whom it is found supremely and in overflowing abundance. In the words of Karl Barth, it is to be warmed and illumined by the radiance of his joy,[58] or, as C.S. Lewis put it, it is to be splashed by a fountain of joy spurting up at the very center of reality.[59] It is, as the Psalmist sang, to feast from the abundance of *his* house, and to drink from the river of *his* delights.[60]

Questions for Thought and Discussion

1. Can you imagine a supremely joyful God? If not, why not?

2. Have you ever experienced the joy of God's presence in your life? If so, try to describe what it was about the joy that seemed to connect you with God.

3. What difference does joy make for your understanding of the Trinity?

4. Can you imagine God rejoicing in you? What difference does that make in the way you approach him in prayer and in worship?

5. What adjustments will you have to make in your theology to come fully to grips with God's sorrow?

CHAPTER 5

JOY INCARNATE

Some people read the Gospels and see a joyless Jesus there. They see no smile on his face. They hear no crackle of laughter in his voice. They see no humor in his words or playfulness in his interactions. They imagine no joy in the Father, no gladness in the Spirit, no celebration of life, no gaiety in company, no delight in children, no pleasure in the beauty and wonders of creation. As they see it, the man who exhorted others to be of good cheer never was.

If you ask why they hold such a dismal view of the most important man in history, they respond that their gloomy Jesus is what the prophet Isaiah told us we would get in a Messiah: "He was despised and rejected by men; a man of sorrows, and acquainted with grief."[1] Never mind that this was not a psychological profile of the Anointed One, but a prophetic portrait of his redemptive suffering. Never mind that the oracle went on to say that the sorrows were not his own, but ours, borne for us in his death.[2] Never mind that for Jesus it was for the "joy that was set before him" that he endured the Cross.[3] They say of him, as Pascal did, "Of all that is on earth, He partakes only of the sorrows, not of the joys."[4]

Read on only if you are prepared to see something very different.

THE OIL OF GLADNESS

Our understanding of the joy of Jesus must first be framed by our understanding of who he is.[5] The man whom we meet in the Gospels is authentically human, and yet so much more. Though it staggers our imagination and beggars our words, the claim of the New Testament is that in Jesus the God of Abraham, Isaac, and Jacob has drawn near to us, so near that he became one of us, so intimately involved in human life that he made it his own. In Jesus we see God-focused-in-humanity.[6] This means that everything we have said about the joy of God we must now bring to our understanding of the joy of Jesus. It is the preface to the Gospel narratives of his life and ministry.

The fellowship of the Trinity was not broken in the Incarnation. The Son's song of love to the Father and Spirit may have been sung to the cadence of creation, but it echoed the music of eternity. His dance of delight with his triune Partners may have slowed to a mundane beat, but it was the same rhythmic reveling that had moved through countless aeons when the morning stars joined with their song and angels shouted for joy.[7]

The writer of Hebrews framed the joy of Jesus in this high Christology:

> But of the Son he says,
> "Your throne, O God, is for ever and ever,
> and the scepter of uprightness is the scepter of your kingdom.
> You have loved righteousness and hated wickedness;
> therefore God, your God, has anointed you
> with the oil of gladness beyond your companions." (1:8-9, ESV)

He is the Son. He is hailed as God. His throne is God's own, with no beginning and no end. He wields a scepter and rules a kingdom. As he had embraced the Father's will through numberless ages past, so he did when he strode the earth. With the Father he loved righteousness and hated wickedness. And he did so perfectly. In response, the Father granted him a joy beyond any other. The same joy he had always known, now distilled in human experience.

JOY OF HEAV'N TO EARTH COME DOWN[8]

Long before the air was pierced by infant cry that first Christmas morning, patriarchs, prophets, and poets scanned the horizon of history in search of the One who would come to fulfill God's plan of redemption. Even what they saw dimly from a distance brought them great joy. Jesus said, "Abraham rejoiced that he was to see my day; he saw it and was glad."[9]

The words "For to us a child is born, to us a son is given; and the government will be upon his shoulder" introduce a well-known prophecy of the Messiah. What is often missed is its centerpiece of joy:

> The people who walked in darkness
> have seen a great light;
> those who dwelt in a land of deep darkness –
> on them has light shone.
> You have multiplied the nation,
> *you have increased its joy;*
> *they rejoice before you*
> *as with joy at the harvest,*
> as they are glad when they divide the spoil. . . .
> For to us a child is born,
> to us a son is given;
> and the government shall be upon his shoulder,
> and his name shall be called
> Wonderful Counselor, Mighty God,
> Everlasting Father, Prince of Peace. (Isaiah 9:2-3, 6, ESV)

As the coming of the Messiah drew near, the joy of those who watched, or would play a part in the drama, grew to a crescendo. We have Luke to thank for preserving these memories. Upon hearing the greeting of Mary, he wrote that Elizabeth, her kinswoman, "exclaimed with a loud cry, 'Blessed are you among women, and blessed is the fruit of your womb. . . . For behold, when the voice of your greeting came to my ears, the babe in my womb leaped for joy!"[10] In response to this, Mary sang out, "My soul magnifies the Lord, and my spirit rejoices in God my Savior."[11]

On the eve of the Messiah's birth, Luke tells us that shepherds, watching over their flocks nearby, were hailed by a host of angels:

> "Be not afraid; for behold, I bring you good news of a great joy which will come to all the people; for to you is born this day in the city of David a Savior, who is Christ the Lord. . . ." And suddenly there was with the angel a multitude of the heavenly host praising God and saying, "Glory to God in the highest, and on earth peace among men with whom he is pleased." (Luke 2:10-14)

If all we knew about the Christ at this point were the words of those who heralded his coming, we would expect joy to feature prominently in the story. In fact, this is exactly what we find.

THE MESSIAH AND HIS FORERUNNER

In some ways Jesus was like John the Baptist. Like John, he emerged from a wilderness experience to begin his public ministry.[12] Like John, he abstained from marriage to fulfill God's calling in his life. Like John, he proclaimed the Gospel of the Kingdom to the multitudes. Like John, he urged baptism and repentance in view of what God was doing in history. Like John he was a popular but controversial figure who stood the religious establishment on its head, challenged the rulers of his day, and met a violent death for doing so.

The similarities end there, however. In fact, the personal differences between John and Jesus are striking. John was known to his contemporaries as a stern prophet, a dour and abstemious character who gathered followers cut from the same camel skin cloth. Not so, Jesus.[13] His enemies found fault with him for being a "glutton and a drunkard."[14] He was neither, of course. It is worth noting, however, that despite the acrimony and exaggeration in the accusation, the Gospels make no attempt to refute or even mute the charge. Jesus was not like his forerunner in this respect. Anyone who knew Jesus knew that he enjoyed the pleasures of food and drink, and enjoyed them even more in the company of others:

> To what then shall I compare the men of this generation, and what are they like? They are like children sitting in the market place and calling to one another, "We piped to you, and you did not dance; we wailed, and you did not weep." For John the Baptist has come eating no bread and drinking no wine; and you say, "He has a demon." The Son of man has come eating and drinking; and you say, "Behold, a glutton and a drunkard, a friend of tax collectors and sinners!" Yet wisdom is justified by all her children. (Luke 7:31-35)

John's disciples fasted regularly as part of their religious devotion. The disciples of Jesus did not. This dissimilarity in discipleship caught the attention of Jesus' contemporaries, who queried him on the matter. Jesus explained, "Can the wedding guests fast while the bridegroom is with them? As long as they have the bridegroom with them, they cannot fast."[15] To do so, he went on, would be like sewing a piece of unshrunk cloth on an old garment, or putting new wine into old wineskins. The incongruity should have been obvious, if only his questioners had known who he was: the Son of God among the sons of Adam and the daughters of Eve. This ought to have occasioned merrymaking, not misery. Happiness, not hunger. The gaiety of full hearts, not the groans of empty stomachs. His ministry was to be characterized by joy. It was to be distinguished by its air of celebration. His disciples were to be known for their festive spirit, not for their fasting, however much this may have set them apart from their religious contemporaries.

Not that Jesus was against refraining from food for spiritual purposes. He fasted at great length before entering his public ministry.[16] He was, however, opposed to the sullen piety it often engendered. Unlike the Pharisees, his disciples were not to make themselves look dismal during their fast. Jesus instructed them to wash their faces and anoint themselves with oil. Even in their discomfort they were to greet others in a way that reflected their joy.[17] As one New Testament scholar put it, "What Jesus in fact wanted was not to revive penitential practices wherever he went, but to spread joy."[18]

JOY IN THE PUBLIC MINISTRY OF JESUS

Jesus claimed that he was the fulfillment of this ancient prophecy:

> The Spirit of the LORD GOD is upon me,
> because the LORD has anointed me
> to bring good tidings to the afflicted;
> he has sent me to bind up the brokenhearted,
> to proclaim liberty to the captives,
> and the opening of the prison to those who are bound;
> to proclaim the year of the LORD's favor, . . .
> to comfort all who mourn;

to grant to those who mourn in Zion –
  to give them a garland instead of ashes,
    the oil of gladness instead of mourning,
  the mantle of praise instead of a faint spirit. (Isaiah 61:1-3; cf. Luke 4:18-19)

What kind of man brings glad tidings to the afflicted, binds up the brokenhearted, opens prison doors, proclaims liberty to captives, comforts those who mourn, strengthens faint spirits, anoints people with the oil of gladness, adorns them with garlands of joy, and clothes them with a mantle of praise? Words like *vitality*, *spiritual robustness*, *courage*, *compassion*, and *joy* come to mind. The prophecy tells us much about the One who would bring its fulfillment – the way he would live before God and among people in desperate need.

When early followers of Jesus told his story, it was not his teaching that came first in their tale, but his ministry of healing.[19] Even if people didn't know what the Rabbi from Galilee taught, they knew that the lives of many had been changed by his restoring touch. Imagine the settings in which these miracles took place. Imagine misery – not momentary, but prolonged, perhaps even for years. Picture pain, suffering, sorrow, the burden of handicaps, the shame of public ridicule, the stares of small-hearted people, the loss of opportunities, oppressive limitations. And then everything changes. Dramatically. Bent bones straighten. Paralyzed muscles flex and move. Unhearing ears hear. Blind eyes see. Diseased skin becomes whole. Now imagine running, jumping, dancing, laughter – gales of laughter – singing, and merriment, and Jesus joining in. Scenes like these played out wherever he went. They should shape our understanding of the kind of man he was.

Jesus once said to a crowd of people, "The Son of man has come eating and drinking; and you say, 'Behold, a glutton and a drunkard, a friend of tax collectors and sinners!'"[20] Whatever else we may say about Jesus, he was no hermit. No one who knew him would have called him an ascetic. He enjoyed the pleasures of creation and the company of others – even those whom the religious establishment considered an unsavory sort. Tax collectors and sinners held the solemn, straightjacketed piety of the Pharisees in disdain. What kind of man would be welcomed in their presence and invited to their gatherings?[21] Not a man of sorrows. Not a wet blanket. Not a spoilsport. Not that he participated in everything that likely occurred at the parties he attended. He was never out of step with the Father's will. Yet this dimension of his life tells us a great deal about the kind of person he must have been. We are compelled to think of him as someone who was attractive to people who had little time for, and less interest in, the somber etiquette of the Pharisees. He was known for his gaiety and gladness of heart, and for his celebration of life with all who would join him. New Testament scholar, Scot McKnight, describes him as a "festive kind of guy."[22] A festive kind of guy!

Children were drawn to Jesus. What does this tell us about him? Little ones sensed in him a kindred spirit. He felt the same toward them.[23] Children would never have been attracted to a man stricken with grief and burdened with sorrow. Gentleness and playfulness are the keys to winning their hearts. They must have seen both in Jesus. The magnetism of Jesus with children was his joy: the inviting sparkle in his eyes that said to them, "Let's play! Let's run and jump and clap our hands and thank the Father for our fun!"

The playful joy of Jesus whispers to us in his interest in children, but speaks in a fuller voice in his relationship with the disciples. There is fun in the nicknames he gave them. The sons of Zebedee were known for a zeal that was often colored by their natural bluster. It was James and John who were prepared to "send down fire from heaven" against the village that had rejected Jesus.[24] Jesus gave them the playful moniker, "sons of thunder."[25]

Or there is Simon, who was nicknamed "Peter" by Jesus. EltonTrueblood wrote:

> Peter got his nickname when, in the district of Caesarea Philippi, he achieved, suddenly, the tremendous insight concerning who his Leader was. Even on this solemn occasion Christ proved that He could joke and He did so by giving Simon the fisherman the most improbable of nicknames. In our terminology, He called the fellow "Rocky" and the name stuck. The paradox is obvious, for Simon was anything but stable or durable, which is what rocky things are supposed to be.
>
> If this was the "Rock" on which the redemptive fellowship had to be built, it certainly seemed to be a shaky foundation. The house was obviously being built on sand, at best, and how, from such an infirm base, would it be possible to penetrate the very gates of hell? Here is paradox on paradox, yet it was more than a joke, though it *was* a joke. Jesus saw more in Simon and the other inadequate men than met the eye. The humorous nickname "Rocky" was a prediction of future stability, even though, at the time, it was patently absurd. At the moment, it must have seemed like our practice of calling the fat man "Slim" and the tall man "Shorty."[26]

In *The Humor of Christ,* Trueblood lists thirty humorous passages in Jesus' encounters with people. [27] There are probably several reasons why contemporary readers miss this dimension of Jesus' ministry. Some puns are lost in the process of translation from Aramaic to Greek to English. More to blame is our familiarity with the Gospels and the cultural image of Christ we bring to the text. We don't expect to find humor in the words of Jesus, and so we don't see it. But it is there. Jesus made others smile and laugh and was the kind of person who delighted in both.

JOY IN THE PASSION WEEK

The joy of Jesus was indomitable, even in the face of ridicule and suffering. When he invited his followers to find joy even in these harsh realities of life,[28] he spoke from his own experience. Strikingly, in fact, it was as he walked through the events that would end in his death that Jesus spoke most of his joy.[29] It is here that his joy comes most clearly into focus.

Jesus entered the Holy City in a great celebration, with throngs of people lining the street, hailing him as the Messiah. How different things were just days later! The curtains lifted on the final act in the drama of redemption. In a small gathering with his friends, knowing that the week would end in his death, Jesus revealed his heart, "Now is my soul troubled."[30] His joy was not a Stoic tranquility shaped by disciplined disengagement from the world! He was fully engaged, every fiber of his being sensitized to the perilous climax of his mission. This soul-trouble will occur again in the upper room and yet again in the garden of Gethsemane.

Without any hint of theological embarrassment (but true to the Gospel narratives), Jonathan Edwards spoke of Jesus' struggle of affections:

> He was the greatest instance of ardency, vigor and strength of love, to both God and man, that ever was. It was these affections which got the victory, in that mighty struggle and conflict of his affections, in his agonies, when he prayed more earnestly, and offered strong cryings and tears, and wrestled in tears and blood.[31]

As we watch this struggle unfold, we see a pattern: Moments of emotional dissonance are resolved in a deeper harmony of joy as Jesus embraces the will of his Father and commits himself to the Father's glory.

The first occasion of his soul-trouble is recorded in John 12:27-28, "Now is my soul troubled. And what shall I say? 'Father, save me from this hour?' No, for this purpose I have come to this hour." His focus shifts from his own distress to the completion of his messianic task, now drawing near. His inner turmoil gives way to the greater goal of his mission, and the greater issue of the glory of God. He consecrates himself with the prayer, "Father, glorify your name."

This pattern of inner turmoil giving way to the Father's glory is repeated in the upper room. Jesus has just washed the feet of his disciples and urged them to follow his example. Judas Iscariot, he knows, will not. After Jesus predicts the treachery of his friend, we are given another glimpse into his inner life, "After saying these things, Jesus was troubled in his spirit."[32] He is troubled by the faithlessness of a friend. He is stung by betrayal. Yet, after Judas departs, triggering a series of prophetic events, Jesus once again turns his focus to the glory of God: "When he had gone out, Jesus said, 'Now is the Son of man glorified, and in him God is glorified; if God is glorified in him, God will also glorify him in himself, and glorify him at once.'"[33]

Joy begins to dispel the darkness of the hour. Moments later Jesus says to his disheartened disciples: "Let not your hearts be troubled."[34] His commitment to the Father's will and the Father's glory has conquered the trouble of his own heart, and he is able in this resolve to encourage his followers, upon whom the realization is now dawning that this trip to Jerusalem will end not with a coronation, but a cross.

In this struggle of affections Jesus has gained the high ground. His focus is not on the trouble of his own soul, but on the glory of God: what that meant for him, and what it would mean for his disciples. He talks about obedience: his in his relationship to the Father, and theirs in their relationship with him. And he talks about joy: his own, and theirs, as they give themselves fully to him:

> By this is my Father glorified, that you bear much fruit, and so prove to be my disciples. As the Father has loved me, so have I loved you; abide in my love. If you keep my commandments, you will abide in my love, just as I have kept my Father's commandments and abide in his love. These things I have spoken to you, that my joy may be in you, and that your joy may be full. (John 15:8-11)

In a world filled with danger for those who followed him, this joy would find its source in his own triumphant joy: "In the world you have tribulation; but be of good cheer, I have overcome the world."[35]

In the next recorded scene we find Jesus praying: “Father, the hour has come; glorify your Son that the Son may glorify you. . . . I glorified you on earth, having accomplished the work that you gave me to do. And now, Father, glorify me in your own presence with the glory which I had with you before the world existed.”[36] He focuses again on the glory of the Father, and shortly after we find him speaking of his joy and the joy of those who followed him, "But now I am coming to you; and I speak these things in the world so that they may have my joy made complete in themselves."[37]

With this we come to the final move in the thrust and parry of spiritual battle as Jesus faces the horrors of the Cross. Matthew, Mark, and Luke record the memories of the innermost circle of apostles of Jesus’ prayer in Gethsemane. Just before this prayer he is deeply distressed. His voice trembles with words that they would long remember, "My soul is very sorrowful, even to death."[38] He enters into earnest prayer, with tears of agony as he looks death in the face, and considers the prospect of enduring it alone, without his familiar and cherished intimacy with the Father.

There is great pathos and poignancy here. But no one who knows this prayer can forget that it ended far from where it began, in a calmed, ready submission to the Father's will. "Yet not what I want, but what you want.”

From this point on we see nothing but determination and courage on the part of Jesus. As the scenes play out there is no focus on his plight. No struggle with his emotions. He gives not an inch to his accusers and assassins. They take nothing that he does not willingly give. They do nothing without his sovereign permission as he yields to the Father's will and seeks the Father's glory. Even as he hangs by nails piercing his flesh, he encourages the penitent thief beside him, whose life is ending with excruciating pain: "Be of good cheer!"[39]

This triumphant joy was so striking that it lived on in the memory of those who knew him. They passed the story to the next generation of Jesus-followers, and in doing so left it for us: "Let us run with perseverance the race that is set before us, looking to Jesus the pioneer and perfecter of our faith, who for the joy that was set before him endured the cross, despising the shame, and is seated at the right hand of the throne of God."[40]

JOY IN THE TEACHING OF JESUS

As he came to the end of his ministry and his departure from the little band of followers who would carry on the mission of the Kingdom, Jesus focused on the things that would be most important for them to remember. Twice in the Gospel of John he summarized the purpose of his teaching, bringing the entire body of his instruction into the clearest possible focus. The first of these summary statements comes in his discourse on the vine and the branches, "If you keep my commandments, you will abide in my love, just as I have kept my Father's commandments and abide in his love. *These things I have spoken to you that my joy may be in you, and that your joy may be full.*"[41]

His second summary parallels the first. It appears in Jesus' intercessory prayer in John 17:13-14, "But now I am coming to you; and *I speak these words in the world so that they may have my joy made complete in themselves.* I have given them your word."[42] Here again he says that the words he had given to them (i.e., the whole body of his teaching) faithfully reflected the word given to him by the Father. Here again we see the unity and purpose of his teaching: the fulfillment of his disciples' joy.

If we read the Gospels with anything other than joy in mind, we are misreading them according to Jesus' own words. They are meant to bring joy. They are meant to delight our hearts. This is the "light yoke" that Jesus spoke of. It is the "abundant life" he came to give.[43] Miss this and you will miss the whole point of his teaching. Miss this and you will miss the centerpiece of what it means to be his disciple.

Recovering the good news. When Jesus began his public ministry, he traveled through the land proclaiming the *Gospel of the Kingdom*: the good news that the reign of God was breaking into history in his own words and deeds:

> And he went throughout all Galilee, teaching in their synagogues and proclaiming the gospel of the kingdom and healing every disease and every affliction among the people. (Matthew 4:23)
>
> And Jesus went throughout all the cities and villages, teaching in their synagogues and proclaiming the gospel of the kingdom and healing every disease and every affliction. (Matthew 9:35)
>
> Now after John was arrested, Jesus came into Galilee, preaching the gospel of God, and saying, "The time is fulfilled, and the kingdom of God is at hand; repent, and believe in the gospel." (Mark 1:14-15)

The word "gospel" has become so entrenched in religious tradition that its original meaning has been all but lost to us. We need to hear again (possibly for the first time) that it is about "glad tidings, good news, welcome information, a shout, or something that makes one sing and talk and rejoice."[44] It is "good news of a great joy."[45] This is what characterized the message and ministry of Jesus. Wherever he went, he heralded the Kingdom. He proclaimed its boon, of greater worth than anything we possess. This is the way he described it: "The kingdom of heaven is like treasure hidden in a field, which a man found and covered up; then *in his joy* he goes and sells all that he has and buys that field."[46]

Nor should we see this joy diminished because the Gospel that Jesus preached requires repentance. "The time is fulfilled, and the kingdom of God is at hand; repent, and believe in the gospel."[47] It is possible to think of repentance as a sullen and tearful response to one's past. Many people do. Jesus did not. He told a trilogy of parables about repentance. The first was about a lost sheep,[48] the second about a lost coin,[49] and the third about a lost son.[50] The first two focus on the joy of God over a sinner's repentance. The third parable does, too, but explores the nature of repentance from the sinner's side. We know this as the parable of the prodigal son.

A young man sins against his father to his own injury. He is reduced to poverty of the most demeaning kind after squandering his inheritance in loose living. At length he becomes aware of his sin before heaven and is prepared to confess it to his father.[51] There is no repentance without this. But there is another dimension: the anticipation of his father's goodness. "How many of my father's hired servants have bread enough and to spare, but I perish here with hunger!"[52] He is certain that if he returns to his father, he will be received and cared for. His repentance includes *turning from* his sin and *turning to* the generosity of his father, even the servants of whom enjoy plenty. His repentance is then joyfully consummated in a feast filled with gifts, dancing, gladness and merrymaking. The father (who stands for God in the story) explains, "*But we had to be merry and rejoice*, for this brother of yours was dead and has begun to live, and was lost and has been found."[53]

For Jesus, spiritual life begins when we exchange the sorrow of sin for the joy of salvation. Those who experience this joy discover the blessings of God's Kingdom and treasure them more than any earthly possession.[54] Like Zacchaeus, they welcome Jesus with joy, and gladly embrace the transformation he brings to their lives:

> So he made haste and came down, and received him joyfully. And when they saw it they all murmured, "He has gone in to be the guest of a man who is a sinner." And Zacchaeus stood and said to the Lord, "Behold, Lord, the half of my goods I give to the poor; and if I have defrauded any one of anything, I restore it fourfold." And Jesus said to him, "Today salvation has come to this house, since he also is a son of Abraham. For the Son of man came to seek and to save the lost." (Luke 19:6-10) [55]

In the teaching of Jesus, life with God begins with joy and ends there, as well. If hell is a place of "weeping and gnashing of teeth,"[56] a place of ultimate sorrow and grief, heaven is a place of sheer and unimaginable bliss. Those who cross that threshold enter into the joy of their Master.[57] As someone from another country might describe her homeland to one who had never been there by using familiar analogies, Jesus taught that heaven is more like the merriment of a marriage banquet than anything else we know.[58]

Happy are those! The teaching of Jesus was punctuated with exclamations we have come to call "beatitudes."[59] He would focus on a character quality, or a dimension of living well before God, and then say, "Blessed are those" who know this to be true in their own lives. In Greek, the word of blessing is *makarios*. It is an important word in the vocabulary of happiness.[60] A.M. Hunter wrote, "'Blessed' means 'Ah, the happiness of,' and beatitude is the happiness of the man who, in communion with God, lives the life that is life indeed."[61]

The beatitudes are collected in sermons in the Gospels of Matthew and Luke,[62] and were no doubt featured in Jesus' teaching whenever crowds gathered. It is probably also true that they found their way into many conversations and teachable moments with his disciples. Jesus spoke often of a blessed, happy life.[63]

When Jesus called the poor in spirit "blessed," he was not merely saying that God commends this trait. Poverty of spirit and the riches of joy are companions of the heart. When our vessel is empty we are in a position to be filled. When Jesus pronounced the meek "blessed," he was not merely saying that God endorses this quality in us. There is a spiritual truth here: In meekness we discover the majesty of God. Our meekness enables us to rejoice in his greatness. These virtues are not ends in themselves; they position our hearts before God so that we can receive and delight in the blessings he gives. When Jesus blessed the meek and the poor in spirit, he had in mind the prophet's promise of joy:

> The meek shall obtain fresh joy in the LORD,
> and the poor among men shall exult in the Holy One of Israel.
> (Isaiah 29:19)

The beatitudes of Jesus include the way we view ourselves before God,[64] our posture before others,[65] our pursuit of righteousness,[66] the way we treat people who are in need,[67] a compassionate use of our resources,[68] the way we face opposition and difficulties in life,[69] living unashamed of Christ,[70] and knowing and doing the will of God.[71] People who walk the path of blessing flourish joyfully in life.

THE JOY OF JESUS

We might miss this centerpiece in the life and teaching of Jesus. We might fall short of the great pleasure he knew in life and wanted for his followers. We might wander from its path. We might fail to plumb its depths, scale its heights, or slake our thirst in its liquid refreshment. If we do so, we may not, however, lay the deficiency at his feet. Jesus modeled the greatest of all joys, taught it, and offers it to all who will follow him in the path he knew so well. Peter Kreeft was right:

> The man who said he was God also said he was our joy. If this claim is not true, it is the most blasphemous, egotistical, and insane thing ever spoken by human lips. If it is true, then God's single gift for all our desires is his Son. He *is* joy, joy alive and wearing a real human face.[72]

The most significant thing that I can do is to direct the longings of your heart to him.

Questions for Thought and Discussion

1. Before you read this chapter, how did you imagine Jesus? Did you see him as a joyful person? If not, what do you think influenced your image of him?

2. As you re-think the Gospels with joy in mind, do you see things you hadn't seen before?

3. What difference does the social life of Jesus make for your understanding of holiness?

4. Now that you have read this chapter, would you describe your understanding of piety as being closer to John the Baptist, the Pharisees, or a joyful Jesus?

5. What difference does joy make in the way you understand the teaching of Jesus?

Chapter 6

The Joyful Spirit

A Trinitarian Perspective

The Trinity will always be a mystery to us. It is beyond the reach of our undersized understanding. We attempt to formulate it, though we cannot fathom it. We confess it, though we don't fully comprehend it. We include it in our creeds, though we cannot frame an image of it in our minds. We celebrate it in our hymns, but with the humble recognition that we never wholly capture its truth.

In the word *Trinitas*[1] Christians affirm that there is one God, but this is not a strict mathematical unity. Within the oneness of God we are compelled from the witness of Scripture (confirmed by centuries of worship) to recognize three personal distinctions, between Father, Son, and Holy Spirit. They are not three different ways or modes in which the one God reveals himself to the world. Nor are they three Gods. They represent a Trinity of Persons within the singular essence of the living and true God. This is what Christians believe, but do not pretend fully to understand.

To the extent that the Trinity is an enigma, it is safe from my study. I will attempt no ascent of its shrouded peaks. With Calvin I wish to avoid any "subtle prying into a sublime mystery." With him I wish only to learn "what is useful to be known."[2]

In search of an analogy. As a university student thinking seriously about God for the first time, I encountered C.S. Lewis' geometric analogy of the Trinity:

> In God's dimension, so to speak, you find a being who is three Persons while remaining one Being, just as a cube is six squares while remaining one cube. Of course we cannot fully conceive a Being like that: just as, if we were so made that we perceived only two dimensions in space we could never properly imagine a cube. But we can get a sort of faint notion of it. And when we do, we are then, for the first time in our lives, getting some positive idea, however faint, of something super-personal – something more than a person. It is something we could never have guessed, and yet, once we have been told, one almost feels one ought to have been able to guess it because it fits in so well with all the things we know already.[3]

While I found this helpful at that point in my life, it does not do justice to Lewis' belief that the Triune nature of God is something we encounter in Christian experience, and that the goal of our theology is "being actually drawn into that three-personal life."[4] Geometry cannot help us here.

Closer to our experience, and more profound, is Dorothy Sayer's reflection upon human creativity:

> The Christian affirmation is . . . that the Trinitarian structure which can be shown to exist in the mind of man and in all his works is, in fact, the integral structure of the universe, and

> corresponds, not by pictorial imagery but by a necessary uniformity of substance, with the nature of God, in Whom all that is exists.[5]

Every work of creativity, according to Sayers, is an earthly trinity matching the heavenly. The image of the Father is seen in the Creative Idea, "passionless, timeless, beholding the whole work complete at once, the end in the beginning." The image of the Son is present in the Creative Energy or Activity "begotten of that idea, working in time from the beginning to the end, with sweat and passion, being incarnate in the bonds of matter." The image of the Spirit can be seen in the Creative Power, "the meaning of the work and its response in the lively soul."[6]

Closer still to our experience, and more fruitful as a result, is Augustine's analogy from love. Love is three-faceted, he says. There is always a lover, a beloved, and love itself.[7] In Trinitarian terms, the Father is the Lover, the Son is the Beloved, and the Holy Spirit is the Love shared between the Father and the Son. For Augustine, love implies a Trinity.[8] If love is ultimate, there must be a personal God, since only persons can love. If God is love,[9] we are compelled by the nature of love to posit a personal distinction in the divine life, between Lover and Beloved.[10] Add the bond of Love itself and the Trinity is faintly illumined against the landscape of our experience.[11]

Not only does this have the stamp of experience, it has the warrant of Scripture. There we discover that God is love,[12] that the Son is the Beloved of the Father,[13] and that the Spirit is the agent of God's love in human hearts.[14] This is a helpful way of approaching this high mystery. We encounter this love in spiritual experience. We are drawn into its Trinitarian dimension in all true Christian living.

Joy, too, can help us understand God in a Trinitarian way. The Father is the joyful One, the Source of all joy. The Son is the One in whom the Father delights. The Spirit is the Joy shared between the Father and the Son. He is "the *ecstasy of the divine life*, the bond of love in the Trinity."[15] We see this pattern in the Scriptures, as well: The Father gifts the Son with joy,[16] the Son is the delight of the Father,[17] and the Son rejoices in the Spirit.[18] Our joy is a connection with the relational joy of God. It is a participation in this joy. We are drawn into this joy in a Godward life.

Theological pedigree. If novelty in theology is usually another name for heresy, allow me to allay any fears you might have. If this is the first time for you to entertain such ideas about God, let me give you a glimpse of their rich history. Drawing upon the work of Hilary, the fourth century bishop of Poitiers, Augustine wrote:

> Therefore that unspeakable conjunction of the Father and His image [the Son] is not without fruition, without love, without joy. Therefore that love, delight, felicity, or blessedness, if indeed it can be worthily expressed by any human word . . . is the Holy Spirit in the Trinity, not begotten, but the sweetness of the begetter and of the begotten, filling all creatures according to their capacity with abundant bountifulness.[19]

Philip Melanchthon, Luther's comrade in the Protestant Reformation, and considered by some to be the greatest Lutheran theologian of all times, wrote:

> The third person in the divine Being is called the Holy Spirit . . . who proceeds from the Father and the Son, and essentially is the love and joy, like a flame, in the Father for the Son and in the Son for the Father. And he is revealed to us as the person who is sent into the hearts of the faithful to sanctify them, to kindle joy and love of God.

> The Father is the procreator, the Son is begotten of the Father and out of the Father's being . . . the essential and full Image of the Father. The Holy Spirit proceeds from the Father and Son and is the love and joy in the Father and Son. . . . The particular work of

> the Holy Spirit is to strengthen us in heartfelt joy and love toward God. . . . Through the Holy Spirit we feel joy, know that we live in grace.[20]

In the late seventeenth century, Anglican Bishop George Bull wrote that since God is characterized by "self-sufficiency and most perfect bliss and happiness in himself alone, before and without all created things . . . it plainly appears, that himself alone is a most perfect society, the Father, the Son, and the Spirit eternally conversing with and enjoying one another."[21]

In the eighteenth century Jonathan Edwards wrote:

> So the Holy Spirit does in some ineffable and inconceivable manner proceed, and is breathed forth both from the Father and the Son, by the Divine essence being wholly poured and flowing out in *that infinitely intense, holy and pure love and delight that continually and unchangeably breathes forth from the Father and the Son*, primarily towards each other, and secondarily towards the creature, and so flowing forth in a different subsistence or person in a manner to us utterly inexplicable and inconceivable, and that this is that person that is poured forth into the hearts of angels and saints.[22]

The Holy Spirit is the Joy of the Father in the Son, the Joy of the Son in the Father, and the overflow of their Joy that splashes and soaks angels and mortals alike!

THE JOYFUL SPIRIT AND CHRISTIAN EXPERIENCE

Whatever you think about this way of understanding the Trinity, it is clear from the Bible that there is an essential connection between the Spirit and joy. Let's explore this.

The Christian life is life in the Spirit. He is the tacit presence of God in the world.[23] He is the wind of God, creating and renewing life.[24] He is the indwelling one, turning unresponsive hearts of stone into hearts of flesh, alive, awake and sensitive to the will of God.[25] He is the holy fire that purges sin and kindles courage in the human spirit.[26] He is the heavenly rain, poured out upon God's people, transforming all upon whom he falls.[27] He is the living water welling up and overflowing in the heart of those who believe.[28] He is the agent of spiritual birth and the dynamic of spiritual life.[29] He is the garment of power from on high.[30] He is the presence of the Incarnate One in the mode of spirit, freeing, guiding, teaching and revealing.[31]

In the stories of the early Church there is an unbreakable link between the Spirit and the joy of those who followed Jesus. He is the genesis of joy, its creative agent, its catalyst. The disciples were filled "with joy and with the Holy Spirit."[32] They knew that their joy was inspired by the Holy Spirit.[33] It was a fruit of the Spirit's presence in their lives. They saw joy in the Spirit as a token of God's Kingdom among them.[34] Even when they were persecuted for bearing the name of Christ, they rejoiced, not only because this marked their union with him, and secured a future joy with him, but because the Spirit of God rested upon them.[35]

We are not in a position to appreciate the role of the Spirit in our joy as the ancients would have. When the early Church taught that the Spirit of God was the agent of its joy, it heralded a monumental message to its contemporaries.[36] In the first century Greek-speaking world, happiness was thought to be the influence of a "good demon" in a person's life.[37] The demonic was not strictly evil, as it was in Christianity. Demons were thought to be spirits: intermediaries between humans on one side, and the gods and the Supreme Deity on the other.[38] To have the fortune of a benign spirit, or demon, in one's life was the key to happiness. Plutarch, the Greek historian who wrote during the time in which the New Testament was taking shape, said, "The words of the daemons are borne through all things, but they sound only for those who have the untroubled nature and the still soul – those, in fact, whom we call holy and happy."[39]

For Calvin, this would have been a sinful corruption of the truth.[40] C.S. Lewis would have seen it as a "good dream" given by God to the pagan world, waiting to be fulfilled by the Christian faith.[41] In either case, the pagan world was right in perceiving the spiritual dimension of happiness, but wrong in not seeking it in the Spirit of the Most High God. What the ancient world longed for in the experience of happiness, Christianity possessed in the many-faceted pleasures of joy. What its pagan contemporaries sought vainly in finite spirits, the Church knew richly and deeply in the Joyful Spirit of the Infinite God.

Christianity conquered its pagan rivals.[42] Its power to transform lives vanquished its foes. Its alluring taste to the soul made everything else seem insipid. The beggarly spirits of paganism gave way before the imperial Spirit of the true God. The meager morsels they paraded as spiritual food were swept under the table like so many crumbs, as thousands upon thousands crowded the burgeoning ranks of the early Christian movement to enjoy the exquisite, bountiful and soul-satisfying feast of the Spirit of the Living God. A feast to which we have been invited.

Questions for Thought and Discussion

1. In what ways have you attempted to understand the Trinity in the past? What analogies have been fruitful? Which have not been?

2. Have you tended to view the Trinity as something that is hopelessly abstract, or something that can touch your actual experience in life? Do you see this as something significant or secondary? Why?

3. How do the analogies of love and joy change the way you think of a Triune God?

4. How does your understanding of the Spirit as the agent of joy in the Trinity (in Edwards' words, "that infinitely intense, holy and pure love and delight that continually and unchangeably breathes forth from the Father and the Son) affect your understanding of joy as a fruit of the Spirit in your own life?

5. How do you think joy and the Spirit might be relevant to quests for spirituality among your friends and peers? With the American "pursuit of happiness"?

Part Three

The Ethics of Joy

CHAPTER 7

THE JOYFUL HEART

If we give an account of a life that is pleasing to God, how do our hearts fit into the accounting? For many, God's moral design boils down to this: He gives us commands; it is our duty to obey them.[1] In this understanding, God is mostly concerned about regulating our behavior, which he does through laws. The Christian life is a rule-oriented project, and Christian ethics, the task of creating a system of rules and resolving dilemmas that arise when rules seem to conflict.

I cut my teeth in that tradition, but I've come to believe that its problems are not few. It is true that commands must be included in our moral reckoning. Again and again in the biblical narrative God makes demands of his people and expects them to obey. But there is much more to the story. God is not interested in obedience alone, but in the quality of our obedience. The Bible has much to say about the moral agents who are expected to obey commands: their desires, values, motivations, dispositions, and character traits. "Oh, that their hearts would be inclined to fear me and keep all my commands always!"[2] God cares about the inclination of our hearts in obedience, and not mere compliance.

Rules point us to actions that are right and wrong, but the Scriptures evaluate our moral life in other ways, as well. We can be good or evil, just or unjust, righteous or unrighteous, wise or foolish, responsible or irresponsible, courageous or cowardly. We can be worthy or unworthy, commendable, lamentable, or deplorable. Our values, decisions, and actions can be good, better, or best, or bad, worse, or worst of all. Rules by themselves fail to capture these dimensions of a moral life. It is like looking at a two-dimensional black and white picture, and then walking into the same scene in a three-dimensional world of color, texture, fragrance, taste, and sound.

Giving priority to commands and our duty to obey them assumes that we can do what is right merely by being told what it is.[3] But we never act in a moral vacuum. Who we are in this moment is who we have become. We make decisions and our decisions make us. The choices we are likely to make now are shaped by all the choices that have brought us to this point. We reap what we have sown.[4] We are not prisoners to our past, but we live in the house that we have built and sleep in the bed that we have made.

Our actions are not only shaped by our moral history, but by our present values, beliefs, and affections.[5] What we do outwardly reflects who we are within. In the words of Jesus, "Every good tree bears good fruit, but a bad tree bears bad fruit. A good tree cannot bear bad fruit, and a bad tree cannot bear good fruit"[6] What we do characteristically flows from who we are. The order is important. It is true to life as God has designed it.

It is possible to do the right thing (publicly) for the wrong reasons (privately), and this is important to God. Ask Ananias and Sapphira![7] Their gift from the sale of their land, which helped to meet the needs of a fledgling Christian community, was a good thing. But they did it not so much to give as to receive. Their motive wasn't neighbor-love, but self-love. It was not inspired by a generous spirit but by envy of the praise that others received for their generosity. Praying is a good thing, but not when it is done to catch the eyes and ears of others,[8] or when it is pursued as a means to a selfish end.[9] Giving alms is a good thing, but not if it is done to be seen and to be praised.[10] Sharing the good news about Jesus is a good thing, but not when it is motivated by envy[11] or a desire for dishonest gain.[12] The heart-factor in our actions qualifies or disqualifies them in the sight of God.

Jesus said that it is a mistake to congratulate ourselves for not breaking a command outwardly if we ignore the intent of the command and its implications for our inner life. The Torah readers of his day knew that adultery was wrong. According to Jesus, what takes place in a lustful heart is kin to that sin.[13] They knew that murder was wrong. Jesus taught them that an angry, hateful heart shares in murder's violent nature.[14] There is a world inside us that is important to our life before God.

It is possible to comply outwardly with God's commands and yet be miles from what he is truly looking for. This was Jesus' complaint against some of the Pharisees of his day. After critiquing the priority they had given to their tradition of rules, he invoked the word of God given through the prophet Isaiah, "The Lord says, 'These people come near to me with their mouth and honor me with their lips, but their hearts are far from me.'"[15] The distance of our hearts from God's is what matters most to him.

THE HEART OF THE MATTER

The heart of the matter is that your heart matters. Your heart is the innermost dimension of who you are. It is the sacred center of your being. It is the place where you think and feel and choose before anyone else ever knows. It's the secret place within, where your values are forged, your priorities are shaped, and your decisions are made.[16]

Your heart is the place where you carry on a constant dialogue. We laugh at people whose inner conversation comes out as they walk down the sidewalk or stand on a street corner. Their lips move. They may even speak out loud and wave their arms and shake their fists, with no one but amused spectators in their audience. But here is the truth: We all talk to ourselves. It's just that most of the time our inner dialogue is hidden to everyone else.

Imagine that we could see a transcript of your heart-talk for a day. A written record of every word, thought, and expression of emotion, from the moment you first realized you were awake until you fell asleep at night. There it is, laid out in one long report. If we had a transcript of this inner dialogue, it would tell us much about your heart. It would be like taking a spiritual X-ray.

I'm glad that you don't know my heart; you are probably relieved that I don't know yours. Ah, but there is One who knows every heart![17] There is One who reads the transcript of your heart-talk and mine every day. The One before whom there are no secrets. The One with whom we have to do, before whom all things are open and laid bare.[18] We may content ourselves with outward compliance with rules, and even think ourselves obedient to God's commands when we do; however, "The LORD does not see as mortals see; they look on the outward appearance, but the LORD looks on the heart."[19] He "searches the heart."[20] He discerns our thoughts "from far away." He knows fully the words that are framed within us before they find their way to our tongues.[21]

The life that is pleasing to God begins within. Deep within, with our thoughts and inclinations, our values and priorities, our hopes and our fears, our secret dreams and aspirations, the things we desire and the things we dread. These inner realities shape the moral quality of our lives. Your heart is the deep fountain from which everything else in your life flows. Solomon wisely wrote, "Above all else, guard your heart, for it is the wellspring of life."[22]

RETHINKING OUR EMOTIONS

In the view of some, emotions belong in the same category as hunger, thirst, and full bladders. The eighteenth century German philosopher, Immanuel Kant, is representative of people who think this way. For Kant, emotions are distinct from our cognitive faculties. They are part of our nature that we share with the animal world. Emotions are impulsive, capricious, and unreliable.[23] They belong to the same group as bodily sensations and even bodily illnesses. On this reckoning, emotions are irrelevant to the moral dimensions of life.

Is this an accurate appraisal of our emotions? I don't think so. Upon closer inspection, emotions are much more than feelings tethered to physical states. Emotions are an intricate fabric, woven from threads of beliefs, feelings, and desires.[24] If I love others I believe that it is good for them to be alive,[25] I experience feelings of warmth and pleasure toward them, and I desire to be with them and to contribute to their well-being. If I am jealous, I believe that my entitlement to the affection of another has been violated, I experience feelings of resentment, and I desire to prevent him from continuing to undermine my rights. If I am anxious, I believe that my future may be imperiled by something over which I have little or no control, I experience feelings of agitation and apprehension, and I desire to avoid or gain control over the uncertainties I envision.

Some emotions take shape so swiftly that we are unaware of the dynamics that create them. They seem seamless. Fear and anger are good examples. They can emerge so quickly that we might not be aware of the beliefs and desires that are involved. If I experience the emotion of fear, I believe that my well-being is threatened, my heart races, I may experience a rush of adrenaline, and I have a strong desire to flee. All of this can happen in a split second. If I experience the emotion of anger, I believe that I have been wronged in some way, I am gripped by painful feelings, and I desire to even the score. The process can be lightning-fast. Emotions like these may not be reflective or deliberative in the same way that other emotions are, but they follow the same pattern.[26] We can have second thoughts about them later only because we had first thoughts when we originally experienced them.[27]

Emotions don't just happen. The values, beliefs, and desires that have shaped our inner life in the past influence *which* emotions – in a range of possibilities – are triggered in a situation in the present. What brings delight to a five-year-old may bring a shrug of indifference to the same person twenty years later. What we believe to be true and to be of value can change over time, with the result that our emotional responses to life change, as well.

When people are confronted with the same factors at the same time and differ significantly in their emotional response, this is so in part because they bring different values, beliefs, and desires to the situation. A football that travels through the uprights with one second left in a game, changing the outcome of the contest, brings tears to some and cheers from others, even though they have seen the same thing take place.

Emotions as we experience them in the moment may give the impression that they are involuntary responses, but there is more to them than seems to be the case. They are the tip of an iceberg. There is much more beneath the surface. And when we explore that territory, we discover that we are active participants and contributors to our emotional states. Even if it seems that we have little control over our feelings *per se*, we do have a say about their entourage of values, beliefs, and desires. We can affirm them or deny them, embrace them or reject them, cultivate them or put them in check. This is what makes it possible for us to "school" our emotions.[28] Wisely or foolishly, in healthy or unhealthy ways, we all manage our emotions. This in turn plays an important role in the formation of our character. And this makes our emotions morally significant.

THE MORAL SIGNIFICANCE OF EMOTIONS

Emotions are powerful forces. They motivate us to act one way or another. They are the energy that moves us from deliberation to decision to deed. Jonathan Edwards wrote, "The Author of the human nature has not only given affections to men, but has made 'em very much the spring of men's actions."[29] If they were taken away, "the world would be, in a great measure, motionless and dead."[30] We have all witnessed the destructive energy of anger and hate, but it is also true that positive emotions are "forces of such raw power as to be able to vitalize and revitalize the lives we live."[31] They provide an energy and inclination to do the things we know are pleasing to God.

Emotions are essential to many of our moral actions.[32] Think for a moment about courage and compassion. If I see someone drowning in a lake, calling out for help, fear for my own safety will prevail and the person in the lake will drown unless my fear is trumped by the stronger emotion of courage.[33] Without courage, the action of jumping into the lake will likely never happen.[34] If I see someone whose home and possessions have been destroyed by fire, feeling compassion (literally, suffering with them) is essential to acting in ways that will meet them in their need. Without the emotional connection, I will probably go on my way and hope that someone else will help them.

Or there is the love of a husband and wife. Edward John Carnell wrote:

> Suppose a husband asks his wife if he must kiss her good night. Her answer is, "You must, but not that kind of must." What she means is this: "Unless a spontaneous affection for my person motivates you, your overtures are stripped of all moral value."[35]

> Suppose a husband celebrates a wedding anniversary by bringing home a dozen dew-laden, American Beauty roses. His elated wife throws open the door and cries, "Honey, you remembered! Oh, thank you — thank you very much!" To which he dryly responds, "Don't mention it; it's my duty." With this single word, all moral worth vanishes."[36]

Especially in relationships (and most of life is relational), our actions have emotional dimensions, and this makes our emotions morally significant.

One of the most important things we can say about God is that he is not apathetic.[37] The Bible does not shrink from attributing emotions to him. He hates the wicked (with respect to their wickedness) and those who love violence (with respect to their perverted love).[38] He hates divorce.[39] He hates spiritually empty religious festivals.[40] He abhors pride.[41] He detests lying lips.[42] God does not only act in mercy, he desires mercy.[43] He does not only act justly, he loves justice.[44] He does not merely practice steadfast love, justice and righteousness; he delights in these things.[45]

So it is with those who live close to the heart of God. Their emotions are fully engaged in a life that is pleasing to him. They hate what God hates and love what he loves. They delight in his word.[46] They delight in his commands.[47] They delight to fear him.[48] They love mercy.[49] They rejoice in the truth.[50] They are lovers of goodness.[51] They are zealous for good deeds.[52] The Bible takes this emotional dimension of life seriously, which is why love and hate, courage and fear, anger and compassion, sorrow and joy, pride and humility, shame and honor, and thanksgiving and ingratitude, are featured prominently in its stories. Robert Roberts goes so far as to say:

> Whatever else Christianity may be, it is a set of emotions. It is love of God and neighbor, grief about one's waywardness, joy in the

> merciful salvation of our God, gratitude, hope and peace. So if I don't love God and my neighbor, abhor my sins, and rejoice in my redemption, if I am not grateful, hopeful and at peace with God and myself, then it follows that I am alienated from Christianity.[53]

VIRTUE AND OUR EMOTIONS

Aristotle taught that virtue is not just doing the right thing; it includes having the right emotions about doing the right thing.[54] Imagine two people. Both know what they should do, and both do it. However, one takes pleasure in doing it, and the other does not. One does it, desiring to do what is right, and the other does it, subjugating, or acting against, his true desires. For the first, there is a harmony between desires and actions, with a resulting experience of pleasure; for the second there is an internal conflict over doing the right thing, even if in the end the right thing is done. The first person is virtuous; the second is not yet. The difference between the two is not an outward act, but the way in which their acts are shaped by their affections. The difference between them is the way in which their emotions align with their actions.

Virtue has to do with the enduring quality of our inner life. It is moral excellence that becomes characteristic of our hearts and is expressed outwardly in a way of living in the world.[55] It involves our emotions, motives, intentions, values, and desires, and then the consistent, habitual manner in which we live with them in our day-to-day lives. Virtue is what is in view in the commandments to love God and to obey him with *all of our heart* and *all of our soul.*[56] It is the whole package of our inner life brought into harmony with God and his design for life.

VIRTUE AND VIRTUE'S PLEASURE

For Aristotle, pleasure in virtue is the mark of true virtue: "Just acts give pleasure to a lover of justice."[57] For Kant, such pleasure is morally irrelevant:

> To be beneficent when we can is a duty; and besides this, there are many minds so sympathetically constituted that, without any other motive of vanity or self-interest, they find a pleasure in spreading joy around them, and can take delight in the satisfaction of others so far as it is their own work. But I maintain that in such a case an action of this kind, however proper, however amiable it may be, has nevertheless no true moral worth.[58]

Aristotle was right; Kant was wrong. If there is no pleasure in moral action, there is no virtue. Sheer grit and determination to do what is right is better than nothing, but that's about all that can be said for it. Its true moral worth is very small in the economy of heaven. In fact in heaven it can't be found at all! Triumph following an inner struggle is laudable. If I have never had an addiction to alcohol, I will never know, but may nevertheless appreciate, an alcoholic's victory over that chemical dependency. There is something heroic about it. There is an inner battle, and a final victory. We should celebrate this. But what about the person who enjoys without excess, who consistently exercises discipline and restraint, who takes pleasure in that way of life, and who, as a result, is not vulnerable to an alcoholic addiction in the first place? I would say that there is greater virtue here. And there is even greater virtue in the person who so enjoys God and takes an appropriate pleasure in his good gifts, that drunkenness holds no appeal whatsoever. (And greater virtue here than for someone who refrains from a sense of duty to a moral code.) This deserves even greater celebration.

There is greater virtue in the integrity of our hearts, when our desires and deeds sing in harmony and dance in step. There is greater virtue in loving virtue and enjoying its pleasure. In fact Augustine went so far as to say that there is no devotion, no good life "unless it be also delighted in and loved."[59] If we don't find pleasure in it, it is not the good life we think it is. *This is an important dimension of joy.* (You knew it was leading here.) Jonathan Edwards wrote, "And in every degree of an act of the will, wherein the soul approves of something present, there is a degree of pleasedness; and that pleasedness, if it be in considerable degree, is the very same with the affection of joy or delight."[60]

JOY AND THE TRIUMPH OF GRACE

The emphasis on duty as the chief motivating factor in our moral life has much more to do with the influence of the Stoics in the ancient world, and Immanuel Kant in the modern, than the Bible.[61] I love what Robert Roberts says about this: "We have duties only because we are *not* yet completely moral. The perfected saint feels no duties, only joys and sorrows."[62] I would only add that this is not an all-or-nothing kind of thing. It is not for perfected saints only. It is what God wants to bring about now, from one degree to another, wherever we are in our lives before him. It is the nature of joy to transform duty into delight.

C.S. Lewis described life in Eden this way:

> Now Paradisal man always chose to follow God's will. In following it he also gratified his own desire, both because all the actions demanded of him were, in fact, agreeable to his blameless inclination, and also because the service of God was itself his keenest pleasure, without which as their razor edge all joys would have been insipid to him. The question, "Am I doing this for God's

> sake or only because I happen to like it?" did not then arise, since doing things for God's sake was what he chiefly "happened to like." His Godward will rode his happiness like a well-managed horse, whereas our will, when we are happy, is carried away in the happiness as in a ship racing down a swift stream. Pleasure was then an acceptable offering to God because offering was a pleasure.[63]

God's goal in our transformation is to make it possible for us to live before him this way once again.

We pray, "Your kingdom come, your will be done on earth as it is in heaven."[64] It is worth asking how God's will is done in heaven. It is done completely. Perfectly. And it is done joyfully. Can we even imagine grumbling obedience in heaven? I don't think so! That is the place of perfected saints for whom duty has no meaning. There, doing the will of God is pure joy. When God answers our prayer, he works within us so that increasingly what is true in heaven becomes true of us on the earth. It is an ascent that looks something like this:

Joyful Obedience

Eager Obedience

Willing Obedience

Mere Consent

Grudging Consent

Complete Resistance

Apart from grace we live in a state of spiritual resistance, justly deserving condemnation because we do not embrace God's will with joy. Martin Luther wrote, "How much the law demands; in particular, a heart that is free and eager and joyful,"[65] and "The law issues in wrath rather than in grace, for no one fulfills it willingly and with joy."[66] This is where we all begin, but it is not where God intends to leave us.

A process of change begins in us when the Spirit of God persuades us to embrace Heaven's offer of salvation. Jesus told a parable about this: "The kingdom of heaven is like treasure hidden in a field, which someone found and hid; then *in his joy* he goes and sells all that he has and buys that field."[67] The joy of salvation begins here. The work of God within us enables us to see his Kingdom as a treasure worth pursuing. He captures our hearts, and it becomes a pleasure to say "Yes!" to him.[68]

The renovation of our hearts continues as we live in grace. We might, but God never loses sight of his goal to make us people after his own heart.[69] Not even for a second. We may grow weary, but he never tires of sculpting our hearts to make us more like Christ. Ever. We might hold him at arms length and even seek to push him away, but there never is a moment when God isn't pressing forward in his gracious work so that we come to rejoice in him and his will for our lives.[70]

As God overcomes our opposition to his will, and we affirm and embrace new desires and aspirations, we come more and more to "serve the LORD with gladness."[71] We "gladly do right."[72] We find that the yoke is easy and the burden is light.[73] We become "cheerful givers" of our time and treasure and talent, no longer reluctant or needing compulsion to invest in what God is doing in the world.[74] This is what God is seeking to bring about in us. It is the heart of a life that is pleasing to him.[75]

JOY AS THE REWARD OF VIRTUE

Aristotle taught that pleasure is the perfection of an activity.[76] Every activity has a pleasure that is suitable to it and that arises from the action itself. We talk about this kind of pleasure when we say that we *enjoy* doing something. Intellectual pleasures arise from intellectual pursuits. Aesthetic pleasures arise from artistic pursuits. Athletic pleasures arise from athletic endeavors. (For Christian athletes there is an even greater pleasure. Eric Liddell, missionary and Olympic runner, says to his sister in the movie *Chariots of Fire*, "Jenny, I believe that God made me for a purpose, for China. He also made me fast, and when I run I feel *His* pleasure!")[77]

Joy is the pleasure of virtuous action in God's world.[78] But it is more than that: It is a reward. When we do the will of God from the heart, joy is the reward he gives for our obedience.[79] This reward is not an alien pleasure, as physical pleasure or wealth would be; it arises suitably and congenially (and can never be separated) from our heart's obedience to God's commands.[80] It is God's approval. It is his "Yes!" to us.

Christ provides the paradigm:

> But of the Son he says,
>
> "Your throne, O God, is forever and ever,
>
> the scepter of uprightness is the scepter of your kingdom.
>
> *You have loved righteousness and hated wickedness;*
>
> *therefore God, your God, has anointed you*
>
> *with the oil of gladness beyond your companions.*" (Hebrews 1:8-9)[81]

This is why Jesus could say to his disciples, "If you keep my commandments, you will abide in my love, just as I have kept my father's commandments and abide in his love. I have said these things to you so that my joy may be in you, and that your joy may be complete."[82] The joy he knew in obedience to his Father's commands becomes ours as we obey his. And the joy God gives to us now as the fruit of whole-hearted obedience is a foretaste of the far greater joy that will be ours when, after our last breath, we hear his voice say, "Well done, good and faithful servant. . . . Enter into the joy of your Master!"[83]

Questions for Thought and Discussion

1. If your understanding of the life that is pleasing to God has centered on rules, commands and duties, does this chapter challenge you to re-think this view? If so, how? If not, where do you find yourself in disagreement? If you are part of a church or Christian community, what views do you see there?

2. How do you see your emotional life playing into a life that is pleasing to God? Have you over-emphasized them in the past? Under-emphasized them? Considered them irrelevant? If you are part of a church or Christian community, what views do you see there?

3. Read Isaiah 29:13 (cf. Mark 7:7-8) and talk about the moral distance of our hearts from God's heart and how that relates to your understanding of the life that is pleasing to God.

4. In the section entitled "Joy and the Triumph of Grace" you were introduced to a stair-step progression from complete resistance to joyful obedience. Where do you see yourself in different areas of your life?

5. Read John 15:10-11 and discuss how joy and obedience are related in God's design for our lives.

Chapter 8

Joy and the Theological Virtues

Before we move on, let's review. Joy is found in our heart's inclination to say "Yes" to God. The person who says "No!" to the will of God will never experience joy doing it, but neither will the one who grudgingly yields to it, or who consents from a sense of duty. Joy begins when our hearts are ready to obey God, grows as we become eager to obey, and reaches its fullness when, with the Psalmist, we can say, "I delight to do your will, O my God; your law is within my heart."[1]

From a Christian perspective, virtue represents all that we have been designed by God to be. It is a way of describing the fullness of our potential as his image-bearers. Ultimately, the goodness God has in store for us is a reflection of who he is.[2] It was embodied for us perfectly in Jesus.[3] He is our model for understanding what virtue is and what it looks like in real-life, human dimensions. He is the epitome of emotional health. He is the perfect example. His character is our ideal, and his life the essence of a life that is fully pleasing to God.[4] He is the standard of what it means to be fully and authentically human. Becoming virtuous, as the New Testament understands it, is the same as being transformed into the image of Christ.[5] It is entering into "maturity, to the measure of the full stature of Christ."[6]

Christ-likeness represents the triumph of grace as God conquers the resistance, and captures the affections, of our hearts. It is what God is pursuing when he works within us "to will and to work for his good pleasure."[7] It is an answer to our prayer, "Your kingdom come, your will be done on earth as it is in heaven."[8] "Joy is what humans experience when the way the world is and the way the world ought to be converge. For Christians joy is love's delight in God and God's promised kingdom, when the way the world is and the way God wills the world converge."[9] Joy is a deep delight in God's dominion. It is a taste of heaven on earth.[10]

We have also seen that joy is the reward of virtue. It is God's way of saying, "Well done, good and faithful servant!" God does not bribe us to pursue his will with money, or sensual pleasure, or anything else that might capture our hearts apart from actually doing his will. The pleasure of joy-as-a-reward arises (and only arises) from the activity of wholehearted obedience itself. It is one and the same as enjoying obedience, and delighting in God's reward for doing so.

We are now ready to explore joy's relation to essential virtues in the Christian life. They are known as the *theological virtues*: faith, hope, and love.[11]

Joy is foundational to these virtues.[12] A virtue is present only to the extent that we take pleasure in it. To the degree that we are at odds with a trait of moral excellence, and move toward it only grudgingly, or reluctantly, or from a sense of duty, it is not yet a virtue in us. Joy is the pleasure that emerges from a harmony of desires and dispositions, inclinations and intentions, and affections and actions. If we are clear-sighted, we will see that it is not possible for us to be people of faith, hope, and love, without also being joyful.[13] Faith, hope, and love are only words if they are not accompanied by joy. They are husks. Parodies of true virtue.

JOY AND THE VIRTUE OF FAITH

Paul offered this prayer for Christians in Rome, "May the God of hope fill you with all *joy* and peace *in believing*."[14] It is God who fills us with joy, and faith that receives the filling. Faith is the soil in which joy is planted, flourishes, and grows. It is the cup into which the liquid refreshment of joy is poured. Paul described his pastoral ministry as helping followers of Jesus in their "progress and *joy* in the *faith*."[15] We can think of joy and faith apart from each other, but in experience they never are.

Josef Pieper wrote, "Man can (and wants to) rejoice only when there is a reason for joy. And this reason, therefore, is primary, the joy itself secondary."[16] We enjoy God *because* we believe that he is our Creator and Redeemer. We enjoy the world *because* we believe it to be the amazing work of our amazing God. We rejoice in our circumstances *because* we see them as the work of a sovereign Lord for our good. We rejoice in our salvation *because* we regard it as the highest and best gift that could ever be given to us in our plight. These are the reasons for joy. Take them away, or prove them false, and joy would disappear with them.[17]

This is the pattern of joy as early Christians saw it:

> More than that, we *rejoice* in our sufferings, *knowing that* suffering produces character. (Romans 5:3)

> You *joyfully* accepted the plundering of your property, *since you knew* that you yourselves had a better possession and an abiding one. (Hebrews 10:34)

> *Count it all joy*, my brothers, when you meet trials of various kinds *for you know* that the testing of your faith produces steadfastness. (James 1:2-3, ESV)

Do you see the condition for joy in these texts? It is described as a kind of knowing. This is another way of talking about faith. It is an orientation of our hearts that results from habituating our thoughts and affections in the truth that the hand of God is at work in every situation, shaping our character and fitting us for life in his Kingdom. Joy is secondary in the sense that it follows this. It cannot take the lead.[18]

The kind of knowing we are talking about in the virtue of faith is not familiarity with information, or even an intellectual assent. James saw this with an ironic twist when he wrote, "You believe that God is one; you do well. Even the demons believe – and shudder!"[19] You can quote verses about joy from memory, say that you believe them, and still remain a stranger to joy. Why is that? Because it is one thing, as Jonathan Edwards saw it, to have a "mere notional understanding," and another for knowledge to become a "sense of the heart,"[20] when truth not only illumines our minds, but kindles our affections, and engages our wills.

All beliefs are not equal. Some are trivial and others are crucial. For instance, I believe this statement to be true: "Water boils at 212 degrees Fahrenheit at sea level." Unless you are trying to boil water on an ocean beach, a yawn might be an appropriate response. I also believe that this statement is true: "It is God's design to transform our hearts through the circumstances of our lives." If it is true it is also important! But what if this belief is no more significant to me than my belief about the boiling point of water? For some people this is so.

The knowing that creates conditions for joy is not merely affirming truth, but treasuring truth. Look at these texts again:

> More than that, we rejoice in our sufferings, *knowing* that suffering produces character. (Romans 5:3)

> Count it all joy, my brothers, when you meet trials of various kinds, *for you know* that the testing of your faith produces steadfastness. (James 1:2-3, ESV)

The explicit condition for joy is knowing that God intends to shape your heart in positive ways through difficult circumstances in life. The implicit condition is that this is important to you. You must understand the significance of trials, but this, in turn, must be significant to you! If you don't value the development of your character in a Godward life, you will never experience joy in trials that come your way. It doesn't matter how many verses you can recite from memory. Faith-as-a-way-of-knowing involves embracing and treasuring truth from God. If this is yours, you will be transformed and find joy in the transformation.

A second issue is closely related. It is not about the status of beliefs, but their role. Some beliefs play a small role in our lives. They are part of our *noetic structure* – the total package of all that we believe – but they have little bearing on the way we see and respond to situations in life.[21] "George Washington was the first president of the United States." Even if you believe this to be true, it isn't likely that it will impact the way you live.

Other beliefs have greater power. They are "control beliefs."[22] They govern our readiness to accept other claims to truth, they direct our values, priorities, and actions, and shape the way we interpret and respond to situations in life. Let me illustrate. If I believe that my wife is faithful to me, this will govern the way I interpret seeing her talking to a tall, dark handsome man in the produce section of the grocery store. I will probably think that he is asking for her advice on kumquats, and even if I suspect that he is attempting to flirt with her, I won't readily believe that there is anything suspicious happening on her side. I will trust her and commit myself to her even if I encounter circumstances, which, at first glance, challenge my belief. Control beliefs work this way.[23]

Let me illustrate again, returning to the way we see God at work in the ordeals of life. His presence in our circumstances and his providence over them must be control beliefs for joy to be ours. It is only as they play this role that they create an existential context for joy. They must shape the orientation of our hearts. They must engage us deeply. They must illumine our thoughts, kindle our affections, and govern our wills for joy to be ours in the circumstances of life.[24] It is not enough to have true information. We must embrace the truth disclosed to us, and let it rule the way we interpret and respond to life as it unfolds.[25] This is the kind of knowing that we are talking about in the virtue of faith, and the kind of faith that is essential to joy.

JOY AND THE VIRTUE OF HOPE

It shouldn't be surprising that if joy is related to faith, it is also related to hope, since hope is another way of talking about faith as it faces the future.[26] Faith, hope, and joy are currents that flow together in the stream of a Godward heart. They are interwoven threads in the fabric of a Godward life: "May the God of *hope* fill you with all *joy* and peace in *believing*, so that by the power of the Holy Spirit you may abound in *hope*."[27]

Hope is not an optimistic outlook on life. It is not a confidence gained by projecting human strengths, abilities, and resources into the future. It is a God-centered vision of life and a God-given virtue for life. The God of hope fills us with joy, and this positions us to abound in hope. Let's look at Paul's prayer again, "May the God of hope fill you with all joy and peace in believing, so that by the power of the Holy Spirit you may abound in hope." If we take Paul's words as our guide, the spiritual dynamics of hope look something like this: As we incline our hearts toward God in faith, God fills us with joy and peace – tokens of the Spirit's presence and activity in our hearts. As the Spirit has free reign in our hearts, he strengthens us with a God-centered hope as we face the future.

Joy is a prerequisite to hope.[28] Hearts that delight in God are confident as they face the future. To use Paul's words, those who know "joy and peace in believing" also "abound in hope." It is also true that hope brings joy. Paul also wrote, "Let hope keep you joyful."[29] The more we fan the embers of hope in our hearts, the greater our joy as we anticipate what God has in store for us.

Joy is drawn to the future.[30] There is a deep truth here: Joy longs to find its fulfillment in the consummation of God's purposes, when his Kingdom comes and his will is done on earth as it is in heaven. When the apostle Paul pulls back the curtains to let us glimpse something of the Kingdom of God, we see "righteousness and peace and joy in the Holy Spirit."[31] Hope is drawn to this. It longs for the undiminished and undiluted experience of these wonders that will one day be fully ours.

The joy in our present experience longs for and anticipates the consummation of joy in the Kingdom to come. Or perhaps the joy of the future Kingdom beckons our present joy, as "deep calls to deep."[32] Hope connects the two. Hope is the Christian's way of living in the world while we wait for God's plan for the ages to be fully realized. We live each day with a sense of great things waiting to happen. We live with the *alreadiness* of our present joy and the *not-yetness* of our future joy in the Kingdom. Because we already know something of the joy God wants for us, we can wait, but because our future joy will be so much greater, we can hardly wait![33]

JOY AND THE VIRTUE OF LOVE

If love is the greatest virtue, and crowns all of God's commandments, finding joy here brings us to summit of living well before God.[34] We should begin by getting clear about what we mean by *love.* At one end of the spectrum of public opinion, love is sentimentalized and reduced to mere feeling. Either we have it or we don't. We can talk about "being in love," but not about love as a duty, and still less about love as a virtue. This is the concept of love that rules pop culture today. It is reduced to eroticism in movies, television shows and pulp fiction, romanticized as the basis for many modern marriages, and not surprisingly (but sadly) is the rationale behind millions of divorces, when one or both partners claim no longer to be in love. Love is not a virtue here. It cannot be.

At the other end of the spectrum love is a sheer act of the will, which we may well have to exercise in opposition to our emotions. Here love is all duty. This is love in the Kantian tradition. James Gilman comments:

> Kant insists that those portions of "Scripture that command us to love our neighbor and even our enemy" cannot mean that we should have a feeling for them. For love that can be commanded "is practical love, not pathological love; it resides in the will and not in the propensities of feeling, in principles of action and not in tender sympathy; and it alone can be commanded."[35]

Love is not a virtue on this accounting either, since virtue is the concord of our values, desires, motives, emotions, inclinations, and choices. Acts of volition are single notes – and not a harmony – in the musical score of life.

Love at its highest and best engages our affections and our wills. This is true of God's love, which we are called to take as our model.[36] It is an affectionate love that expresses itself in loving choices and loving actions. We see this in Moses' description of God's love for Israel. Note the progression from affections to choices to actions:

> The LORD set his affection on your forefathers and loved them.
>
> He chose you.
>
> He defends the cause of the fatherless and the widow, and loves the alien, giving him food and clothing.
>
> He is your God, who performed for you those great and awesome wonders.
>
> Now the LORD your God has made you as numerous as the stars in the sky. (Deuteronomy 10:15ff., NIV)

When it is all that it can be and ought to be, our love, like God's, stirs deep affections within us, engages our wills in the choices we make, and is given practical expression in actions that seek the wellness of others.

In *The Four Loves*, C.S. Lewis makes a distinction between "Need-love" and "Gift-love." Drawing an illustration from a man's love for a woman, Lewis explains the differences this way:

> Need-love says of a woman, "I cannot live without her." Gift-love longs to give her happiness, comfort, protection – if possible, wealth. Appreciative love gazes and holds its breath and is silent, rejoices that such a wonder should exist even if not for him, will not be wholly dejected by losing her, would rather have it so than never to have seen her at all.[37]

Let's put this distinction into the following table, using the commands to love God and our neighbor as a guide for our exploration:

	God	**Neighbor**
Need-love	Need-love for God	Need-love for Neighbor
Gift-love	Gift-love for God	Gift-love for Neighbor

Need-love for God. Need-love arises from our finitude. It is a dimension of creaturely dependence. It is a brute fact of our existence that we are incomplete on our own. We have needs that can only be met by others, and desires that match our needs. God designed the life of creatures to be this way. At the most fundamental level, this begins with our relationship with him. Lewis wrote, "But man's love for God, from the very nature of the case, must always be very largely, and must often be entirely, a Need-love."[38] This love becomes a virtue in us when it is habituated in humility, when we see ourselves as radically dependent upon God, and we are happy to have it that way. It becomes a trait of moral excellence in us when we shun all other gods, forsake all other rivals, and seek and find the fulfillment of our desires in the living and true God.[39]

Listen to the words of the prophet, Jeremiah:

> Be appalled, O heavens, at this;
> be shocked, be utterly desolate,
> declares the LORD,
> for my people have committed two evils:
> they have forsaken me,
> the fountain of living waters,
> and hewed out cisterns for themselves,
> broken cisterns that can hold no water. (Jeremiah 2:12-13, ESV)

If it is evil to forsake God and to seek fulfillment in someone or something other than God, then it is good for us to cleave to him and to seek the satisfaction of our souls in him. This is the virtue of Need-love for God.

When Need-love for God becomes a virtue in us, joy follows as the enjoyment of God. It is the pleasure we experience when our need for God is met by God. It is like the pleasure of cool, crystalline water slaking our thirst, or the pleasure of eating our favorite food when we are hungry:

> Come, everyone who thirsts,
> come to the waters;
> and he who has no money,
> come, buy and eat!
> Come, buy wine and milk
> without money and without price.
> Why do you spend your money for that which is not bread,
> and your labor for that which does not satisfy?
> Listen diligently to me, and eat what is good,
> and delight yourselves in rich food. (Isaiah 55:1-2, ESV)

If those "who choose another god multiply their sorrows,"[40] those who seek their fulfillment in the living and true God discover the greatest joy possible.

Gift-love for God. At first glance this seems odd, and even incoherent. What can we give to a God who has everything? What do we give to a God who is "not served by human hands, as though he needed anything, since he himself gives to all men life and breath and everything"?[41] The answer is surely "Nothing!" If it is true, however, that God rejoices over us and delights in us, then the surprising implication is that we can contribute to his joy.[42] We are not meeting a need or removing a deficit, we are adding to a surplus.

God has no needs for us to meet, but he does have desires for us that we can fulfill.[43] We bring pleasure to God when we pray with an upright heart.[44] We contribute to his joy in our thanksgiving and praise.[45] When we bow before him in reverential awe, he looks on in delight.[46] Children bring pleasure to God when they obey their parents.[47] Our gifts to others are "a fragrant offering, an acceptable sacrifice, pleasing to God."[48]

How is joy related to the virtue of Gift-love for God? It is the same kind of joy I experience when I give a present to my wife and see the delight in her eyes. There is pleasure in knowing that I have brought pleasure to her. Flames of joy are lit in my heart from the embers of her joy. Her joy kindles my own. If God delights in the gifts we bring, our joy in giving them is the resounding of his joy within us. Our cup is filled from the overflow of his.

Need-love for our neighbors. We all know that it is possible to use people to meet our needs, advance our interests, or satisfy our desire for pleasure. Others become a means and our interests the end. This is not a virtue, but a vice. However, if our wellness is supported and enhanced by others *by design*, then there must be ways to direct this Need-love toward our neighbors in morally and spiritually healthy ways.

We can learn from the apostle Paul and his letter to the church at Thessalonica. He wrote, "So, being affectionately desirous of you, we were ready to share with you not only the gospel of God, but also our own selves, because you had become very dear to us."[49] There was a desire in Paul's heart for these men and women. They touched his affections deeply. But it was not a selfish desire. In fact it motivated him to share himself with them.[50] It was not a desire to acquire and possess, but to value and enjoy. It was a love that affirmed their worth, not as a means to something else, because they had become precious to him.

This is what Need-love/neighbor-love looks like as a virtue. It desires, but does not take advantage. It delights, but does not use. It enjoys, but does not exploit. It finds pleasure in others without seeking to possess them.[51] It honors and values those who enrich our lives. It appreciates those who give to us and is thankful for their gifts. When Paul describes this kind of love for the church at Philippi, we see how joy is interlaced in the weave, "Therefore, my brothers, whom I love and long for, my joy and crown, stand firm thus in the Lord, my beloved."[52] He longs for them: They are his desire. They are his beloved: precious to his heart. He honors them: They are his crown. He delights in them: They are his joy. This pleasure is God's gift. It is a sign that our relationships fit his design and enjoy his blessing. Here we truly flourish in life.

Gift-love for our neighbors. This love begins with the affirmation, "It is *good* that you exist; how wonderful that you are!"[53] It treasures another person as a unique creation of God. But it does more than this. Gift-love moves from affirmation to action, from appreciation of our neighbors to an active commitment to their good. It seeks to meet their needs and to help them flourish in life. Its domain is the whole of life: physical health, emotional wholeness, financial wellness and spiritual growth.[54]

Since joy is their highest good (whether they know it or not), Gift-love for our neighbors is always a commitment to their joy. Paul wrote to the church in Corinth, "We are workers with you *for your joy*."[55] And since joy is found in a relationship with God, Gift-love for our neighbors will always seek to point others to him. To quote Augustine:

> Now you love yourself suitably when you love God better than yourself. What, then, you aim at in yourself you must aim at in your neighbor, namely, that he may love God with a perfect affection. For you do not love him as yourself, unless you try to draw him to that good which you are yourself pursuing.[56]

To seek the highest and best for our neighbors is to seek joy-in-God for them.[57]

As we seek the joy of others, we discover greater joy for ourselves. As Jonathan Edwards saw it, love not only seeks to promote the happiness of others, it also *rejoices* in their happiness.[58] Our joy is the pleasure of loving others this way. If we think about love clearly, we will see that "love without joy is impossible."[59] The more we give ourselves lovingly to others for their joy, the more we enjoy loving. "We love to love!"[60] When the apostle Paul wrote of the fruit of the Spirit and thought of love, joy came next to his mind.[61] Joy grows fruitfully in a loving heart.[62]

VIRTUE AND THE FRUIT OF THE SPIRIT

As we conclude this part of our study, it is important to say that in a Christian vision of life virtue is the fruit of the Spirit. The Greeks thought of virtue as the development of human potential through our own habit-forming efforts. Many Christians – Protestants in particular – have been less than enthusiastic about virtue ethics for this reason. They fear that it will lead to a life-project that centers on *works*, that it understates our need for God's grace, and thinks too highly of what we can do as sinful human beings. Jonathan Wilson comments:

> Evangelical theology has been rightly wary of some aspects of virtue ethics . . . being rooted in the doctrine of justification by grace through faith, has asserted that virtue ethics undercuts grace. It sees virtue ethics as placing too much within the power of humanity and as verging on salvation as a human achievement – the ancient heresy of Pelagianism.[63]

We can learn from the ancient Greek philosophers where their thinking aligns with the New Testament understanding of a life that is pleasing to God. Where it does not, however, we must part company with them. This is one of those places. The Greeks were right in seeing virtue as the ideal of our humanity. As Christians, however, we do not arrive at this vision of virtue through a calculation of a middle point between two extreme character traits, as Aristotle did. We look to Christ. (As Ambrose said, "When we speak about virtue, we speak about Christ.")[64] He is our model. Our example. Our moral hero, whose way of living embodies all that we seek to emulate. His life epitomizes the life that is fully pleasing to God. To become virtuous is to become like him.

This is not something that we can do on our own.[65] Here again we must part company with the Greek philosophers. To use technical language, our role is a *necessary condition*, but not a *sufficient condition*, for becoming virtuous. We must be involved because it is our virtue that we are talking about. It is our heart. Our character. Our values and priorities. Our hopes and desires. Our inclinations and motivations. Our decisions and actions. But this is not enough to get the job done, so to speak. God's role in making us virtuous is what makes the project possible. As we have seen, virtue represents the triumph of God's grace in our lives as he conquers the resistance, and captures the affections, of our hearts.

The apostle Paul put it this way in his letter to the Philippians, "Work out your own salvation with fear and trembling." This is our part, the necessary condition of virtue formation. Then he adds, "For God is at work in you, both to will and to work for his good pleasure."[66] This is God's part, the sufficient condition that makes it all possible. We participate in the process, but the deeper truth is here: The life that is fully pleasing to God is from him, through him and to him.[67] He is its creative Source, empowering Agent and final Goal. There can be no virtue apart from the transforming grace of God in action.[68]

Paul saw joy as a fruit of the Spirit.[69] It is the *natural* outcome of a *supernatural* presence and power in our lives. Joy lies in the interface between the Spirit's presence and our hearts, when they are open, receptive and responsive to him as he seeks to bring about the transformation of our character.[70] It can never be reduced to human factors alone.

Those who find any infringement of their (illusory) personal independence and autonomy distasteful will no doubt object to this *God-factor.* ("I'd rather do it on my own, thank you!") Those who know God and have experienced his presence and work in their lives would have it no other way. It is all joy.

Questions for Thought and Discussion

1. As you think about faith as a way of knowing, discuss Jonathan Edwards' distinction between a "mere notional understanding" of Scripture, and a "sense of the heart." How do you think you could move from the first to the second?

2. Discuss this quote from the chapter:

   > [God's] presence in our circumstances and his providence over them must be control beliefs for joy to be ours. It is only as they play this role that they create an existential context for joy. They must shape the orientation of our hearts. They must engage us deeply. They must illumine our thoughts, kindle our affections, and govern our wills for joy to be ours in the circumstances of life. It is not enough to have true information.

3. How does joy, as the fulfillment of hope, challenge and connect with the yearning and desires of our culture?

4. How does joy, as a virtue, challenge the notions of love as a feeling and love as an act of the will? And how does this challenge the way you view the commands to love God and your neighbor?

5. How do you see Need-love and Gift-love for your neighbor playing out in your own quest for joy?

CHAPTER 9

JOY AND THE GOOD LIFE

Why should we pursue virtue? If we say that we should because God commands us to, that alone warrants an obedient response. (Theology 101: God is God and we are not.) But that answer, at least for a curious mind like mine, suggests other questions: Is there a rationale behind God's commands? Does he have reasons for commanding us to pursue some things and to avoid others? Does the Bible allow us to ask these kinds of questions? If we do ask them, does it give us answers, or clues that point us in the right direction?

Many of us are accustomed to seeing God's commands in light of his sovereign right to oblige us to conduct our lives in certain ways. You will get no argument from me. But is there more to the story? If we say that we should obey God's commands because God says so, there isn't much more that can be said. But if we say that God's commands reflect his goodness (his commitment to our well-being), and his wisdom (his design for a life well lived), this opens new terrain for us to explore.

It will be helpful for us to make a distinction between a *reason* and an *incentive* for doing something. If we ask why we should pursue virtue, and a reason is what we are looking for, the answer is that we should because God commands us to. But if we ask again, looking for an incentive, the answer is that it is in our best interests to do so.[1] The path of virtue leads us to God's wisdom and his desire to see us flourish in life.

DESIGNED FOR US

Scientists and philosophers who think about the natural world sometimes speak of an "anthropic principle" at work in the development of our solar system and life on our planet. It is as if human life was the goal. Everything is finely tuned, down to the smallest detail, so that if the system had been tweaked at all – say, for instance, the distance of the earth from the sun – another outcome would have resulted that would not have been hospitable for humans. I would not be here to write this and you would not be here to read it.[2] Science points to this, Genesis tells the story, and Christians believe it to be so.

There is an anthropic principle in Christian ethics as well. The first and most important thing we can say about God's moral law is that it bears the imprint of his character. It is grounded in his own moral excellence. But it is also significant to say that as it has been given *to* us it is designed *for us*. It is congenial to who we are as God's image-bearers. It is ideally suited to our nature and his purposes for us. It is a reflection of his wisdom: It fits the world as he created it, and perfectly matches his purposes for created life. It is an expression of his goodness: his commitment to our wellness and his desire to see us flourish in the world he has made.[3]

Why should we pursue a path of virtue? Because God commands us to do so? Yes, but this is only part of the answer. Lewis Smedes wrote that God's commands are not "barked at us by a capricious heavenly staff sergeant."

They "match the configurations of life as God created it."[4] They fit God's design, and his desire to see us flourish in life. Arthur Holmes wrote:

> This is . . . a teleological universe [If you aren't familiar with the word *teleological,* Holmes will now define it], one designed and guided for the achievement of intended ends. It is not the impersonal teleology of immanent forces limited to processes already given to us in the world as it is, such as some of the Greeks and nineteenth-century evolutionary thinkers asserted. Rather, it is a personal teleology, a transcendent Creator's active pursuit of good ends for his own creation.[5]

JOY AND THE *TELOS* OF LIFE

If you came to the word *teleological* above and found a question mark forming in your mind, let me introduce you to a very important concept. The word *telos,* given to us by the Greeks, means, literally, *an end.* The word *telescope* comes from two Greek words meaning, "to see" and "an end." It is an instrument that allows us to see the farthest reaches of our visual field. *Telos* also refers to a goal: the *end* of a race is the runner's *goal.* It suggests purpose. The purpose of running a race is to reach the goal. The goal gives meaning and intentionality to the endeavor.

When the Greeks thought of our *telos,* they were thinking about the meaning or purpose of human existence. To fulfill this purpose, to reach this goal, is to flourish in life. It is to live well, as life is meant to be lived. Some saw the *telos* of humanity as pleasure. This approach to life is known as hedonism. We will explore this more fully in the next chapter. The path we will follow here will take us in a different direction.

While some in the ancient world saw pleasure as the *telos* of human existence, another school of thought saw it as happiness.[6] This was Aristotle's understanding of the good life. Happiness is flourishing in life as we pursue a life of reason and virtue.[7] In Aristotle's vision of life, the answer to the question, "Why should we pursue a path of virtue?" is that it enables us to fulfill the *telos* of human existence. It puts us in a position to realize our human potential.[8] This is the happy life.

It seems to me that we can learn from this approach to life, even if in the end we must let the Bible speak for itself. The ancient Hebrews envisioned life differently than the Greeks did. To them, life is like a journey. Living is like walking.[9] If we take a journey we must choose a path. The path we choose depends on the destination we wish to reach. The path one takes in the journey of life (as opposed to a trip to a neighboring village) is the "path of life." In many ways it comes to the same thing as the Greek's *telos*: It's about direction and a destination in life. Its concern is the meaning, purpose, and goal of life. Unlike the Greeks, however, Jewish people believed that the path of life is revealed. Reason does not discover it; God makes it known. Nor is the path of life about human potential and achievement. It is not about happiness as Aristotle understood it. It is about a relationship with God and the life-encompassing joy we discover there:

> You show to me the path of life.
> In your presence there is fullness of joy;
> in your right hand are pleasures forevermore. (Psalm 16:11, NRSV)

In a biblical vision of life, joy is our final end. Our *telos*. A life well lived is about the enjoyment of God and all of life before him.[10]

Augustine believed that the quest for happiness was fulfilled in the Christian experience of joy. The pagan world was right to pursue happiness, but wrong in the way it pursued this goal, as well as where it thought this happiness could be found. It is ours in the enjoyment of God:

> In so far as all men seek the happy life they do not err. But in so far as anyone does not keep to the way that leads to the happy life, even though he professes to desire only to reach happiness, he is in error.[11]

> Is it, perchance, that as one joys in this, and another in that, so do all men agree in their wish for happiness, as they would agree, were they asked, in wishing to have joy – and this joy they call a happy life? Although, then, one pursues joy in this way, and another in that, all have one goal, which they strive to attain, namely, to have joy.[12]

> Following after God is the desire of happiness; to reach God is happiness itself.[13]

> How, then, do I seek You, O Lord? For when I seek You, my God, I seek a happy life.[14]

> The greatest commandment, therefore, which leads to a happy life, and the first, is this: "You shall love the Lord your God with all your heart, and soul and mind."[15]

Aquinas saw a kinship between Aristotle's view and a Christian understanding of life. His was a *double-decker* approach to happiness. At a purely human level, he believed that Aristotle was right in seeing happiness as an end, and virtue as a necessary means to that end. Seeking to be true to the biblical witness, however, he also believed that there was a higher happiness possible for those who were rightly related to God:

> Man is perfected by virtue, for those actions whereby he is directed to happiness. . . . Now man's happiness is twofold. . . . One is proportionate to human nature, a happiness . . . which man can obtain by means of his natural principles. The other is a happiness

> surpassing man's nature, and which man can obtain by the power of God alone.[16]

For Aquinas this *supernatural happiness* is another name for joy:

> Happiness is called man's supreme good, because it is the attainment or enjoyment of the supreme good.[17]
>
> God alone constitutes man's happiness.[18]
>
> Joy itself is the consummation of happiness.[19]

The 17th century Westminster Shorter Catechism sees life in the same way when it asks, "What is the chief *end* of man?" The question means, "What is our purpose? At its highest and best, what is life all about?" Its answer is that our end, our *telos* as human beings, is to "glorify God and to enjoy him forever."[20]

If we look at life this way, it is important to say that virtue is a means to our end, or *telos*. Not in the sense, however, that once the end has been achieved, we can dispense with the means. We can never say, "Now that I have joy, I no longer need the things that made it possible." Means and end belong together and cannot be separated.[21] To put this into a New Testament vision of life, joy is found – and only found – in a harmony between God's heart and ours. The joy we seek and for which we have been created comes only in a triumph of God's grace, as our resistance is conquered, our affections are captured, and the Spirit of God shapes our character into the likeness of Christ.

JOY AND THE *SUMMUM BONUM* OF LIFE

Another way of talking about the good life frames the discussion in terms of our *summum bonum*, or our highest good. There are many goods in the world: food, clothing, friends, knowledge, and health. A good is anything that has positive value for human life. What is it that distinguishes our highest good from other goods? Aristotle taught that a final good is one that is desired for its own sake, and not for the sake of anything else. Other things may be related to it as means, but it will never be a means to anything else because there is nothing higher or better. Augustine believed that two conditions must be met for something to be our highest good: It must be a "good than which there is nothing better," and "it must be something which cannot be lost against the will."[22] Aristotle believed that only one thing meets his criterion: happiness. All other goods are a means to this end. Because they saw themselves living in a theistic universe, Augustine and Aquinas believed that our *summum bonum* must be found in relation to our Creator.

As Christians we say that God is the Highest Good, but we must add that there are objective and subjective dimensions to this. There are two sides of this coin, so to speak. Objectively, God is the highest good in this world, and must be in any world that he creates. But if we are talking about the highest good *for us*, it involves an enjoyment of that good on our part. Augustine put it this way:

> No one can be happy who does not enjoy what is man's chief good, nor is there any one who enjoys this who is not happy.[23]

> The happy life . . . (occurs) when that which is man's chief good is both loved and possessed.[24]

> No one is blessed who does not enjoy that which he loves. For even they who love things that ought not to be loved, do not count themselves blessed by loving merely, but by enjoying them. Who, then . . . will deny that he is blessed, who enjoys that which he loves and loves the true and highest good?. . . He who loves God is blessed in the enjoyment of God.[25]

Similarly, Aquinas wrote, "Man's last end may be said to be either God who is the Supreme Good absolutely; or the enjoyment of God, which denotes a certain pleasure in the last end."[26] God is *the* Highest Good; the enjoyment of God is *our* highest good. Seeking this is the good life; finding it is life at its very best.

THE GLORY OF GOD AND THE GOOD LIFE

Let's return to The Westminster Shorter Catechism. It approaches the good life by asking the question, "What is the chief end of man?" and then answering, "Man's chief end is to *glorify* God, and to *enjoy* him forever."[27] Many centuries before, prophets, poets, and apostles understood that there is a close connection between God's glory and our joy:

> Shout for *joy* to God, all the earth;
> sing the *glory* of his name. (Psalm 66:1-2)
>
> Let the faithful exult in *glory*;
> let them sing for *joy* on their couches. (Psalm 149:5)
>
> The wilderness and the dry land shall *be glad*,
> the desert shall *rejoice* and blossom;
> like the crocus it shall blossom abundantly,
> and *rejoice with joy and singing*. . . .
> They shall see the *glory* of the LORD,
> the majesty of our God. (Isaiah 35:1-2)

> Let the LORD be *glorified*, that we may see your *joy*." (Isaiah 66:5)
>
> We *rejoice* in our hope of sharing the *glory* of God. (Romans 5:2)
>
> And though you have not seen Him, you love Him, and though you do not see Him now, but believe in Him, you greatly rejoice with *joy* inexpressible and full of *glory*. (1 Peter 1:8, NASB)
>
> . . . that you may also *rejoice* and be glad when his *glory* is revealed. (1 Peter 4:13)
>
> Now to him who is able to keep you from stumbling and to present you blameless before the presence of his *glory* with great *joy*. (Jude 24, ESV)
>
> Let us *rejoice* and be glad and give him *glory*! (Revelation 19:7, NIV)

What is the link between God's glory and our joy, and how does it help us understand and pursue the good life? Although the word *glory* can be used of the revelation of God's presence in the world, in its primary theological sense glory characterizes God-as-he-is-in-himself. [28] It is his majesty, his magnificence, his infinite worth and unlimited power. It is all that God is in his transcendence over his creation. Like the holiness of God, the glory of God is not a single attribute, but his very essence. It is his nature in its totality. In all that he is he is glorious. The Biblical writers tried to capture something of this when they called him "the King of glory,"[29] "the God of glory,"[30] the "Father of glory,"[31] and "the Majestic Glory."[32]

The fitting response to the glory of God is reverence, wonder, and awe: a shudder at our own smallness, a shivering sense of the magnitude of God, and a trembling delight in his unbounded greatness and grandeur. Hearts that have been gripped by glory know the tremulous joy that so great a Being exists, and astonishment-that-takes-one's-breath-away that so great a God would invite us to know and enjoy him. It is a pleasure that is at once dread and delight, fear and fascination, amazement and adoration. To glorify God, first and foremost, is to acknowledge, confess, celebrate, and live our lives in light of God's glory. This is where joy is found. This is where our hearts discover pleasure in God.[33]

The glory of God has implications for what we value in life. The Hebrew word for glory, *kabod,* has the root meaning of heaviness or weight.[34] It was used, for instance, of wealth or riches.[35] In antiquity wealth was not measured artificially by numbers on paper, but by the weight of one's silver or gold. *Kabod,* or glory, then, speaks of a person's wealth, or worth. By analogy, when it is used of God, it refers to his supreme worth or worthiness. He is the Supremely Valuable One. This is an important part of what we mean when we attribute glory to God.

The appropriate response to God's glory/supreme value is worship (from the old English word, *worthship*): declaring and delighting in the infinite worth of God. The halls of heaven ring with the refrain, "You are *worthy*, our Lord and God, to receive *glory* and honor and power, for you created all things, and by your will they existed and were created."[36] Heaven celebrates the worthiness of God with or without our assent. None there wait in silence for us to join them. We experience joy, however, only when he is supremely worthy *to us*, when we honor him above all else, esteem him most highly, give him first place in all that we treasure and hold dear, find ourselves enriched by his infinite worth, and then revel in this greatest of all goods.

Glorifying God brings us back to the pursuit of virtue. We glorify God when we mirror his glory in our lives, when the radiance of his moral excellence is reflected in the transformation of our character. Paul put it this way, "And we all, with unveiled face, beholding the glory of the Lord, are being changed into his likeness from one degree of glory to another; for this comes from the Lord who is the Spirit."[37] To know the glory of God, to behold his glory, is to be wonderfully transformed. It is a life-long process of transformation, from "one degree of glory to another." It is not something we bring about on our own, "for this comes from the Lord who is the Spirit." We are invited to fix our gaze upon his glory: to be absorbed with his honor, his majesty, his worthiness, his loveliness, and to set ourselves to live in harmony with this. It is God who then brings about the wonderful change in us.

Once again (and we should not find this surprising at this point) we see that the *good life* turns out to be very much about God making *our life good.* It is about God making *us* good. At its heart it is about our hearts. It is about a pursuit of moral excellence that puts us into alignment and harmony with God's wise design for life, and his commitment to our well-being. Its outcome is a way of living that glorifies God and flourishes in joy.

THE BIBLE AND FLOURISHING IN LIFE

Torah. The Bible encourages us to embrace God's commands as expressions of his benevolent commitment to us and his wise design for life. As the people of Israel prepared to enter Canaan, Moses rehearsed the commands God had given to govern their lives in a new land. It was important for them to understand that these imperatives were not just a matter of divine fiat, but reflected God's plan for blessing them: "See, I am setting before you today a blessing and a curse: *the blessing, if you obey the commandments of the LORD your God that I am commanding you today*; and the curse, if you do not obey the commandments of the LORD your God."[38]

To say that obedience is a condition for God's blessing implies that God's purpose for giving commands in the first place is to provide a way of living that enjoys his good hand. God wants to bless his people; his blessings become ours through obedience.[39] We see the connection between God's commands and his commitment to our well-being in passages like this:

> So now, O Israel, what does the LORD your God require of you? Only to fear the LORD your God, to walk in all his ways, to love him, to serve the LORD your God with all your heart and with all your soul, and to keep the commandments of the LORD your God and *his decrees that I am commanding you today, for your own well-being.* (Deuteronomy 10:12-13, NRSV)

The phrase "that it may go well with you," is given again and again as a rationale for obeying God's commands.[40] The message is clear: God wants us to live robustly. His commands are a means to this end.

Wisdom. Living well is a prominent theme in the wisdom literature of the Old Testament (Proverbs, Ecclesiastes and many Psalms[41]). We learn from these books that wisdom enables us to flourish in life before God. It teaches us how to live in harmony with God, the world, and others.[42] The law of the LORD is central to this. To have one's heart shaped by God's Word, to meditate on it, and to delight in it, is to put oneself in a position to prosper in life. Psalm 1 says it well:

> Blessed is the one
>   who does not walk in step with the wicked
> or stand in the way that sinners take
>   or sit in the company of mockers,
> but whose delight is in the law of the LORD,
>   and who meditates on his law day and night.
> That person is like a tree planted by streams of water,
>   which yields its fruit in season
> and whose leaf does not wither —
>   whatever they do prospers.
> Not so the wicked!

They are like chaff
  that the wind blows away.
Therefore the wicked will not stand in the judgment,
  nor sinners in the assembly of the righteous.
For the LORD watches over the way of the righteous,
  but the way of the wicked leads to destruction. (Psalm 1, NIV)

Prophets. We often think of the Hebrew prophets as messengers of doom, but they were compelled to speak and write by a burning desire to see the people of God return to their covenant with God, and to the blessings that were promised there. It was the prophets who developed the important notion of *shalom*, or peace. It is a prominent theme in Isaiah:

For to us a child is born,
  to us a son is given;
and the government shall be upon his shoulder,
  and his name shall be called
Wonderful Counselor, Mighty God,
  Everlasting Father, Prince of *Peace.*
Of the increase of his government and of *peace*
  there will be no end,
on the throne of David and over his kingdom,
  to establish it and to uphold it
with justice and with righteousness
    from this time forth and forevermore.
      The zeal of the LORD of hosts will do this. (9:6-7, ESV)

You keep him in perfect *peace*
  whose mind is stayed on you,
because he trusts in you. (26:1, ESV)

O LORD, you will ordain *peace* for us,
  for you have indeed done for us all our works. (26:12, ESV)

And the effect of righteousness will be *peace*,
  and the result of righteousness, quietness and trust forever.
My people will abide in a *peaceful* habitation,
  in secure dwellings, and in quiet resting places. (32:17-18, ESV)

Oh that you had paid attention to my commandments!
Then your *peace* would have been like a river,
  and your righteousness like the waves of the sea; (48:18, ESV)

How beautiful upon the mountains
  are the feet of him who brings good news,
who publishes *peace*, who brings good news of happiness,
  who publishes salvation,
  who says to Zion, "Your God reigns." (52:7, ESV)

For the mountains may depart
  and the hills be removed,
but my steadfast love shall not depart from you,
  and my covenant of *peace* shall not be removed,"
  says the LORD, who has compassion on you. (54:10, ESV)

"For you shall go out in joy
  and be led forth in *peace*;
the mountains and the hills before you
  shall break forth into singing,
  and all the trees of the field shall clap their hands. (55:12, ESV)

I have seen his ways, but I will heal him;
  I will lead him and restore comfort to him and his mourners,
  creating the fruit of the lips.
Peace, peace, to the far and to the near," says the LORD,
  "and I will heal him. (57:18-19, ESV)

For the prophets, *shalom* is a gem with many facets, a color with many hues, a bouquet with many nuances. It pictures life at its best under God: health, well-being, fulfillment, harmony, and an environment of joy for all. Cornelius Plantinga writes:

> The webbing together of God, humans, and all creation in justice, fulfillment, and delight is what the Hebrew prophets call *shalom.* We call it peace but it means far more than mere peace of mind or a cease-fire between enemies. In the Bible, shalom means *universal flourishing, wholeness and delight* – a rich state of affairs in which natural needs are satisfied and natural gifts fruitfully employed, a state of affairs that inspires joyful wonder as its Creator and Savior opens doors and welcomes the creatures in whom he delights. Shalom, in other words, is the way things ought to be.[43]

Gospels. We should not be surprised to see the Torah, Wisdom, and Prophetic traditions reflected in the teaching of Jesus. The Jewish Scriptures were his sustenance in life.[44] More than that, he believed that they were fulfilled in him.[45] When he summarized the purpose of his teaching to his disciples, Jesus made it clear that their joy was at the heart of it all.[46] This is what he meant, I think, when he said that he came to give an "abundant life" to those who followed him.[47] He said that his yoke is easy and his burden, light. In taking them we will find rest for our souls.[48] He said that those who embrace and practice his teaching are "blessed" or happy.[49] Behind the teaching of Jesus – which gave them a new focus, shape, and power – we see the ancient and rich traditions of understanding God's commands as the path to a robust life.

Epistles. The followers of Jesus saw themselves at the convergence point of redemptive history. Everything that God had said and done in the past pointed to and met in the life, death, and resurrection of Jesus. The apostle Paul put it this way: "All the promises of God find their Yes in him."[50] The blessings of the Torah, the wisdom of the Sages, and shalom of the Prophets found their fulfillment in Christ. They were fulfilled and raised to new heights, so that flourishing in life from that time to ours is best described as a "joy inexpressible and full of glory."[51]

The followers of Jesus saw themselves living not only at a convergence point, but a pivotal point. In the life, death, and resurrection of Jesus, history moved in a new direction. A new era dawned. A new epoch began. They saw themselves living in the inauguration of the Kingdom: the reign of God breaking into history, conquering evil, setting captives free, liberating from sin, healing broken bodies and wounded hearts, bringing reconciliation with God, and restoring fractured relationships among all who share our humanity. In its sum, the Kingdom of God is about "righteousness and peace and joy in the Holy Spirit" – the boon of his empire.[52] This is now the best way to describe what it means to flourish in life. God's aspirations for us are possible in ways that could only be hinted at in the past. Our dreams come true in God's dreams for us, as we awaken to them in the glory of his Kingdom.

Questions for Thought and Discussion

1. How does it change the way you look at the Christian life to see it against the background of his goodness and wisdom?

2. How does the "anthropic principle" challenge the way you have thought about God's commands in the past? How would you communicate this to an interested friend who thinks that God's commands are arbitrary and oppressive?

3. How does a Christian view of the *telos* of life compare with rival understandings in our culture today?

4. How does a Christian view of our *summum bonum* compare with rival understandings in contemporary culture?

5. Discuss the relationship between our joy and God's glory. How will this shape your pursuit of joy?

Chapter 10

Joy and the Pursuit of Pleasure

(An Exploration of Christian Hedonism)

Joy is the highest and best of life's pleasures. It is our *summum bonum*, our highest good. It is essential to our *telos*, the end for which we were created. If you think about this long enough, the word *hedonism* will surely come to mind. Some have suggested, in fact, that if we are serious about pursuing pleasure in God and enjoying life before him, we should think of ourselves as *Christian hedonists.*[1] Even if this seems at first glance to be a case of strange bedfellows, it is worth exploring. At the very least it will help us think clearly and take better aim at a life of joy.

There were hedonists in the ancient world. Among Greek philosophers, the Cyrenaics believed that human knowledge is limited to present sensory experience, that a present-tense experience of pleasure is the only intrinsic good, and that life at its best is a matter of squeezing maximal pleasure from each and every moment.[2] (Anyone who knows university dormitories, fraternities, and sororities knows that the Cyrenaics are alive and well and walk among us today!) Even if it is not always that crass, hedonism has become the frontrunner among life-quests in contemporary Western society. What was a cultural drift in this direction in the last century is a frenzied chase in ours. Our world is crowded with people who believe that sensual pleasure is the bullseye on the target of life.

Jesus had this philosophy in mind in his parable of the rich man, whose aim in life was summed up in the words, "Take your ease, eat, drink, and be merry!" We see what God thinks of this in the parable's stinging words of indictment, "Fool! This night your soul is required of you!"[3] The apostle Paul called hedonists "lovers of pleasure rather than lovers of God,"[4] and said of them, "Their end is destruction, their god is the belly, and they glory in their shame, with minds set on earthly things."[5] If this is what we are talking about, we can end our exploration here. *Christian hedonism* is a contradiction in terms.

That isn't the only kind of hedonism for us to consider, however. Enlightened hedonists seek to maximize pleasure and minimize pain (pleasures of the palate without nausea, intoxication without a hangover, sex without pregnancy or sexually transmitted disease), and to balance the present and future in their calculus. In the ancient world, Epicurus held that the quest for pleasure should consider a lifetime, not just the present moment, and should include intellectual, social, and aesthetic pleasures, as well as pleasures of the senses.[6] There are advocates of this kind of qualitative hedonism in our day.[7] If we broaden the parameters of pleasure along these lines, and fill it with the nuances of joy, can we make a case for Christian hedonism? Let's try.[8]

A THOUGHT EXPERIMENT

We should start by asking what makes one a hedonist. If I enjoy pleasure, does that make me one? No, no more than I am a Marxist if I am concerned about the plight of the poor, or a feminist if I am interested in the rights of women in the work place, or an environmentalist if I fill my recycling bin and put it at the curb in front of my house every Monday morning. It takes more than just enjoying pleasure and seeing it as part of a positive vision for life to make one a hedonist. But how much more?

Philosopher Rem Edwards identifies three beliefs that are essential to *normative* hedonism:

1. Pleasure, or happiness defined in terms of pleasure, is the *only* thing which is intrinsically good; and pain, or unhappiness defined in terms of pain, is the *only* thing which is intrinsically evil.

2. *Happiness*, hedonistically defined, consists of a positive surplus of pleasure over pain through an extended period of time; *unhappiness*, hedonistically defined, consists of a surplus of pain over pleasure through an extended period of time.

3. I *ought to act* to maximize pleasure or happiness and to minimize pain or unhappiness.[9]

Let's conduct a thought experiment. We will use this as a paradigm, substitute joy for pleasure, and see if we can make a case for Christian hedonism. Let's start with Edwards' first requirement. Can we say that joy is the only thing that is intrinsically good in our experience? If it is our highest good (which we have already seen), it is also an intrinsic good. If it is the first, it must be the second.[10] Since the highest good brooks no rivals, joy is the only thing that is intrinsically good.[11]

How would we translate the belief that pain is the only thing that is intrinsically evil into the language of Christian hedonism? If the pleasure we are talking about is first and foremost the enjoyment of God, then we should think of pain as spiritual *dis*pleasure, or soul-sorrow.[12] If joy is the pleasure of our hearts in God, then pain is an experience of spiritual discomfort or distress. If joy is the pleasure of God's presence,[13] then pain is the sting of separation from God (or a painful awareness of the absence of God) from a temporary departure to a profound and permanent parting of the ways. We are not required to see this as the only evil in the universe. It is the only thing that is *intrinsically* evil. All other evil leads to it or flows from it. The intrinsically good is experienced most fully in heaven, and the intrinsically evil most fully in hell.[14]

Let's move on to Edwards' second requirement. If we replace happiness with joy, and unhappiness with *unjoy*, does this fit well with a Christian vision of life? We would have to say something like this: "Joy consists of a positive surplus of pleasure (in God) over pain (soul-sorrow) through an extended period of time." And "*Unjoy* consists of a surplus of pain (soul-sorrow) over pleasure (in God) through an extended period of time."[15]

The first difficulty we encounter is one of lifespan. Hedonism is entirely *this-worldly* and a Christian vision of life is not. Even if we stretch the boundaries of "an extended period of time" as far as our mortality allows, it is not the same as eternity, and this makes a world of difference. The Puritan, Richard Baxter, wrote, "The work of godliness is a living unto God, and preparing for everlasting life, by foreseeing, foretasting, seeking, and rejoicing in that endless happiness which we will have with God."[16] This is essential to a Christian vision of life. We can't compromise here and call it a *Christian* vision.

Another problem is hedonism's notion of a surplus of pleasure over pain, or pain over pleasure. This implies an ability to measure pleasure and pain, or what is known as a "hedonistic calculus."[17] Even if there are degrees of pleasure in our enjoyment of God (from a mild euphoria to an intense ecstasy) and varying degrees of soul-sorrow (from discomfort to the depths of agony), it is difficult to see how we could quantify them in any meaningful way and then correlate intentional acts with them. If we are to base our actions on a surplus of pleasure over pain, this requires some way of measuring and forecasting the consequences of our actions. And this is a necessary dimension of acting morally according to this system: "Whatever its difficulties may be, the hedonistic calculus is essential to hedonism. Happiness cannot be the greatest possible balance of pleasures over pains unless there is such a balance, and it cannot be achieved unless this can be calculated and distinguished from lesser sums."[18]

Our thought experiment is breaking down. Edwards' third requirement only makes matters worse. Consider this proposal: I *ought to act* in ways that maximize my pleasure in God (joy) and minimize painful states of soul-sorrow (*unjoy*). Even if there is some wisdom in this, a calculating approach to God is doomed from the start. God cannot be calculated or controlled. He cannot be subjected to any formula we create. God is the biggest problem for Christian hedonism, and they don't get any bigger! But joy is also problematic. It is a gift. It is the God of joy giving himself to us. Joy is a pleasure that God bestows, not something that we generate and control, or manage and predict.

What about when God seems distant or even absent? It is true that sin is disruptive to our relationship with God,[19] and we are responsible for the rift. But there are also times when, for his own reasons, God veils himself to our hearts. Christian mystics call this the "dark night of the soul." Luther called God in this mode, *Deus absconditus*, or the Hidden God.[20] If we are unable to manage these dimensions of our relationship with God, we are never in a position to calculate the spiritual pleasure or pain we may experience as a result of the choices we make.

The more serious difficulty is that we are talking about a *moral* calculation: seeking to determine what we *ought* to do in every situation in order to bring about the greatest pleasure (even if it is joy) and the least pain (even if it is the absence of joy). It doesn't matter how accurate the calculation is, *it is the calculating itself that is a problem.*

Let me explain by introducing you to two sets of Latin terms. The first tandem is *frui* and *uti,* used by Augustine to talk about our love for God and our love for things.[21] *Frui* refers to an enjoyment of something, and *uti* refers to a use of something as a means to something else. The proper ordering of our affections, according to Augustine, is an enjoyment of God (*frui*) and a use of things (*uti*). We ought to love and enjoy God and use things. But what happens if we do the opposite? What if we attempt to use God and love and enjoy things? This seems to characterize "Name it and Claim it" Christianity. Prayer is treated as a form of magic (though its proponents would not call it that), with God (supposedly) bound to answer and give the supplicant whatever he or she wants. This, in effect, makes God a means to another end that is valued more highly. And that is idolatry (having other gods before the true God).[22]

Read this carefully: If, in our calculations, we use God for the sake of our joy, it comes to the same thing. Jonathan Edwards wrote of some Christians in his day:

> Instead of rejoicing in Christ Jesus, they rejoice in their admirable experiences. Instead of feeding and feasting their souls in viewing the innate, sweet, refreshing amiableness of the things exhibited in the gospel, they view them only as it were sideways. The object that fixes their contemplation, is their experience; and they are ever feeding their souls, and feasting a selfish principle with a view of their discoveries.[23]

This may seem more noble or spiritual than attempting to use God to gain material things, but it is not. As C.S. Lewis noted, "theological hedonism is still hedonism" whether one is seeking "heaven or a hundred pounds."[24]

Now for the second set of Latin terms. They were used by Edwards to promote moral clarity. A *bonum utile* is a *profitable good* to us, which, he says, serves our interest, and so suits our self-love. A *bonum formosum* is a *beautiful good* in itself, and is, according to Edwards, part of the moral and spiritual excellency of the divine nature.[25] If we calculate joy in God as a *bonum utile* and devise a way to bring it about, we put our own interests before God. This is self-love, dressed in religious clothing. It is idolatry: having another god (self) before the true God. No, we should seek joy in God as a *bonum formosum*. The enjoyment of God is a *beautiful good* to us because God is beautiful, and he is worthy of our heart's adoration.

Using Edward's distinctions, there is a paradox here: If we seek joy as a *profitable good* for ourselves, it will escape us; if we seek it as a *beautiful good* in God, we are then, and only then, in a position to experience it as something *good for us*. Here is the important point for our discussion: This paradox destroys the possibility of any calculation.[26] If calculating pleasure and pain as a moral compass is essential to the ethics of hedonism, then it is neither useful nor appropriate for Christian ethics, even if we are talking about the pleasures of joy.

Our thought experiment has failed.[27] This is disappointing to me, because I would love to be a Christian hedonist! If I were reading this book, however, I would underline the other side of this colon: While it is true that we can't embrace Christian hedonism as a normative approach to life and at the same time be true to God's Word, this is not a loss, or even a weakness. It is an offer of redemption. By refusing to make a god of pleasure, we honor the true God and enjoy the gifts of pleasure as he intends them in his wise and good plan for life. A joy-centered life is the only way to redeem hedonism. Instead of trying to bend our vision of life to fit pagan parameters, we ought instead to invite the hedonists of our day to join us in a much healthier, more satisfying way of living.[28]

To borrow inspired figures, trying to fill hedonism with Christian content is like pouring new wine into old wineskins. Trying to superimpose

Christian commitments onto the world's quest for pleasure is no more likely to succeed than patching a moth-eaten, threadbare cloak with a new piece of cloth. The attempt can only fail.[29] The idea of Christian hedonism may be intriguing and provocative; at the end of the day, however, we must conclude that we are better off (because we will be truer to the Scriptures, and therefore closer to the heart of God) to let joy chart its own course.

A QUEST FOR JOY

It is one thing to make joy the sum of a calculation, and another to make it the quest of a lifetime. A quest is very different from a calculation, and is a better way of understanding how to discover joy in life. Calculation seeks to predict and control. A quest involves intentionality, passion, and the pursuit of an objective, but embraces uncertainties along the way. A quest involves a journey and a path, not a formula and a method. Those who are on a quest know that they do not control much that will happen, but they are convinced that the possible rewards outweigh the likely risks. They embrace the fact that their mission is something greater than their ability to manage and scheme outcomes, but they are willing to give everything for the sake of their heart's desire.

The primary conviction in a quest for joy is that the enjoyment of God is our highest good. There is nothing better for us. It is the one thing that is intrinsically good. The pure, undimmed, and unbroken enjoyment of God is another way of describing heaven. The pain of separation from God is the one intrinsic evil in the universe, whether it is something we experience as a temporary, broken fellowship with God, or the ultimate, unmitigated, and unending suffering experienced by those who reject God and his ways, which is what we mean by hell (joy refused and forfeited with finality).

We cannot create or control joy, but we can position ourselves for it.[30] We can prepare ourselves for joy. We can ready ourselves for it. It isn't a matter of calculating means and measuring outcomes. It is walking the path that God himself has made for us, and wandering neither to the right nor to the left.

In our quest for joy we will seek to avoid things that disrupt or weaken our fellowship with God and our enjoyment of him – which is another way of saying that we will resolve to avoid sin. We will endeavor to stay away from anything that develops our character in unhealthy, ungodly ways. We will resist anything that creates a moral distance between God's heart and ours. We will resolve to avoid anything that violates his will. As *characentric* Christians,[31] we will commit ourselves to act in ways that prepare our hearts for joy – not that we calculate and forecast the consequences of our actions and then choose only those things that will best serve our own interests – even if it is our interest in joy.[32] Rather, we will seek to become all that God wants us to be, to harmonize our hearts with his, and to delight in obeying his commands, knowing that this is the path he has prepared for his glory and our good.[33]

WHOSE PLEASURE SHOULD WE SEEK?

If we say that pleasure is the highest good, it still makes sense to ask whose pleasure we are talking about. Whose pleasure ought we to seek? Most forms of hedonism (ancient and modern) assume that we have our own pleasure in mind. It is our own pleasure that we should seek. This is sometimes called "egoistic hedonism." But this isn't the only possible answer to the question we are posing. In the eighteenth century a number of philosophers espoused an ethical theory known as utilitarianism, a kind of "altruistic hedonism," in which acting morally is always a matter of seeking the greatest pleasure for the greatest number of people.

Although utilitarianism has its flaws,[34] bringing the pleasure of others into an accounting of the good life moves us in the right direction. It isn't that our own pleasure is illegitimate or unimportant; it's just that in our quest for joy we will seek to please God supremely, and we will seek the joy of others before our own.

The heart of a joy-quest is aiming first and foremost at a life that is fully pleasing to God, pursuing a life over which God rejoices. This was perfectly realized in the life of Christ, who could truthfully say of his relationship with the Father, "I always do what is pleasing to him."[35] His life is our model. We seek to bring pleasure to God and discover our own joy as we do.[36]

Pleasing God is central to a New Testament vision of life:

> Therefore, I urge you, brothers, in view of God's mercy, to offer your bodies as living sacrifices, holy and pleasing to him - this is your spiritual act of worship (Romans 12:1)
>
> We make it our aim to please him. (2 Corinthians 5:9)
>
> (I pray) that you may be filled with the knowledge of his will in all spiritual wisdom and understanding, to lead a life worthy of the Lord, fully pleasing to him (Colossians 1:9-10).
>
> Finally, then, brothers, we ask and urge you in the Lord Jesus, that as you received from us how you ought to live and to please God, just as you are doing, that you do so more and more. (1 Thessalonians 4:1, ESV)
>
> (May he) equip you with everything good that you may do his will, working in you that which is pleasing in his sight. (Hebrews 13:21)

In our pursuit of joy, we will also seek the joy of others. We will delight in spreading the pleasures of joy far and wide.[37] Joy always looks for company. It seeks camaraderie. But we must say more than this if we are to be true to the teaching and example of Jesus. In our pursuit of joy we will seek the joy of others *before* our own (even if, paradoxically, we discover joy ourselves by doing this). Karl Barth wrote, "It must be said that we can have joy . . . only as we give it to others."[38] The currents of joy flow over this riverbed:

> It is more blessed to give than to receive. (Acts 20:35)
>
> Let each of us please his neighbor for his good, to build him up. (Romans 15:2, ESV)
>
> Let no one seek his own good, but the good of his neighbor. (1 Corinthians 10:24)
>
> Consider others better than yourselves. (Philippians 2:3, NIV)

Augustine was right: "Now you love yourself suitably when you love God better than yourself."[39] And we love ourselves suitably when we love others better than we love ourselves. In a joyful vision of life, a commitment to our own pleasure will always be a humble affair by the standards of the world. We will seek the pleasure of God above everything else, seek the joy of our neighbors, and then revel in the enjoyment of God and our neighbors.

Let's be candid: Seeking our own joy, even if it is third, is an expression of self-love. What should we think of this? When loving God and loving others is subordinated to loving ourselves, it is not a virtue, but a vice. Paul had this moral defect in mind when he condemned those who were "lovers of self."[40] Luther called the person who lives this way, *homo incurvatus in se* – man curved in upon himself, like a shriveled leaf. It is the essence of sin: a self-seeking, self-preferring, self-exalting way of living before God and others.[41]

In the right order, however, loving ourselves is a good and healthy thing. It is integral to the second greatest commandment, "You shall love your neighbor as yourself."[42] Paul understood this when he argued from the premise of a husband's love for himself to the conclusion that he has a moral responsibility to love his own wife in the same way.[43] It is impossible to affirm the goodness of creation[44] without affirming the goodness of our own existence, and affirming ourselves as God's handiwork.[45] Augustine said, in fact, that you cannot love God without loving yourself: "For it is impossible for one who loves God not to love himself. For he alone has a proper love for himself who aims diligently at the attainment of the chief and true good; and if this is nothing else but God . . . what is to prevent one who loves God from loving himself?"[46]

Seeking our own joy, when it follows love for God and love for others, not only has God's permission, but his blessing. Even if it is upside down from the world's approach to hedonism, this is God's design for pleasure at its highest and best. When we pursue our own joy third, we are given a key that unlocks a treasure chest filled with pleasures in God and his good gifts. This is pleasure at its best: cultivating a way of life in which we enjoy God as our highest good, in the overflow of that joy, give ourselves to the joy of others, and then, in these first two commitments, discover a greater joy for ourselves than we could ever have known if we had put our own pleasure first.

VIRTUE AND THE QUEST FOR JOY

Hedonism subordinates all other moral considerations in its pursuit of pleasure. Pleasure is the only *intrinsic* good. Insofar as anything else is good, its value is *extrinsic*, or instrumental. Its worth lies only in its ability to bring about a positive balance of pleasure over pain. Loving another has value only if it puts us in a better position to receive the benefits of love. Patience has value only if waiting increases the likelihood of a pleasurable reward. And so on.

We have already seen that in a Christian vision, virtue is never merely a means to the good life; it is essential to the good life. Means and end are bundled together in the package of life. Virtue can never be regarded as a means and then treated as a matter of prudential reckoning with another end in view. That would fundamentally change the nature of our acts.[47] Having said this, however, it is important to add that there is great joy in pursuing a path of virtue. Virtue is not merely a means to our end, but it is a means. A Christ-like character leads to a greater enjoyment of God, and a greater enjoyment of life before God. They are coincidental (happening at the same time), and this is not coincidental (happening by chance). It is God's design.

HYPHENATED JOY

John Piper warns that seeking a subjective experience of joy will end in frustration, and in fact dishonors God.[48] I agree, but would say, more fundamentally, that it is a misunderstanding of joy to think that such a thing is even possible. Joy engages us as subjects, but it is never merely subjective. It is the enjoyment of someone or something.[49] It always has an outward look. It is always attached. In this sense, there is no such thing as joy in itself. You can't extract joy, as you might cinnamon from a cinnamon tree, and then enjoy the taste in itself. Joy is governed by its objects.[50]

Joy must always be hyphenated in our thinking. It is always joy-in-God or joy-in-his-gifts or joy-in-our-neighbors. Joy in God's creation, for instance, is our pleasure in a rainbow or the song of a nightingale. Joy may linger beyond the encounter, and may even return in memory; it is still, however, attached to an object. In its highest sense, it is impossible to talk about joy without also talking about God. Joy cannot be separated from the enjoyment of God. As Dr. Piper tells us:

> We are commanded by the Word of God, "Delight yourself in the LORD." This means: Pursue joy in God. The word "joy" or "delight" protects us from a mercenary pursuit of God. And the phrase "in God" protects us from thinking joy somehow stands alone as an experience separate from our experience of God himself.[51]

You will never find joy by looking for it in itself. It is always found in an outward look, in an engagement with God, his world, and the people he has created. It can't be found anywhere else. The focus of joy is not inward, toward the soul's entertainment of pleasure. It is outward, toward its Object. Its interest is never merely the experience of delight; it is always the One in whom our souls find delight. The difference makes a very significant difference. It will not only make a difference in your life, but in the world as it is filled with people who pursue this joy.

Questions for Thought and Discussion

1. *Christian hedonism* is a provocative way of thinking about a life that is pleasing to God. When we began our exploration of this path, did you find yourself hoping that it would work out? If so, why? Or did it seem too startling and unsettling to your understanding of the Christian life? If so, why?

2. How does the joy of God's presence and the pain of separation from God help you to think about the Christian doctrines of heaven and hell?

3. How do you think life as a joy-quest could speak to contemporary versions of hedonism in our culture?

4. How does seeking the pleasure of God help you understand the command to love God?

5. How does seeking the pleasure or joy of others help you understand the command to love your neighbor as yourself?

CHAPTER 11

JOY AS AN IMPERATIVE

In the Bible joy is often dressed in the language of command:

> Rejoice before the LORD your God, you, your sons and daughters! (Deuteronomy 12:12)
>
> Rejoice in the LORD and be glad! (Psalm. 32:11)
>
> Serve the LORD with gladness! (Psalm 100:2)
>
> Be glad and rejoice! Surely the LORD has done great things. (Joel 2:21)
>
> Rejoice and be glad, because great is your reward in heaven. (Matthew 5:12)
>
> Rejoice in the Lord always. I will say it again: Rejoice! (Philippians 4:4)
>
> Let us rejoice and be glad and give him glory! (Revelation 19:7)[1]

How should we understand these imperatives? It is one thing to experience joy, but another to be intentional about it. It is one thing to be enriched by joy when it comes, for as long as it lasts, but another to embrace joy as a mandate from our Creator. You are not alone if you aren't sure how to make sense of joy-imperatives in the Scriptures. Yet the commands to rejoice and be glad look like any other commands that we are expected to obey. Do we take them at face value? If we don't, do we risk missing out on something God wants for us and expects from us? If we do, how do we say "Yes" to them?

THE SERIOUS BUSINESS OF HEAVEN

There is a tradition which says that it is a mistake to use the language of command with our emotions. They are beyond our control. They are givens that we must take into account, but they have no moral significance. Bible scholars who have been influenced by this view think we should probe beneath the surface meaning of the imperatives to rejoice (since they can't really mean what they seem to be saying) to see their real significance. Commands to rejoice and be glad end up being mere affirmations that joy is a good thing if it happens to come to us.[2]

I choose to take my stand with those who believe that the language of command, which makes the pursuit of joy a moral obligation, should be taken literally and seriously. If you join me, we will be in good company. Martin Luther wrote, "A Christian should and must be a cheerful person. If he isn't, the devil is tempting him."[3] Karl Barth wrote, "The man who hears and takes to heart the biblical message is not only not permitted but plainly forbidden to be anything but merry and cheerful."[4] Here is Henri Nouwen:

> Joy does not simply happen to us. We have to choose joy and keep choosing it every day.

> It is important to become aware that at every moment of our life we have an opportunity to choose joy.[5]

We can add C.S. Lewis:

> My own idea, for what it is worth, is that all sadness which is not either arising from the repentance of a concrete sin and hastening towards concrete amendment or restitution, or else arising from pity and hastening to achieve assistance, is simply bad; and I think we all sin by needlessly disobeying the apostolic injunction to "rejoice" as much as by anything else.[6]

Lewis wrote, "Joy is the serious business of heaven."[7] Making it the serious business of our lives here and now begins when we face the command to be joyful, refuse to water it down or maneuver around it, and accept the challenge of harmonizing our wills with God's will for us. Our first response to God should be "Yes!" even if our second response is "How?"

APPROACHING JOY INDIRECTLY

One mistake we might make is to think in terms of direct cause-and-effect relationships: If *a* results in *b* and we want *b*, we must do *a*. Life is rarely that simple. Many of the objectives we pursue don't fit that model. They are complex, multi-faceted projects: gaining admission to the college of one's choice, earning the respect of a boss at work, winning someone's heart in a romance, becoming debt-free, or putting oneself in a position to retire.

Many of our practical goals can only be approached indirectly. Let me give you two examples. Suppose that I make a New Year's resolution to get rid of my "love handles." I go to the local gym where I am told that spot reducing is a myth. The trainer tells me that if I want to get rid of that corpulence, I will have to lower the number of calories I consume (which, in turn, will involve many decisions every day), and burn calories through an overall regimen of strenuous exercise. I can wear a shorter belt, but not the way I initially thought. I will have to approach the goal indirectly. There are things I must stop doing, and other things that I must start doing and continue doing if I want to reach it.

Or there is the challenge I often face falling asleep at night. It seems to me that I don't control this. When I'm lying in bed staring at the ceiling, I really don't! I can give myself the command, "Go to sleep!" but that has yet to work. That doesn't mean, however, that I can't approach the problem indirectly with a positive result. I have learned, for instance, that there are things I should avoid if I want to fall asleep at night. I should avoid sugar and caffeine in the afternoon and evening hours. As I approach the time to retire, I shouldn't allow my mind to continue in the highly active state it has been in all day. I shouldn't go to bed too early or too late, and I shouldn't go to bed at a different time every night. On the positive side there are things that I should do. I should exercise earlier in the day. I should try to establish rhythms and patterns in preparing for sleep. I should wind down with pleasant conversations with my wife and children, leave the challenges and cares of the day behind with a chapter in a novel, and then close my eyes with a prayer of thanksgiving. What seems at first to be beyond my control turns out to be something that I can influence in significant ways by approaching it indirectly.

Obeying the command to be joyful looks something like this.[8] Even if we don't have direct control over joy, there are still many choices that we can and must make if we resolve to pursue this pleasure. We will move closer to the intent of the joy-commands by choosing to say "No" to the things that will keep us from joy, and "Yes" to those things which move us toward joy.[9]

BEGIN WITH CONFESSION

It may seem that I am only stating the obvious, but to find joy we must first be open to it. Karl Barth wrote:

> We can close ourselves to joy. We can harden ourselves against it. We can try to be merely busy and therefore slothful in the expectation of fulfillments. We can regard life as such a solemn matter that there is no desire for celebration. We can look upon icy seriousness as the highest duty and virtue. On the basis of experienced disappointments we can try to establish that our only right is to bitterness. Is it not obvious that we can never really have joy? Does not joy really consist only in the joy of anticipation? But the fact that we actually become joyless is only a symptom that in self-embitterment we do violence to life and to God as its Creator.[10]

Opening ourselves to joy will require adjustments in the way we think. If God commands us to rejoice – not just occasionally, but always – it means that joy is essential to God's design for our lives. It means that joy, from the perspective of the Creator, is normative for us. A joyful heart is normal, and an absence of joy is abnormal or deviant. I'm not sure that many Christians see life or live life this way. I'm not sure that many are taught from the pulpit or encouraged in the pew to evaluate their lives this way. As long as we see joy as something that is optional or peripheral to God's design for our lives, we are not open to what God wants for us.

Obedient joy begins with confession. The Greek word translated "to confess" means, literally, "to say the same thing."[11] If I confess my sin to God, I am saying the same thing about my sin that God says about it. Confessing is agreeing with God. It is embracing his view of things. Openness to joy begins when we say the same thing about it that God does, regardless of what others may think. It is a choice you must make. You will have to take sides on this.

Jonathan Edwards wrote, "That religion which God requires, and will accept, does not consist in weak, dull, and lifeless wishes, raising us but a little above a state of indifference."[12] But let's be honest. Many Christians seem to be satisfied with that kind of life. They rationalize their plight and insist that theirs is a more "realistic" view to take. They may even dress it in religious language and have proof-texts from the Bible to bolster their position. You can go with the flow of this false piety, with its pleasure-denying, delight-disapproving, joy-stifling approach to life, or you can begin swimming with the currents of joy. You must choose. One way or another, you must respond.

If God commands joy, and it is central to his design for life, then it is a genuine possibility. It can happen. Not just for someone else, but for you! Are you open to that? As Barth observed, you can close your heart to joy. You can rule it out in advance, either because you don't think that it is possible, or because you don't see how it can be possible for you. If you find yourself there, let me encourage you to drop to your knees before God, confess it as disobedience, and pray, "I believe; help my unbelief!"[13]

QUENCHING AND GRIEVING THE SPIRIT

Joy is the fruit of the Spirit.[14] It is not an exotic fruit, any more than an apple is an exotic fruit for an apple tree. It is the natural result of the Spirit's presence and work in our lives. If it doesn't happen, something is wrong.[15] If we shift the metaphor from fruit to fire, we can discover what that might be. We cannot control the Spirit, but we can quench the Spirit. We are not responsible for generating the glow of the Spirit's presence (a good way of thinking about joy), but the apostle Paul said that we can put out the flames.[16] If we look at the flow of exhortations, which includes quenching the

Spirit, we will find contextual clues to help us understand what Paul had in mind: "Rejoice always, pray without ceasing, give thanks in all circumstances; for this is the will of God in Christ Jesus for you. Do not quench the Spirit. Do not despise prophecies, but test everything; hold fast what is good. Abstain from every form of evil."[17]

We douse the Spirit's fire when we ignore prayer and live as if we didn't need it, when we take the good things in life for granted and fail to give thanks, when we are not open to the Spirit's voice, but at the same time uncritically open our hearts to the world's version of a good life, when we loosen our grip on what God says is good for us, and when we entertain what God says is evil as a real possibility for ourselves. If we do these things, we are simply not in a position for joy. We disqualify ourselves. Doing these things numbs our spiritual senses, obstructs our spiritual vision, weakens our spiritual appetite, and dulls the edge of spiritual desire. Joy is not possible when this happens.

The Spirit is not just a Fire whose flames we can extinguish; he is a Person whom we can grieve.[18] If the Spirit who dwells within us is grieved by the way we live our lives, we should not expect him, at the same time, to bestow joy.[19] Sin grieves the *Holy* Spirit. If the Spirit is mourning sin in our lives, we ought to expect conviction, admonition, and reproof, but we should not expect joy. In his lament he seeks to woo us back through a painful sense of joy-lost, joy-forfeited, and joy-abandoned. Joy will not return, however, until we repent of the things that have grieved our heavenly Guest, and we again seek the things that are pleasing in his sight.

REMOVING EMOTIONAL BARRIERS TO JOY

In an earlier chapter we explored the emotional dimensions of joy. There we discovered that joy often accompanies and enriches other emotions. It can be a nuance of peace, a dimension of gratitude, a hue of hope, a facet of reverential fear and even a feature of godly sorrow. We also learned that joy is incompatible with some emotions. Bitterness and anxiety are two examples. Bitterness is an unhealthy emotional response to the past, and anxiety is an unhealthy emotional anticipation of the future. Both will keep you from joy. It is not possible to let yourself become bitter about things that have happened to you or to others, and experience joy at the same time. It is not possible to live in a state of anxiety as you face the future and to be joyful at the same time. They are not just contrary emotions; they are contradictory. Bitterness and joy, and anxiety and joy, cannot exist in the same heart at the same time. If joy is a river, bitterness and anxiety are boulders that block its course. They must be removed before the currents of joy can flow again.

Bitterness and anxiety are both cultivated ways of seeing life. If I am bitter, I have formed habits in the way I look at things that have happened to me. I believe that I have been wronged, I nurse the pain, and I instinctively desire to balance the scales of justice. I cultivate the emotion of bitterness by replaying a video or audio of the past, rehearsing my side of the story, feeling the pain all over again, and nurturing the desire to get even – which I attempt to do (even if I am not consciously aware of doing it) by focusing and directing negative emotional energy toward others. I convince myself that I am punishing the offender with my negative emotions (though, ironically, I am the one who is hurt by them).

In the case of anxiety, I cultivate this emotion by playing the "if-game." I think to myself over and over, "If this happens, then this could happen. And if that happens, then that could happen," and so on, piling *ifs* on top of each other. Anxiety is the emotional friction between our *ability to imagine* the future, and our *inability to control* the future. Anxiety is not a momentary wave of concern that washes over the shore of my soul. It is a river that carves banks and bed through a ceaseless process of spiritual erosion. It is a cultivated disposition. It is a way of habituating my heart in a worried interpretation of life.

If you want joy, but you struggle with bitterness, you must begin with the way you think and feel about your past. You must look at it again through a new set of spiritual lenses, affirming that God is good: He is committed to what is best for you. He is wise: He knows how to accomplish it. He is all-powerful: He is able to bring it about.[20]

The way out of bitterness and into joy involves revisiting and revisioning your past (seeing it again in a different way). If you struggle with bitterness, you are already revisiting the wrongs you have suffered. The way out begins when you revisit them, but change the direction and outcome by seeing everything that has happened to you through the lens of the goodness, wisdom, and power of God. It is in revisioning your life through faith that you weaken the control of bitterness in your heart. The more you do this, the weaker its grip will be. When you can say, as Joseph did to his brothers, "You meant this for evil, but God meant it for good,"[21] you will begin to remove the chains of bitterness from your soul. When you can finally forgive and release them from the punishment you have been trying to inflict on them in your heart, you will walk out of that emotional prison. As you cultivate a heart of praise to God for his goodness, wisdom, and power, and thank him for what he is seeking to do through the events and experiences of your life, you will step into the exhilarating, triumphant freedom of joy.[22]

If you want joy, but you struggle with anxiety, you must begin with the way you think about the future. If forgiveness is the antidote to bitterness, trust is the cure for anxiety. The same truths are relevant here. Like forgiveness, trust is made possible by affirming and embracing the goodness, wisdom, and power of God, only here it is brought to bear on the way you face life's uncertainties. Let these faith-commitments be the place where you begin thinking about the path that lies before you. Whatever may come, God will work with you for your good. He is committed to it. He knows how to bring it about. And it is fully within his reach. As Paul put it, when you present your requests about the future to God, and you thank him in advance for what he is going to do, you will experience a peace that "passes all understanding," guarding your heart and mind.[23] The peace of God will protect you and joy will be your companion as you venture into the days to come.

REFUSE TO SETTLE FOR LESS

Before we move to the positive side of obedient joy, there is one more thing that we should not do if we wish to become joyful people: We should not settle for anything less than joy. Aquinas wrote, "No one can live without delight and that is why a man deprived of spiritual joy goes over to carnal pleasures."[24] If we do not cultivate joy in our lives, we will seek to fill that spiritual void with surrogate pleasures. It is a spiritual law. It is not only nature that abhors a vacuum. Deprived of joy, we will seek substitutes.

The ancient adversary of God is ever vigilant and eager to exploit this. He is a master counterfeiter. He cannot create genuine pleasures. Only God can. But he can corrupt them. He can twist them. He can make his imitations attractive and plausible to the unsuspecting. In *The Screwtape Letters*, C.S. Lewis has Screwtape, a veteran demon, give this advice to Wormwood, his apprentice:

> Never forget that when we are dealing with any pleasure in its healthy and normal and satisfying form we are, in a sense, on the Enemy's [God's] ground. I know we have won many a soul through pleasure. All the same, it is His [God's] invention, not ours. He made the pleasures; all our research so far has not enabled us to produce one. All we can do is to encourage the humans to

> take the pleasures which our Enemy [God] has produced, at times, or ways, or in degrees, which He has forbidden.[25]

Satan can make the "fleeting pleasures of sin"[26] seem appealing and convince us that we are better off with his offer and its easy and instant gratification than with God's. The Bible is filled with stories of men and women who were ensnared by that trap to warn us how easily it can happen.

Tempting us to pursue bad things to satisfy our desire for joy is only one of hell's strategies. It has much greater success convincing us to pursue good things in bad ways. God has made us creatures with needs and desires that he delights to satisfy, first by giving himself, and then by opening the storehouse of his world to us. It is possible to have all of our desires satisfied and to want nothing badly.[27] That will be the hallmark of heaven. The success of the advertising industry in our day, however, demonstrates how very far we are from that. Madison Avenue cares for nothing more than profit. Satan cares for nothing more than seeing us become sated with good things that are wanted wrongly.[28]

One of the truly haunting passages of the Bible is Deuteronomy 28:47-48. If its truth were fully grasped and fully embraced on a large scale (say, for instance, in the Church!) it could deal a deathblow to our narcissistic culture of consumption:

> Because you did not serve the LORD your God with joyfulness and gladness of heart, by reason of the abundance of all things, therefore you shall serve your enemies whom the LORD will send against you, in hunger and thirst, in nakedness, and in want of all things; and he will put a yoke of iron upon your neck, until he has destroyed you.

God said that he would judge his people for not serving him with joyfulness and gladness of heart. This tells us how seriously Heaven takes the business of joy! But the reason for their failure to live joyfully in service to God was the culture of abundance they had created for themselves. It was God who had given them the blessing of prosperity,[29] but they had forgotten that (as he said they would), and turned their hearts away from him to the gifts he had given. When what God intends for our joy is valued more highly than God, and is pursued apart from him, it becomes a pseudo-joy, a substitute for joy, and even a rival to joy, because it becomes a rival to the God of joy.

C.S. Lewis wrote, "We are half-hearted creatures, fooling about with drink and sex and ambition when infinite joy is offered us."[30] It is an absurdity, but one that we readily embrace. The Creator is stunned by the idols we create:

> For cross to the coasts of Cyprus and see,
> or send to Kedar and examine with care;
> see if there has been such a thing.
> Has a nation changed its gods,
> even though they are no gods?
> But my people have changed their glory
> for that which does not profit.
> Be appalled, O heavens, at this,
> be shocked, be utterly desolate,
> says the LORD,
> for my people have committed two evils;
> they have forsaken me,
> the fountain of living waters,
> and hewed out cisterns for themselves,
> broken cisterns,
> that can hold no water. (Jeremiah 2:10-13)

Through the prophet Isaiah, he pleads with us:

> Come, everyone who thirsts,
> come to the waters;
> and he who has no money,
> come, buy and eat!
> Come, buy wine and milk
> without money and without price.
> Why do you spend your money for that which is not bread,
> and your labor for that which does not satisfy?
> Listen diligently to me, and eat what is good,
> and delight yourselves in rich food.
> Incline your ear, and come to me;
> hear, that your soul may live; (Isaiah 55:1-3, ESV)

To say that our Creator is also our highest good is to say that he has made us so that our deepest desires can only be fulfilled in him. In the words of Pascal:

> There once was in man a true happiness of which now remain to him only the mark and empty trace, which he in vain tries to fill from all his surroundings, seeking from things absent the help he does not obtain in things present. But these are all inadequate, because the infinite abyss can only be filled by an infinite and immutable object, that is to say, only by God himself.[31]

This is where we meet the command to rejoice in the Lord and say "Yes" or "No." Our *highest good* becomes *our* highest good only when we embrace it as the very best in life *for us*. In countless choices we make in the course of life, we seek to fill the "infinite abyss" with something other than God, or we invite him to fill the void that he alone fits. We content ourselves with a "mark and empty trace" of true happiness, or we pursue our greatest joy in God and protect its highest place in all that we treasure and hold dear. God has given us that choice, and we make it many times every day. Joy or a substitute. Joy or a surrogate. A feast or a morsel. Bread or dirt.

POSITIONING OURSELVES FOR JOY

One of the things we have learned about joy that might keep us from thinking that we have responsibilities for it is that joy is not something we can bring about ourselves. It is the gift of God. It is the fruit of the Spirit, and the Spirit's work, like the wind, will always seem surprising to us. It isn't the kind of thing we can plan and organize, or regulate and control. We can't *produce* joy, but we can *position* ourselves for it. We can't bring it about on our own, but we can open our hearts and be receptive to it. We can make ourselves ready for joy.

Suppose I know that friends will visit from another state, but I don't know when they will arrive. When I will greet them at my front door is not something that I control. But I can put myself into a state of readiness for their visit. If I do that I will anticipate the possibility that the doorbell will ring at any moment, announcing their arrival. I will prepare for their coming. I will make adjustments in my schedule to accommodate them, and I will do my best to help keep the house clean, and the coffee pot ready, in expectation of their stay.

In this sense, joy is like the return of Christ. He will come like a thief in the night, he said. We cannot know and cannot control the time of his arrival, but we can, and ought to, keep ourselves in a state of readiness for his return.[32] In the same way, banking on the goodness of God, and knowing that he wants us to be joyful, we should look for joy. We should not only be open to the possibility of joy, we should be ready for it. We should eagerly await it. We should hopefully anticipate it as we move through the day. Karl Barth wrote, "Our first point in this respect is that it is certainly required of man that he should continually hold himself in readiness for joy."[33] Joyful people do this. It is the daily disposition and discipline of their hearts.

SEEK GOD, FIND JOY

> Glory in his holy name;
> let the hearts of those who seek the LORD rejoice!
> Seek the LORD and his strength;
> seek his presence continually. (Psalm 105:3-4)

Let's unpack these verses. Those who seek God find joy. It is like finding water and getting wet, or finding fire and basking in its warmth. Now, it is possible to think that we are seeking God, but to be mistaken about this. It is possible to confuse religious activity with pursuing God. Some are led into this confusion by people to whom they look for spiritual guidance who, in some way, benefit from religious activity. It happened in Jesus' day.[34] It happens in ours. People who seek God might do these things, but seeking God should not be confused with going to church, attending Bible studies, or going to Christian conferences, retreats, and concerts. You can put these activities on a list and check them off as you go, and still not pursue God and find joy in the pursuit.

The kind of seeking the Psalmist has in mind is a matter of the heart. "Seek the LORD and his strength," he says. It begins with a painful sense of our weakness in the face of life's challenges. We know our need for God's empowering presence, and we refuse to pretend otherwise. We long to be "strong in the Lord and in the strength of his might."[35] We refuse to flee hardship and challenge, or to act from the fund of our resources alone. Neither is acceptable to us. We take intentional steps of faith beyond the boundaries of our ability, asking God for his strength with each step we take.

As we do this, this is what we discover: The joy of the Lord is our strength.[36] Joy makes us strong. It enables us to face life with greater courage and confidence, and to see possibilities under God that we never saw before.

What looked so daunting on the front side of seeking the Lord and his strength looks small and unimposing on the other side, and we laugh at ourselves for not seeking and trusting God sooner. It is the triumphant laughter of joy.

The Psalmist links joy with seeking the Lord, and seeking the Lord with seeking "his presence continually." To rehearse an earlier lesson, "Where God is, there is joy."[37] This is bedrock spiritual reality. If God is everywhere present, then we can experience the joy of his presence wherever we are, and cultivate this joy in all that we do.

Seeking the presence of God does not make him present; it opens our hearts to the God who is there. It is like cultivating an aesthetic sense: becoming alert to beauty, attentive to its subtle nuances, and delighting in details that others hurry past and never notice. The truth is that we live in the context of the Divine. Every moment of every day, we are either aware of this or we are not. We are either mindful or forgetful of God's presence. We say "Yes" or "No" to Jesus' view of the world:

> To his eyes this is a God-bathed, and God-permeated world. It is a world filled with a glorious reality, where every component is within the range of God's direct knowledge and control – though he obviously permits some of it, for good reasons, to be for a while otherwise than as he wishes. It is a world that is inconceivably beautiful and good because of God and because God is always in it. It is a world in which God is continually at play and over which he constantly rejoices.[38]

In this vision of life, God is an enveloping, enchanting, and endowing Presence. He is the Power that configures all things into a pattern that covers the cosmos and spans the ages. He is the Light that illumines every path. He is the relentless Love that beckons our hearts and pursues us through the course of life. We cannot escape him. We would perish in the attempt. Running into his embrace, we discover our heart's desire and the joy for which we were made. Escape or embrace: They are the only options we have. The first is futile because it is impossible.[39] The second is the best decision we can ever make.

Finally, the verses that exhort us to find our joy in seeking God, his strength, and his presence, begin by exhorting us to "glory" in our God. This is another way of talking about worship. It is a way of living before God. It is a way of enthroning God in our lives and celebrating his reign. It includes everything we do. Everything. "Whether you eat or drink, or whatever you do, do all to the glory of God."[40] Doing this is worship. Thomas Howard writes:

> It is our task in this shrine to take these ordinary things and, by lifting them up in oblation, to hallow them to the service for which they were given us here, which was to bring us to the habitation of God where we are set free to live in the splendor where eating and drinking and working and playing are known for what they really are, forms of perpetual worship and therefore bliss.[41]

If we glory in God, all of life becomes an expression of worship and an opportunity for joy.

Worship is meant to engage our voices as well as our hearts as we put into words our heart's adoration and delight. When worship is authentic, praise is the overflow of enjoying God. C.S. Lewis put it this way, "All enjoyment spontaneously overflows into praise." And, "I think we delight to praise what we enjoy because the praise not merely expresses but completes the enjoyment; it is its appointed consummation."[42] This completes our worship and so completes our joy.

If we do not worship well on Sundays (if ceremony becomes a substitute for celebration), it is because we have not worshiped well during the week. If we do not worship well in the company of others (if ritual becomes a substitute for reveling), it is because we have not worshiped well in the secret places of our heart. If we worship as a way of life, seeking God, communing with him, honoring him, and enthroning him in all that we do, say, and think, our worship with others becomes the crown of joyful living. We come to love everything about worship.[43] If we love to worship God, we will love to worship him with his people. If we enjoy him when we are alone, we will revel in a shared joy with others (and a greater joy because it is shared) as we celebrate our life together in God.

PURSUE MORAL EXCELLENCE

Jonathan Edwards wrote, "True happiness consists in the possession and enjoyment of moral good, in a way sweetly agreeing with God's moral perfections."[44] This is another way of saying that joy and virtue are woven together in the fabric of life.[45] Joy is a sign that our hearts are functioning the way God intends them to, with a harmony between our desires and decisions and deeds, and the congeniality of our hearts with his. This is essential to our understanding of joy as a mandate. C.S. Lewis wrote:

> Every time you make a choice, you are turning the central part of you, the part that chooses, into something a little different from what was before . . . you are slowly turning this central thing either into a heavenly creature or a hellish creature . . . to be one kind of creature is heaven; that is joy and peace and knowledge and power. To be the other means madness, horror, idiocy, rage, impotence,

> and eternal loneliness. Each of us at each moment is progressing to one state or the other.[46]

Let's frame this in a positive way: We make many choices in the pursuit of virtue. The sign of true virtue is our pleasure in it. This pleasure is another way of talking about joy. To know joy and its virtues perfected is heaven.

CULTIVATE COMMUNITY

The biblical commands to rejoice are found in the second person plural.[47] If we were to use a southern idiom, we would translate them, "Y'all, rejoice in the Lord!" Now, the obvious thing is that a congregation is being addressed. But there is more to it than this. The joy that God has for us is not something we can realize on our own, in isolation from others. It is found in community. This is so because God made us relational beings. He created us to live in relationship with him and with others. The command to live joyfully meets us in the interface between our lives and the lives of others who are walking the same path of faith, moving in the same direction, pursuing the same end.

It is the nature of joy to be this way. Joy always has an outward look. It is always found in an engagement with God, his world, and our neighbors. Kierkegaard was right: While grief is "secretive, silent, solitary and seeks to retire into itself," joy is "communicative, social, open-hearted, and desires expression."[48] The good news about Jesus Christ at one and the same time creates fellowship with God and fellowship with others who have been drawn into a relationship with him. When we are united to Christ through faith we are at the same time included in a fellowship with those who are likewise united with him. As Augustine put it, our joy becomes "the joy of God and the enjoyment of each other in God."[49]

In the community of faith we discover shared joy. The Greeks had a special word for this: *sunchairein*, "to rejoice with."[50] It is found often in the New Testament:

> And when he comes home, he calls together his friends and his neighbors, saying to them, "*Rejoice with* me, for I have found my sheep which was lost." (Luke 15:6)

> If one member suffers, all suffer together; if one member is honored, all *rejoice together*. (1 Corinthians 12:26)

> Even if I am to be poured as a libation upon the sacrificial offering of your faith, I am glad and *rejoice with* you all. (Philippians 2:17)

We see this shared joy in the early Church: "Breaking bread in their homes, they partook of food with glad and generous hearts."[51]

There is another way in which the community of faith is essential to a life of joy. I have tried to impress upon you the importance of virtue in the pursuit of joy. But virtue is best understood as a community project.[52] God's design for transforming our character includes sharing a vision of life with others, sharing life's experiences with them, seeking to act (even if we fail) on the commitments we share, encouraging each other, holding each other accountable, learning from each other, correcting each other, teaching each other, coaching each other, and modeling for each other the traits that we are pursuing in life. It is God's intention to make us like Christ through relationships: marriage, family, friendships, small groups of Christians meeting together, and the larger community of Christian faith, the local church. Saying "Yes" to this is essential to obeying the command to become joyful people.

ENJOY!

The musician who has given himself fully to his art is in the best position to enjoy sitting at a piano and playing a masterpiece. The athlete who has devoted herself to her sport knows most fully the pleasure of playing it well. If you commit yourself to the way of life that I have described in this chapter, you will be in the best position to enjoy the good gifts of our good God. The apostle Paul wrote, "God . . . richly furnishes us with everything to enjoy."[53] He wants you to say *yes* to his provision. *Yes* to his invitation.

As you consider the words "everything to enjoy," it may seem that this is too good to be true. You may feel like a one-year-old on her first birthday, seated before a frosting-laden cake, hopeful and yet apprehensive, with her mother inviting her, "Go ahead! Put your fingers into the frosting and eat!"[54] We are invited to enjoy all that God has created, with the only qualification that we do so with thanksgiving: "Everything created by God is good, and nothing is to be rejected, if it is received with thanksgiving."[55] Everything. Everything! It is not too good to be true. It is incredibly good and amazingly true. Your invitation is from God himself.

GETTING PERSPECTIVE

You may have begun this chapter not understanding how to obey the command to be joyful. My fear, now that we have come to its end, is that you will see obedient joy as a lengthy list of do's and don'ts. It isn't that at all. Think of it, rather, as a multi-faceted way of living before God as we seek to harmonize our hearts with his and make him the center of all that we do. It is like learning to ride a bicycle. This is actually a complex task. If you were a beginner and were presented with a list of all the things involved in mastering this skill, you could easily be overwhelmed. But once you learn to ride, it no longer seems complicated or demanding at all. You simply find yourself rolling along. Or we might liken it to learning a new language. At first the vocabulary and grammar seem complicated and impenetrable. But when you become fluent in that language, you no longer think about grammar and vocabulary. You find yourself thinking and speaking in a new tongue. Give yourself fully to the grammar and vocabulary of joy, and in time it will become the language of your life.

Questions for Thought and Discussion

1. Before you read this chapter, how did you interpret the commands to rejoice and be glad in the Bible? In what ways was this view shaped by your experience with other Christians and their approach to joy?

2. Discuss this statement from the chapter: "Joy, from the perspective of the Creator, is normative for us, so that to be joyful is to be normal, and that an absence of joy is abnormal or deviant." If this is true, what difference does it make for you in your life?

3. Are there ways in which you might be quenching or grieving the Spirit in your life? Do they tend to be isolated events, or are they part of a recurring pattern that you may need to deal with?

4. Can you identify any substitutes for joy in your life? How has this come about? What will you now do about this?

5. Where is the Church or community of faith in your life? How important are these relationships to you? How has the Church contributed, or been an obstacle, to your joy? What kind of things in your involvement in a faith community might change the outcome in a positive way in your pursuit of joy?

CHAPTER 12

JOY AND THE WORLD'S TRAVAIL

There is one more issue that we must address in this volume. We can frame it as a question: Is it morally responsible for us to pursue joy in a world in which there is so much suffering? How can we pursue joy when others live in poverty, are victims of violence and oppression, are ravaged by disease, or have been crushed beneath the weight of life? If a quest for joy meant flight from the world, I can't see how it would be permissible for us, and even less how it could be praiseworthy.

Whether it is entirely true or not, a common complaint against Christians is that we are "so heavenly minded" that we are of "no earthly good." (In our day it would be truer to say that we are so earthly minded that we are of no earthly or heavenly good.[1]) Because some who profess Christian faith show little interest in making the world a better place, it is at least tempting to see a pursuit of joy as an explanation for their apathy toward the world in its distress.[2]

Let me say as clearly as I can that those who flee the world and its problems to gain joy are not pursuing joy, but a counterfeit. Retreating from the world and its sorrow will not help them find the joy they are looking for.

They won't find it because it can't be found that way. Joy is not a grail whose quest takes us away from others in their need; it is more like a magnetic force that draws us into their plight. But I'm getting ahead of myself.

We must start further back if we are to understand how joy relates to our troubled world. It begins here: God has not instructed us how to live in the world from a position of ignorance about the world, disinterest in the world, or detachment from it. The world does not exist, nor does history move an inch in any direction, apart from his all-inclusive knowledge and sovereign purposes.[3] This includes the rise and demise of nations[4] as well as the sparrow that falls lifelessly to the ground.[5] The right place to begin is the observation that the God who commands us to live joyfully in the world is the same God who is sovereign over the world and its travail. Our pursuit of joy and our involvement in a suffering world are united under God.[6]

REALISTIC JOY

If we seek joy by ignoring or refusing to come to grips with suffering, whether it is our own or the pain of others, we will never find what we are looking for. Joy does not sacrifice realism for personal peace or pleasure. In the words of Archbishop Temple, "Christian joy and hope do not arise from an ignoring of the evil in the world, but from facing it at its worst."[7] When we turn to the pages of the New Testament, we see Jesus teaching his disciples to face adversity squarely and with joy, "Blessed are you when men revile you and persecute you and utter all kinds of evil against you on my account. Rejoice and be glad."[8] When they faced the persecution that Jesus said would come, we find his followers rejoicing "that they were counted worthy to suffer dishonor" for the name of Christ.[9] We learn from Paul's experience, "I rejoice in my sufferings."[10] We read James' words, "Count it all joy, my brothers, when you meet trials of various kinds."[11] We see Peter approaching life the same way, "Rejoice in so far as you share Christ's sufferings."[12]

Joy does not look away from suffering. It faces it head-on, without flinching, and then looks through it. Suffering is not entirely opaque; it is partly transparent. There is much that we cannot see, but we can see enough for joy.[13] Joy looks through the lens of suffering to see what God is seeking to do, and exults in this:

> More than that, we rejoice in our sufferings, knowing that suffering produces character. (Romans 5:3)

> You joyfully accepted the plundering of your property, since you knew that you yourselves had a better possession and an abiding one. (Hebrews 10:34)

> Count it all joy, my brothers, when you meet trials of various kinds, for you know that the testing of your faith produces steadfastness. (James 1:2-3, ESV)

Joy is ruthlessly realistic about the world we live in, but it refuses to reach the same conclusions drawn by pessimists and fatalists. Because joy is illumined by a Light they do not have, it envisions possibilities for the world that they do not see and cannot entertain.

OUR CAPACITY FOR JOY AND FOR SORROW

Paul wrote to the church at Rome, "Rejoice with those who rejoice; weep with those who weep."[14] Only those who can weep can also rejoice.[15] Sorrow and joy are drawn from the same emotional well. Think of emotions as concerned ways of interpreting and responding to the world.[16] To say that emotions are concerned means that they have something invested in the world. The way things are, and the way things ought to be, matter. When something has gone wrong, the joyful heart weeps, even if, in a larger frame of reference, it sees reasons for joy.

Sorrow and joy are both dimensions of love.[17] To say that God loves the world is to say that he affirms and rejoices in his handiwork, is saddened by our sin, and laments our suffering. He is not the God of Deists, who has removed himself from the world and looks on in transcendent disinterest. He has bound himself to his creation in covenant love. He is passionately interested and actively involved – so much so that he became one of us in Christ. And so it must be for his people, if we seek to love as God does. The Christian path of joy is not the Stoic path of resignation and apathy. It is a life of passion and costly involvement. It ventures everything for joy and risks sorrow in the quest.

If you open your heart to joy you cannot close it to sorrow. If you delight in justice, as God does,[18] your heart will be broken by injustice in the world. If you love mercy,[19] you will be devastated by the world's cruelty. If you rejoice in the beauty and wonder of God's handiwork, you can only mourn the ways in which it is despoiled. If it is a pleasure for you when God is honored, you must also embrace the anguish of seeing you see him dishonored. If you find your joy in the glory of God, you can only be dismayed when others ignore him, treat him irreverently, scorn him or regard him with disdain. Jesus taught his followers, "Blessed are those who mourn."[20] Even if there is beatitude in our lamentation, we must still lament, because we take seriously the evil in our world. Paul understood this well when he characterized his own experience as "sorrowful, yet always rejoicing."[21] In our world, sorrow and joy are often soul mates. They are traveling companions on the path of life.

KINGDOM RIGHTEOUSNESS, PEACE, AND JOY

Jesus said that one day our sorrow will turn to joy.[22] One day, joy will emerge from the chrysalis of the world's travail and fly on sun-gilded wings in the new heavens and the new earth. In that place there will be no sadness.[23] There will be no reason for sorrow. There will be no time or occasion for it. Joy will occupy every waking moment in a land where there is no sleep![24] It will be all joy and joy more glorious than our feeble minds can fathom and our puny imaginations can envision. With so much to break our hearts in this world, how do we keep from losing heart? Part of the answer is nurturing hope in what God will bring about at the end of days. The glory and joy God has promised us far outweighs the struggle and suffering we may now endure:

> So we do not lose heart. . . . For this slight momentary affliction is preparing for us an eternal weight of glory beyond all comparison. (2 Corinthians 4:16-17)

> I consider that the sufferings of this present time are not worth comparing with the glory that is to be revealed to us. (Romans 8:18)

Joy looks through our present suffering and anticipates this future glory.

If this is all there is, however, it is hard to see how it can do much more than give us strength to endure the harsh realities of our world. Should we just twiddle our thumbs and wait for God's Kingdom to come? No – and here is the other part of the answer – because the Kingdom of God is not merely future. In its fullness it is yet to come; however, Jesus came to inaugurate the Kingdom, to bring its blessings into our present experience in advance and anticipation of its consummation when he returns.[25] The Kingdom of God does not force us to choose between heaven and earth. We must choose both if we pray as Jesus taught us, "Your kingdom come, your will be done, on earth as it is in heaven."[26] There is not one Kingdom, which is future; nor are there two Kingdoms, one present and another future. There is one Kingdom, which is present (in inauguration) and future (in consummation), and which reflects God's will for the world.

Paul wrote to the church in Rome, "The kingdom of God is not food and drink but righteousness and peace and joy in the Holy Spirit."[27] The first thing we should note is that he was not forecasting a future state, but describing something in the present.[28] Whether we see it or not, whether we connect with it or not, at this very moment, righteousness, peace, and joy in the Holy Spirit characterize the Kingdom of God. Wherever the Kingdom is, you will find these things. Wherever you find righteousness, peace, and joy in the Holy Spirit, there you will find the Kingdom of God at work.

What are these traits, and how are they related to the Kingdom? Some commentators see them as "the inward graces of the Spirit."[29] You can find that in other places in Paul's writing, but not here. Paul is addressing the way Christians live together in community, and the significance of the Kingdom of God for this. Righteousness, peace, and joy are what the Kingdom is about. They describe the culture of the Kingdom. They are the foreign and domestic policies of the Kingdom. They represent the Kingdom-in-action, empowered by God's Spirit. They are not what we hope to find when we look within; they are what we should expect to find when we see God's people living together – in the power of the Spirit – as representatives of God's Kingdom in the world. They are spheres of service, as Paul says next: "For the one who serves Christ in this is pleasing to God and approved by men."[30] As followers of Christ we are called to be agents of righteousness, ambassadors of peace, and heralds of joy. If we are fighting with each other over scruples, as they were in Rome, we cannot fulfill these Kingdom roles – which is exactly Paul's point.[31]

Kingdom righteousness in this context is not "the status of righteousness before God which is God's gift."[32] It is "righteous action"[33] or what biblical writers referred to as "doing righteousness."[34] It is action taken to promote and protect the well-being of others.[35] The righteousness of the Kingdom is what the Psalmist thought of when he said of God, "Righteousness and justice are the foundation of his throne."[36] God is committed to a world in which his creatures truly thrive. Ancient people of faith often praised God for his commitment to those who were least likely to flourish in a fallen, sinful world. We practice the righteousness of the Kingdom when our hearts align with God's, and we join him in seeking the good of others – especially those who need our help if they are to prosper in life:[37]

> He executes justice for the fatherless and the widow, and loves the sojourner, giving him food and clothing. (Deuteronomy 10:18)

> The LORD works vindication
> and justice for all who are oppressed. (Psalm 103:6)

> Happy is he whose help is the God of Jacob,
> whose hope is in the LORD his God,
> who made heaven and earth,
> the sea, and all that is in them;
> who keeps faith for ever;
> who executes justice for the oppressed;
> who gives food to the hungry.
> The LORD sets the prisoners free;
> the LORD opens the eyes of the blind,
> the LORD lifts up those who are bowed down;
> the LORD loves the righteous.
> The LORD watches over the sojourners,
> he upholds the widow and the fatherless;
> but the way of the wicked he brings to ruin.
> The LORD will reign for ever,

thy God, O Zion, to all generations.
Praise the LORD! (Psalm 146:5-10)

Righteous people are actively committed to the well-being of others:

I delivered the poor who cried,
and the fatherless who had none to help him.
The blessing of him who was about to perish came upon me,
and I caused the widow's heart to sing for joy.
I put on righteousness, and it clothed me;
my justice was like a robe and a turban.
I was eyes to the blind,
and feet to the lame.
I was a father to the poor,
and I searched out the cause of him whom I did not know.
I broke the fangs of the unrighteous,
and made him drop his prey from his teeth." (Job 29:12-17)

The righteous care about justice for the poor. (Proverbs 29:7, NIV)

Then the righteous will answer him, "Lord, when did we see you hungry and feed you, or thirsty and give you something to drink? When did we see you a stranger and invite you in, or needing clothes and clothe you? When did we see you sick or in prison and go to visit you?" The King will reply, "I tell you the truth, whatever you did for one of the least of these brothers of mine, you did for me." (Matthew 25:34-40)[38]

Then I heard what seemed to be the voice of a great multitude, like the roar of many waters and like the sound of mighty peals of thunder, crying out,

"Hallelujah!
For the Lord our God

> the Almighty reigns.
> Let us rejoice and exult
> and give him the glory,
> for the marriage of the Lamb has come,
> and his Bride has made herself ready;
> it was granted her to clothe herself
> with fine linen, bright and pure"—
> for the fine linen is the righteous deeds of the saints.
> (Revelation 19:6-8, ESV)

Daniel Maguire has written, "Healthy joy cannot be full while sisters and brothers are in misery. Joy in a surrounding context of misery is insulted and undone."[39] Those who have been brought into a right relationship with God, and with others under God, long to see the circle of righteousness enlarged to include as many as possible.[40] They long to see others flourish in God's will. They seek the oppressed, the hungry, the poor, the fettered, and the blind, because they know that God is committed to them and their plight. They yearn to see them discover their help in the God of Jacob and their hope in the LORD their God. This is the righteousness of the Kingdom. It must be important to followers of Jesus, because it was important to him. He saw this as the heart of his mission, fulfilling the ancient prophecy:

> The Spirit of the Lord is upon me,
> because he has anointed me to preach good news to the poor.
> He has sent me to proclaim release to the captives
> and recovering of sight to the blind,
> to set at liberty those who are oppressed,
> to proclaim the acceptable year of the Lord. (Luke 4:18-19)[41]

What about Kingdom peace? Again, it is tempting to see this as an experience of inner tranquility. But this moves us further from Paul's thought in this context. There are times when the apostle does have personal peace in mind.[42] Those who know this experience treasure it above all earthly possessions. There are also times when he is thinking about peace between people. Sometimes it is peace between fellow believers.[43] Sometimes it includes all who enter the circle of our lives: "If it is possible, as far as it depends on you, live at peace with everyone."[44] When peace is put into the context of God's Kingdom, however, its parameters are as broad as his reign. It is global in its design and intent. It is a harmony in the world that emerges from right relationships – with God, our neighbor, and the created order in which we have been placed. Those who know something of this peace seek to be peacemakers, bringing health, wholeness, and the possibilities of flourishing in life before God to all whose hearts are open.

There is a progression in this Kingdom triumvirate: righteousness, peace, and joy. If people are living in right relationships with God and with each other under God, peace is the harmony that results, and joy is the pleasure we find in that concord. Kingdom joy is thus the consummation of Kingdom peace. This peace, or *shalom*, is best understood as "the fulfillment of our capacity for rejoicing."[45] It is "a peace which at its highest is enjoyment. To dwell in shalom is to enjoy living before God, to enjoy living in nature, to enjoy living with one's fellows, to enjoy life with oneself."[46] It is "a just peace with joy in God's creation."[47]

The righteousness, peace, and joy of the Kingdom are an indicative and an imperative for the Church.[48] To say that they are indicative of the Kingdom means that they are depictions of the life we enjoy under God's reign (in part now and fully in the future). To say that they are an imperative means that they are objectives which our King commands us to pursue as citizens of his Kingdom. Or we can put it this way: The righteousness, peace, and joy of God's Kingdom are a description and a demand. They are ways of describing the blessings of God's Kingdom we enjoy as its citizens, and at the same time they demand the investment of our lives as agents of the Kingdom in the world. They are both portrait and project. They portray Kingdom life, and are also the chief project, or enterprise, of the Kingdom. Righteousness, peace, and joy in the Holy Spirit will be perfectly realized in God's Kingdom in the age to come. Knowing that they will one day be our full possession, they become our goal in the present as we seek to live under God's sovereign and gracious reign.[49]

HARMONIZING OUR HEARTS WITH GOD'S

You can see now that we are not even within shouting distance of a self-absorbed pursuit of joy that ignores, and isolates itself from, the suffering of our fallen, broken world. This is simply not the kind of joy God offers. He doesn't offer it because it would not be true to his own joy. The gifts of God are always true reflections of the Giver.

If we think of the righteousness, peace, and joy of God's Kingdom as somehow distinct from God himself, it can only be because we are thinking of earthly kings and kingdoms, where a kingdom is a realm that is distinct from its king, and kings come and go while the kingdom remains. But this is not true of the Kingdom of God. The Kingdom of God is a descriptive way of referring to God himself in his sovereign and active reign over human affairs. To say that the Kingdom of God is righteousness, peace, and joy, is to say that these things characterize God's heart, his desires for humanity, and his commitment to bring these things about. They become ours when we harmonize our hearts with God's, tune our wills to his, and align our life-purpose with his purposes. Righteousness, peace, and joy in the Holy Spirit are the answer to our prayer for God's Kingdom to come and his will to be done on earth as it is in heaven.

NO FROWNING SAINTS!

If we are to be agents of joy in the world, this suggests something about us. The joy of others cannot be isolated from our own. It is a shared joy.[50] We can only give what we have. As we give we receive. Not only is it unlikely that we will reach out to others in need if we are strangers to joy,[51] seeking the well-being of others grudgingly and reluctantly is a spiritual contradiction.[52] Paul saw this clearly:

> If you are helping others in distress, do it cheerfully. (Romans 12:8)[53]
>
> Each one must do as he has made up his mind, not reluctantly or under compulsion, for God loves a cheerful giver. (2 Corinthians 9:7)[54]
>
> Their abundance of joy and their extreme poverty have overflowed in a wealth of liberality on their part. (2 Corinthians 8:2)

Perhaps no one in recent memory has exemplified joyful compassion more than Mother Teresa. Malcolm Muggeridge described his experience with her:

> Accompanying Mother Teresa, as we did, to these different activities for the purpose of filming them – to the Home for the Dying, to the lepers and unwanted children, I found I went through three phases. The first was horror mixed with pity, the second compassion pure and simple, and the third, reaching far beyond compassion, something I had never experienced before – an awareness that these dying and derelict men and women, these lepers with stumps instead of hands, these unwanted children, were not pitiable, repulsive or forlorn, but rather dear and delightful; as it might be, friends of long standing, brothers and sisters.[55]

He wrote of Mother Teresa and her co-workers:

> Their life is tough and austere by worldly standards, certainly; yet I never met such delightful, happy women, or such an atmosphere of joy as they create. Mother Teresa, as she is fond of explaining, attaches the utmost importance to this joyousness. The poor, she says, deserve not just service and dedication, but also the joy that belongs to human love. This is what the Sisters give them abundantly.[56]

Imagine a world in which the Church across the globe is filled with joyful, compassionate people: men and women, girls and boys, whose loving action fills them with delight, whose joy overflows the cup of their own lives and spills onto needy people with a life-changing splash of grace. Imagine a world in which the Church in every country is empowered by the Holy Spirit and devoted to righteousness, peace, and joy. Imagine a world in which people from every nation, tribe, and tongue see our good works, done with joyful hearts, and glorify our Father in heaven. Jesus envisioned this for us.[57] How will you respond?

Questions for Thought and Discussion

1. Read the following quote from this chapter:

> Let me say as clearly as I can that those who flee the world and its problems to gain joy are not pursuing joy, but a counterfeit. Retreating from the world and its sorrow will not help them find the joy they are looking for. They won't find it because it can't be found that way. Joy is not a holy grail whose quest takes us away from others in their need; it is more like a magnetic force that draws us into their plight.

How do you see your life in this light? Your local church? Christian groups that you are part of?

2. Read the following quote from this chapter:

> Joy does not look away from suffering. It faces it head-on, without flinching, and then looks through it. Suffering is not opaque; it is partly transparent. There is much that we cannot see, but we can see enough for joy. Joy looks through the lens of suffering to see what God is seeking to do, and exults in this.

How does this relate to painful experiences you have had or that you may be going through now?

3. How will you seek to cultivate a heart that can both weep and rejoice?

4. How does viewing God's Kingdom in the two phases of *inauguration* and *consummation* help you see yourself as an agent of the Kingdom here and now?

5. What steps can you take to pursue righteousness, peace, and joy in the Holy Spirit?

About the Author

In 1983 Rick and Sue Howe moved to Boulder, Colorado, where they raised three children – Amberle, Lorien, and Jamison – and have devoted more than thirty years to campus ministry at the University of Colorado. In addition to writing and speaking, Rick now leads University Ministries, whose mission is to "inspire and nurture a thoughtful pursuit of Christ, one student, one professor, one university at a time." To learn more about Rick, visit his website at www.rickhowe.org. You can also follow him on Facebook at *Rick Howe on Joy* and on Twitter @rickhoweonjoy. To learn more about University Ministries, see www.university-ministries.org.

Endnotes

PREFACE

1 Modernity's vaunted claims about reason are primarily objectivity and certainty. Because we can achieve the first, the second is also within our reach. Postmodernism, on the other hand, sees us entirely embedded in subjective, linguistic, and social situations that result in an all-encompassing relativism.

I find myself agreeing with C.S. Lewis: "For my own part I hate and distrust reactions not only in religion but in everything. Luther surely spoke very good sense when he compared humanity to a drunkard who, after falling off his horse on the right, falls off it next time on the left." C.S. Lewis, *The World's Last Night and Other Essays* (New York, NY: Mariner Books, 2002) p. 94.

Modernity and Postmodernism are the drunken peasant falling off his horse on one side and then the other. I prefer to stay sober and on the horse. On the one hand, the claim of radical relativism, if true, makes its own claims self-defeating. If it were true, on its own terms we could never know it to be true. On the other hand, I believe that it is a healthy move to acknowledge that we are more than "thinking beings"(Descartes), and that there is no such thing as "reason alone" (Kant) – both part of the Enlightenment paradigm.

2 Not just the ancient roots of Western civilization, but anything that is native, indigenous, and pre-colonial anywhere in the world.

3 See Stanley J. Grenz, *Revisioning Evangelical Theology* (Downers Grove: InterVarsity Press, 1993), pp. 137ff.

4 Thomas C. Oden, "So What Happens after Modernity? A Postmodern Agenda for Evangelical Theology" in David S. Dockery, ed., *The Challenge of Postmodernism: An Evangelical Engagement* (Wheaton: Victor Books, 1995), pp. 398ff. See also his book, *After Modernity . . . What? Agenda for Theology* (Grand Rapids: Zondervan/Academie, 1990).

5 Thomas Oden, "The Death of Modernity and Postmodern Evangelical Spirituality" in Dockery, *The Challenge*, p. 28.

6 *St. Thomas Aquinas: Philosophical Texts*, ed. and trans. Thomas Gilby (Durham, North Carolina: The Labyrinth Press, 1982), p. 275.

7 C.S. Lewis, *Mere Christianity* (New York: Simon and Schuster, Touchstone edition, 1996), p. 142.

INTRODUCTION

1 Matthew 21:19

2 See Matthew 21:4-5, ESV

3 John 14:1

[4] John 15:11

[5] See John 16:20, 22, 24, 33.

[6] John 17:13, NRSV

[7] Jürgen Moltmann wrote, "For Jesus, the gospel of the kingdom is a messianic message of joy, not an apocalyptic threat to the world." Jürgen Moltmann, *The Trinity and the Kingdom: The Doctrine of God, trans., Margaret Kohl (San Francisco: Harper & Row, 1981), p. 69.*

Chapter 1: The Highest and Best of All Pleasures

[1] G.K. Chesterton, *The Everlasting Man* (New York: Image Books, Doubleday & Company, Inc., 1955), p. 11.

[2] This understanding of joy lies buried in the etymology of the word in our own language. Our English word "joy" comes from the Latin *gaudium,* which was used not only of joy, delight, and gladness, but of "physical or sensual delight." See *The Oxford Latin Dictionary,* ed., P.G.W. Glare (Oxford: The Clarendon Press, 1982), p. 755. You will see the same thing with the Greek vocabulary of joy in footnote 15 below.

[3] A study of the Hebrew vocabulary of joy reveals that the words often translated as "joy" can also be rendered "pleasure" or "delight," and that these words appear in a wide range of contexts, encompassing the whole of life before God. See, for instance, the following words, as they are found in *A Hebrew and English Lexicon of the Old Testament,* eds., Francis Brown, S.R. Driver, and Charles A. Briggs (Oxford: Clarendon Press, Reprint. 1953):

> *Tov*: The verb may be rendered "be pleasant, delightful," or "be glad, joyful" (p. 373) The adjective, *tov,* may be translated "pleasant, agreeable, good" and as "glad or happy" (pp. 373-374).
>
> *Naem*: The verb means "to be pleasant, delightful" (p. 653). The cognate adjective *naim* ("pleasant, delightful") parallels "joy" as a synonym in Psalm 16:11b.
>
> *Sus*: The verb may be rendered as "to rejoice or exult" (p. 965). It is translated "take delight in", e.g., in Deuteronomy 30:9 (RSV).
>
> *Sameach*: The verb may be rendered "to rejoice, be glad," or "take pleasure in" (p. 970). The noun *simchah* may be translated "joy, gladness, mirth" or "pleasure" (ibid.).

[4] This example is known as "synonymous parallelism." Other kinds of parallelism in Hebrew poetry include "antithetical parallelism," where one line contrasts another, and "synthetic parallelism," where ideas are combined.

[5] NRSV

[6] Psalm 4:7. See also Zechariah 10:7, ESV.

[7] Pascal was right when he said that Christians "give up pleasures only for greater pleasures"! Quoted by Donald Bloesch, *Freedom for Obedience* (San Francisco: Harper & Row, 1987), p. 37.

[8] See Psalm 63:5, ESV.

[9] See Psalm 119:14, ESV, and Isaiah 9:3, ESV.

[10] See Isaiah 61:10; 62:5, ESV.

[11] See Matthew 13:44, ESV.

[12] See Matthew 22:1-10, ESV, and Luke 14:15-24, ESV.

[13] For the series of parables, see Luke 15.

[14] For an excellent treatment of the New Testament vocabulary of joy, see William Morrice, *Joy in the New Testament* (Grand Rapids, Michigan: William B. Eerdmans Publishing Co., 1984), especially Part One.

[15] The writers of the New Testament cautiously avoided any positive use of the word *hedone,* the classic term for sensual pleasure, no doubt because of its keystone position in hedonism – a pagan philosophy which they rightly considered a serious rival to the true Gospel. The noun *hedone* does occur five times in the New Testament, but always negatively, of passions and pleasures pursued in defiance of God, e.g., Luke 8:14; Titus 3:3; James 4:1, 3 and 2 Peter 2:13.

Even with that note of caution, however, some writers used its adverbial forms, *hedeos* and *hedista,* in a positive sense to describe joy. The former is used of the gladness with which a great throng heard Jesus (Mark 12:37), and the latter is used of Paul's pleasure in experiencing the power of Christ in the midst of difficulties (2 Corinthians 12:9), and of his joy in spending himself on behalf of those whom he had led to Christ (2 Corinthians 12:15). There is something almost sensual about this Christ-centered joy! Something tangible. Concrete.

There were other terms that were more congenial to the early Christian description of joy, but they focus no less on joy's pleasure. The words used most frequently in the New Testament are *chara* and *chairo,* a noun and verb related to a Sanskrit word meaning "to take pleasure in." *The New International Dictionary of New Testament Theology*, Gen. ed., Colin Brown (Grand Rapids: Zondervan, 1976) Vol. II, p. 352. *Chara* expresses joy, delight, or pleasure (Liddell and Scott, *Greek-English Lexicon*, Abridged Edition: [Oxford: Oxford University Press, Impression, 1980], p. 777), and *chairo* the action of rejoicing, being glad, delighted, or pleased (Ibid., p. 774.). These were not "sacred "words. Their native home was not the religious world but the world of common pleasures. One scholar calls them, in fact, "intrinsically secular terms" (Morrice, *Joy in the New Testament*, p. 69).

Two other words in the early church's vocabulary of joy were *agalliaomai* and its cognate noun *agalliasis.* The verb appears 11 times in the New Testament (e.g., Matthew 5:12; Luke 1:47; Acts 2:26; 16:34), and the noun five times (e.g., Hebrews 1:9; 1 Peter 1:6, 8; and Jude 24). They were apparently coined by the translators of the Septuagint, and were then used by Jewish and Christian writers who were dependent upon that translation for their reading of

Scripture. They were derived from the Greek *agallo* and *agallomai*, which were used of the rapture and ecstasy of the devotees of Dionysus, the Greek god of wine (Morrice, *Joy in the New Testament*, p. 19). Although they felt compelled to alter these words slightly in order to remove them from a context of debauchery and the worship of a false god, the writers of the Greek Bible clearly felt that these words captured an important dimension of joy in God.

Finally, there are the terms *euphraino* and *euphrosyne*. In classical Greek these were words used of the pleasures of food and drink particularly in the context of a banquet or festivity. They are used that way even in the New Testament: negatively, as in the case of the rich fool in Luke 12:19, and the rich man in Luke 16:19, and positively, as in the case of the banquet held in honor of the prodigal son upon his return (Luke 15:23, 32), and of the gift of gladness bestowed by God even upon the pagan world (Acts 14:17). They are also used of joy in God! Peter used the noun in his citation of Psalm 16:11 in Acts 2:28 – "You have made known to me the ways of life; you will make me full of gladness with your presence." The apostle Paul used the verb of Gentiles who have been included in the promises of salvation (Romans 15:10), and of the cheer experienced in fellowship with other believers (2 Corinthians 2:2). The verbs appear again in Revelation 12:12 and 18:20, referring to the joy of those in heaven.

16 See, for example, Psalm 5:11, and 31:7, ESV.

17 See Song of Solomon 1:4, ESV.

18 See Proverbs 5:18-19, ESV.

19 See Ecclesiastes 11:9, ESV.

20 See Ecclesiastes 3:22, ESV.

21 See Ecclesiastes 5:19, ESV.

22 See Deuteronomy 12:7, ESV.

23 See Deuteronomy 26:11, ESV.

A cognate noun, *simchah*, illustrates the same truth. It is used of the believer's joy in God (e.g., Psalm 16:11), but also of exultation in military victory (1 Samuel 18:6; 2 Chronicles 20:27), the festive gaiety of a coronation (1 Kings 1:40), delight in sensual pleasure and wealth (Ecclesiastes 2:10), and in the pleasures of food and drink (1 Chronicles. 12:38-40; Ecclesiastes 9:7).

24 I know that some readers will say that I have failed to distinguish between "religious" and "other" uses of these words – categories which are fairly commonplace in Bible Dictionaries and Lexicons. However, this is the very distinction I am challenging. My suspicion is that at least in this case it reflects only the theological views and (Platonic) biases of the scholars themselves.

25 See 1 Timothy 4:3-5, ESV.

26 So, Aquinas: "Now whatever we desire naturally, can also be the object of reasoned desire and delight (pleasure), but not vice versa. Consequently, whatever can be the object of

delight (pleasure), can also be the object of joy in rational beings." Thomas Aquinas, *Summa Theologica,* trans. Fathers of the English Dominican Province (London: Burns Oates & Washburn, Ltd., third ed. 1941), I, II, Q. 31, A.3. I would qualify this. For a sensory pleasure to be the object of joy takes more than rationality; it requires the appropriate use of reason, when the mind refers a pleasure back to God in thanksgiving and praise.

27 *Pascal's Pensées*, trans. W.F. Trotter (New York: E.P. Dutton & Co., Inc., 1958), p. 187.

28 C.S. Lewis wrote, "I sometimes wonder whether all pleasures are not substitutes for joy." *Surprised by Joy* (New York: Harcourt, Brace & World, Inc. 1955), p. 170. Although pleasures can be substitutes for joy, Lewis' perspective here is more Platonic than Christian. He was much closer to the truth, I think, in one of his letters to Malcolm, where he says, "I was learning the far more secret doctrine that *pleasures* are shafts of the glory as it strikes our sensibility. As it impinges on our will or our understanding, we give it different names – goodness or truth or the like. But its flash upon our senses and mood is pleasure." C.S. Lewis, *Letters to Malcolm: Chiefly on Prayer* (New York: Harcourt, Brace & World, Inc.: 1964), p. 89. Lewis could also speak of pleasures as "patches of Godlight" and "tiny theophanies" (Ibid., p. 91).

29 Arthur Holmes wrote, "The Old Testament writers rejoice in physical beauty and are awed by its grandeur. They delight in food, drink, sight, sound, sexuality." Arthur F. Holmes, *Contours of a World View* (Grand Rapids, MI: William B. Eerdmans Publishing Co., 1983), p. 111.

30 *St. Thomas Aquinas: Philosophical Texts*, ed. and trans. Thomas Gilby (Durham, North Carolina: The Labyrinth Press, 1982), p. 275.

31 2 Timothy 3:4

32 Titus 3:3

33 While I acknowledge that contemporary genetic evidence and other postulates of evolutionary theory represent a challenge that should engage Christians in serious thinking and dialogue, I did not come to my belief (nor will I abandon my belief) in a historical Adam and Eve, an original Edenic environment in which they lived, and a state of innocence from which they fell, on the basis of scientific inquiry.

The Scriptures are the "norming norm" for my faith. I make no apologies for this. Indeed, it is a great joy to me! Having said this, the ancient texts of Scripture must be read first – as much as possible – with their original audience in mind. We should resist the temptation of importing our interests and concerns into the way we understand them, and forcing them to take up arms in our conflicts.

I recognize that the Hebrew word *adam* was used for humanity as a whole as well as for an individual in the Genesis story (Adam = Mankind). I can also see how Israel, in its exile from the promised land, would have seen itself in Adam and his expulsion from the Garden (Adam = Israel). Neither of these observations, however, negates the possibility that Adam was *also* viewed as a historical figure. (Compare Jacob = Israel.) Neither seems to factor into the canonical context of Jesus' teaching on marriage and divorce in Matthew 19, and Paul's exposition of redemptive history in Romans 5 – both of which posit a historical Adam.

While Jesus does not refer to an original pair by name, his affirmation of the Creator's original intention for marriage clearly has the Edenic couple in mind. ("He who created them from the beginning made them male and female, and said, 'Therefore a man shall leave his father and his mother and hold fast to his wife, and the two shall become one flesh.'" On the matter of divorce, he affirms an original state of innocence from which humanity has lapsed ("From the beginning it was not so.")

In Romans 5, Israel as a nation is not in view, and "the one man" (Adam) is distinguished from all who followed from him ("all men"). In this passage we do observe the Jewish penchant for seeing deeper meanings in their stories. Adam is not an archetype for humanity or for Israel, however, but a "type" of Christ. This is the frame of reference in which we should pursue our interpretation. The parallels are between two men (Adam and Christ), sin entering the world through one and grace through the other, an act of disobedience and an act of righteousness, judgment and justification, death and eternal life. Any other frame of reference is alien to the context. In a grand metanarrative, Paul lays out the themes of Creation, Fall, and Redemption: one man in the beginning from whom humanity sprang and through whose "act of disobedience" sin entered the world, a historical period ("from Adam to Moses"), and God's saving action through the one man, Jesus Christ ("the one who was to come").

I affirm that there is great value in the scientific enterprise, and believe that if we love God with our minds (in fulfillment of the greatest commandment) we will boldly declare that all truth is his – wherever it is found – and we will pursue it to the best of our abilities under God. I also affirm the priority and supremacy of the Scriptures for our faith, and what seems to me to be the clear teaching of Jesus and Paul. This leads me to a confident belief that whatever we may say about the age of the universe and the development of life on our planet, there was an original couple who bore the image of God without flaw, were placed in an Edenic setting of innocence, fell from that state through a primal act of disobedience, and brought sin into the world as well as all future generations of humans who fallibly bear the image of God.

For a contemporary discussion, see Matthew Barrett and Ardel B. Caneday, eds. *Four Views on the Historical Adam* (Grand Rapids: Zondervan, 2013).

34 See Genesis 1:31, ESV.

35 See 1 Timothy 4:1-5, ESV.

36 According to the apostle Paul, the resurrected body of the believer will be a "spiritual body" (1 Corinthians 15:44). While this may, at first glance, seem to teach otherwise, it does not mean that it will be incorporeal, or that we will exist without physical properties. A spiritual body, in Paul's way of thinking, is one that is completely governed by, consecrated to, and infused with, the Spirit.

Augustine wrote:

> The bodies of the saints, then, shall rise again free from every defect, from every blemish, as from all corruption, weight, and impediment. For their ease of movement shall be as complete as their happiness. Whence their bodies have been called spiritual, though undoubtedly they shall be bodies and not spirits.

Augustine, "The Enchiridion" in *Basic Writings of Saint Augustine*, ed., Whitney J. Oates (Grand Rapids, MI: Baker Book House, 1948, reprint. 1980), Vol. 1, p. 711.

See George Eldon Ladd, *A Theology of the New Testament* (Grand Rapids, MI: William B. Eerdmans Publishing Co., 1974), p. 370:

> The spiritual body will be a body so infused with the life-giving Spirit of God that it will be an imperishable, glorious, powerful body. In other words, the complete enjoyment of the life of the Spirit will result in the very transformation of the natural mortal order of bodily existence, so that mortality, weakness, will be swallowed up in the fullness of eternal life.

Anthony A. Hoekema, *The Bible and the Future* (Grand Rapids, MI: William B. Eerdmans Publishing Co., 1979), p. 250, writes:

> But *spiritual* . . . here does not mean nonphysical. Rather, it means someone who is guided by the Holy Spirit, at least in principle, in distinction from someone who is guided only by his natural impulses . . . the spiritual body of the resurrection is one which will be totally, not just partially, dominated and directed by the Holy Spirit.

See C.S. Lewis, *Letters to Malcolm*, p. 122: "At present we tend to think of the soul as somehow 'inside' the body. But the glorified body of the resurrection as I conceive it – the sensuous life raised from its death – will be inside the soul."

See also Lewis' comments in his essay, "The Weight of Glory" in *The Weight of Glory and Other Addresses* (Grand Rapids, MI: William B. Eerdmans Publishing Co., 1949, reprint. 1974), p. 14:

> The faint far-off results of those energies which God's creative rapture implanted in matter when He made the worlds are what we now call physical pleasures; and even thus filtered, they are too much for our present management. What would it be to taste at the fountain-head that stream of which even these lower reaches prove so intoxicating? Yet that, I believe, is what lies before us. The whole man is to drink joy from the fountain of joy. As St. Augustine said, the rapture of the saved soul will "flow over" into the glorified body.

For a clear treatment of Paul's concept of a spiritual body, see William Lane Craig, *The Son Rises: The Historical Evidence for the Resurrection of Jesus* (Chicago: Moody Press, 1981), pp. 110ff.

[37] As Aquinas put it, "Corpulence will be cured, but not corporeity"! *St. Thomas Aquinas: Philosophical Texts*, p. 278.

[38] 2 Peter 3:13

[39] Thomas á Kempis, *The Imitation of Christ* (New York: Grosset & Dunlap, n.d.), p 104.

[40] C.S. Lewis, *The Four Loves* (New York: Harcourt, Brace, Jovanovich, 1960).

---

[41] So Aquinas taught: "If . . . spiritual pleasures be compared with sensible bodily pleasures, then, in themselves and absolutely speaking, spiritual pleasures are greater." *Summa Theologica,* I, II, Q. 31, A. 5. See also Q. 34, A. 3, where Aquinas responds to the question of whether any pleasure can be the greatest good:

> Happiness is the greatest good: since it is the end of man's life. But Happiness is not without pleasure: for it is written (and here he quotes Psalm 16:11, which speaks of the believer's joy in God): Thou shalt fill me with joy with Thy countenance; at Thy right hand are delights (i.e., pleasures) even to the end . . . Accordingly, man's last end may be said to be either God Who is the Supreme Good simply; or the enjoyment of God, which implies a certain pleasure in the last end. And in this sense a certain pleasure of man may be said to be the greatest among human goods.

[42] We started out saying that joy is a kind of pleasure. If the truth were fully known, however, we would see that in a sinless world pleasures are species of joy. That world was once ours, and will be again at the end of days when we and our world are fully redeemed.

[43] J.I. Packer writes:

> I hold the heady doctrine that no pleasures are so frequent or intense as those of the grateful, devoted, single-minded, whole-hearted, self-denying Christian. I maintain that the delights of work and leisure, of friendship and family, of eating and mating, of arts and crafts, of playing and watching games, of finding out and making things, of helping other people, and all the other noble pleasures that life affords, are doubled for the Christian; for, as the cheerful old Puritans used to say . . . the Christian tastes God in all his pleasures, and this increases them.

J.I. Packer, *God Has Spoken* (Downers Grove: InterVarsity Press, 1979), p. 8.

[44] C.S. Lewis, "Transposition," in *The Weight of Glory, p.* 27. Lewis did not apply the concept of transposition to the relationship between joy and other pleasures in general in this essay.

[45] Donald G. Bloeesch writes, "God did not change into a man, as in Greek mythology. Instead the Son of God adopted human nature and united it with his divine nature *in the unity of one person.*" (emphasis added) *Essentials of Evangelical Theology* (San Francisco: Harper & Row Publishers, 1978), Vol. I, p. 128.

[46] C.S. Lewis, *Four Loves,* pp. 25ff.

[47] Ibid., p. 32.

[48] C.S. Lewis, *The Pilgrim's Regress* (Grand Rapids, MI: William B. Eerdmans Publishing Co. 1943, reprint. 1974), p. 7.

[49] Psalm 42:1-2

[50] Jonathan Edwards believed that there are four reasons for the satisfaction of the soul in "spiritual enjoyments." The first two are particularly relevant in this context. First:

> They in their kind and nature, are fully adapted to the nature, capacity, and need of the soul of man. So that those who find them, desire no other kind of enjoyment; they sit down fully contented with that kind of happiness which they have, desiring no change, nor inclination to wander about any more, saying 'Who will show us any good?'

Second:

> They are satisfying also in this respect, that they answer the expectation of the appetite. When the appetite is high to anything, the expectation is consequently so. Appetite to a particular object implies expectation in its nature. This expectation is not satisfied by worldly enjoyments . . . but not so with spiritual enjoyments; they fully answer and satisfy the expectation.

"On Religious Affections," *The Works of Jonathan Edwards,* Perry Miller, Gen. ed., (New Haven: Yale University Press, 1959), Vol. 2, pp. 378-79.

51 To say that joy is an appreciative pleasure is to say that it is a close kin to aesthetic experience. Joy sometimes engages the senses; it always engages the mind. Aquinas called it the pleasure that "follows reason." He wrote, "We do not speak of joy except when delight (i.e., pleasure) follows reason" (Aquinas, op cit., I, II, Q. 31, A. 3).

It is the role of our minds in the experience of joy that parallels aesthetic pleasure. Elton Trueblood, for instance, wrote, "In the appreciation of beauty the physical senses are involved, but they are by no means sufficient to the aesthetic result. Always there is a process of thought." David Elton Trueblood, *Philosophy of Religion* (Grand Rapids: Baker Book House, 1957), p. 120. The same is true of joy. It is the appreciation (a process of thought) of pleasure in its relation to God, and never merely pleasure itself, that is "sufficient" to the joyful result.

Of what he calls "esthetic love," Henry Stob wrote:

> It emerges characteristically in the presence of some value – whether of truth, of beauty, of goodness, or of holiness – when this value appears not primarily as an object of desire but as an object of enjoyment. This love wills not so much to acquire and possess its object, as to contemplate and take delight in it.

Henry Stob *Ethical Reflections* (Grand Rapids, MI: William B. Eerdmans Publishing Co., 1978), p. 118.

This could be said just as well of joy as an appreciative pleasure. It is a reflective delight. I would add only that when we are talking about joy, it is never simply a matter of meditating on an object of enjoyment; the mind's focus is drawn ineluctably to the One whose presence is conveyed, and whose right hand holds the pleasure, in the experience of joy (Psalm 16:11). It beholds him as the Beautiful (Psalm 27:4) and enjoys him as the Source of all that is beautiful and pleasurable in the world.

See, e.g., Edwards, "Religious Affections," p. 250:

> True saints have their minds, in the first place, inexpressibly pleased and delighted with the sweet ideas of the glorious and amiable nature of the things of God. And

> this is the spring of all their delights, and the cream of all their pleasures; 'tis the joy of their joy. This sweet and ravishing entertainment they have in viewing the beautiful and delightful nature of divine things is the foundation of the joy they have afterward in the consideration of their being theirs.
>
> The first foundation of the delight a true saint has in God, is his own perfection and the first foundation of the delight he has in Christ is his beauty; he appears in himself the chief among ten thousand, and altogether lovely. They first rejoice in God as glorious and excellent in himself, and then secondarily rejoice in it, that so glorious a God is theirs.

See also Edwards, "The Nature of True Virtue," in *The Works of Jonathan Edwards*, ed., John E. Smith (New Haven: Yale University Press, 1989), Vol. 8, pp. 550-551:

> For as God is infinitely the greatest Being, so he is allowed to be infinitely the most beautiful and excellent: and all the beauty to be found throughout the whole creation, is but the reflection of the diffused beams of that Being who hath an infinite fullness of brightness and glory. . . . God . . . is the foundation and fountain of all being and all beauty...

52 "Lectures on Galatians," *Luther's Work*, Jaroslav Pelikan, ed., (Saint Louis: Concordia Publishing House, 1963), Vol. 26, p. 230.

Aquinas had something similar to say (Aquinas, *Summa*, I, II, Q. 5, A. 2):

> But as to the attainment or enjoyment of this Good, one man can be happier than another; because the more a man enjoys this Good the happier he is. Now, that one man enjoys God more than another, happens through his being better disposed or ordered to the enjoyment of Him. And in this sense one man can be happier than another.

53 See Philippians 4:10, ESV

54 See Psalm 43:4, ESV.

55 See Matthew 2:10, KJV.

56 See Psalm 16:11, ESV, and John 15:11, ESV:

57 See 2 Corinthians 7:4, ESV.

58 See Psalm 137:6, NIV.

59 See 1 Peter 1:8, ESV.

60 See Psalm 16:11, ESV.

1 This is actually the title and sub-title of a sermon series and book by Warren Wiersby*: Be Joyful: It Beats Being Happy.* (Wheaton: Victor Books, 1974).

[2] See, e.g., Donald Bloesch, *Freedom for Obedience* (San Francisco: Harper & Row, 1987), p. 192:

> Happiness signifies the satisfaction of human desire; joy indicates the surge of transforming power within us that enables us to delight in the presence of God and to serve our neighbor in self-giving love. Happiness is the fulfillment of our dreams and hopes; joy is the breaking in of a new horizon of meaning that relegates our dreams and hopes to insignificance. Happiness is temporal and fleeting ... Joy is eternal and abiding.

See also C.S. Lewis' comment: "Joy . . . is here a technical term and must be distinguished both from Happiness and Pleasure. Joy (in my sense) has indeed one characteristic, and one only, in common with them; the fact anyone who has experienced it will want it again." *Surprised by Joy* (New York: Harcourt, Brace & World, Inc. 1955), p. 18.

In his study of C.S. Lewis, Terry Lindvall writes, "Joy is not the same as unadulterated happiness or uninhibited pleasure. It is not the culmination of these things or the greatest in degree among them, because it is different in kind." Terry Lindvall, *Surprised by Laughter: The Comic World of C.S. Lewis* (Nashville: Thomas Nelson Publishers, 1996), p. 65.

Peter Kreeft also distinguishes between joy and happiness: "It is misleading to speak of joy as 'satisfaction'; that confuses it with happiness or even with pleasure." *Heaven: The Heart's Deepest Longing* (San Francisco: Ignatius Press, Expanded Edition, 1980), p. 124. For a fuller view of his treatment of this topic, read the entire chapter, "The End of the Quest: The Joy of Heaven."

Henri Nouwen wrote: "Joy is not the same as happiness. We can be unhappy about many things, but joy can still be there because it comes from the knowledge of God's love for us." Henri J.M. Nouwen, *Here and Now: Living in the Spirit* (New York, NY: Crossroad Publishing Company, 1994), p. 28.

[3] Aristotle, *The Nicomachean Ethics,* trans. J.A.K. Thompson (Penguin Books, 1976), pp. 66-67.

[4] St. Augustine, "The Trinity," in *Augustine: Later Works,* trans. & ed., John Burnaby (Philadelphia: The Westminster Press, 1953), p. 95.

[5] We often speak of pleasure in the plural, i.e., "pleasures." If happiness and pleasure were interchangeable terms, we should be able to do the same thing with happiness. But can we? "Happinesses" sounds very awkward, at best. We can write it and pronounce it, but I'm not sure that any of us would have a clear picture of what it might mean.

As William Frankena observes, "We must, I think, distinguish between pleasure and happiness. 'Pleasure' suggests rather specific feelings, whereas 'happiness' does not. We can speak of 'pleasures' but hardly of 'happinesses.'" William K. Frankena, *Ethics* (Englewood Cliffs, New Jersey: Prentice-Hall, Inc., 1973), p. 89. The same result occurs when one tries to equate wealth, or fame or power with happiness. These things may make people happy, but they clearly are not the same thing as happiness itself.

[6] According to Aristotle, "The good for man is *an activity of the soul* in accordance with virtue." (emphasis added). Aristotle, *Nicomachean Ethics*, p. 76.

According to one ancient commentator on Aristotle," Happiness is activity (*energeia*) in accordance with virtue . . . happiness is life, and life is the fulfillment . . . of activity." Quoted in Julia Annas, *The Morality of Happiness* (New York: Oxford University Press, 1993), p. 45.

7 Although the Stoics could, with Aristotle, speak of happiness consisting in the active exercise of virtue, they also viewed it as an "*inner state* which, once achieved, cannot be increased," and "a *desirable state* that one would reasonably want to be in." See Annas, Ibid., pp. 408, 409. Emphasis added.

See the article "Stoicism" in *The Encyclopedia of Philosophy*, ed., Paul Edwards (New York: Macmillan Publishing Co., 1967) Vol. 8, p. 21:

> The consequence of such a life (living according to the benevolence and orderliness of the universe) is *apatheia*, or *euthymia*, spiritual peace and well-being; another term for this ultimate desideratum was *eudaimonia*, the happy condition of the daimon, or soul, when it resembles the deity.

The Stoic philosopher, Seneca, wrote, "What is the happy life? Self-sufficiency and abiding tranquility. This is the gift of greatness of soul." Quoted in *The Stoic Philosophy of Seneca, Essays and Letters*, trans. Moses Hadas, (New York: The Norton Library, 1958), p. 239.

While the Stoics viewed happiness as an inner state, it would be a mistake to say that they equated it with feelings. See F.H. Sandbach, *The Stoics* (Indianapolis: Hackett Publishing Company, second edition, 1989), pp. 40-41.

8 Aristotle, *Nicomachean Ethics,* p. 75.

9 Following Aristotle, Aquinas called it the pleasure which "follows reason." Thomas Aquinas, *Summa Theologica,* trans. Fathers of the English Dominican Province (London: Burns Oates & Washburn, Ltd., third ed. 1941), I, II, Q. 31, A. 3.

10 For recent literature from a Christian perspective, see J.P. Moreland, *Love Your God With All Your Mind: The Role of Reason In The Life Of The Soul* (Colorado Springs: NavPress, 1997); James W. Sire, *Habits of the Mind: Intellectual Life as a Christian Calling* (Downers Grove: InterVarsity Press, 2000); and W. Jay Wood, *Epistemology: Becoming Intellectually Virtuous* (Downers Grove, Illinois: InterVarsity Press, 1998).

11 Augustine "Teaching Christianity" in *The Works of Saint Augustine: A Translation for the 21st Century*, ed. John E. Rotelle, O.S.A., trans. Edmund Hill, O.P. (New York: New City Press, 1996), I/11, p. 144. See Arthur F. Holmes, *All Truth is God's Truth* (Grand Rapids: Willliam B. Eerdmans Publishing Co., 1977).

12 See the third section of this book.

13 See Annas, *The Morality of Happiness*, p. 59: "Aristotle famously defines virtue as a state involving choice which is 'in a mean relative to us, a mean defined by reason, i.e., the reason by which the intelligent person would define it.'"

14 James Gilman writes, "Joy is what humans experience when the way the world is and the way the world ought to be converge. For Christians joy is love's delight in God and God's

promised kingdom, when the way the world is and the way God wills the world converge." James E. Gilman, *Fidelity of Heart: An Ethic of Christian Virtue* (Oxford: Oxford University Press, 2001), p. 54.

[15] The distance between Aristotle and the New Testament account of virtue is captured well by Alasdair MacIntyre. After acknowledging some common ground, he comments: "Aristotle would certainly not have admired Jesus Christ and he would have been horrified by St. Paul." See *After Virtue* (London: Duckworth, 1985), p. 172.

[16] The active dimension of joy is found in its cognate verbs: *rejoice* and *enjoy.*

[17] One commentator describes Aristotle's view in these words: "Happiness is thus thought of as active rather than passive, and as something that involves the agent's activity, and thus as being . . . up to the agent." Annas, *Morality of Happiness,* p. 45.

[18] "But the fruit of the Spirit is love, joy, peace, patience, kindness, goodness, faithfulness." (Galatians 5:22, ESV)

[19] New Testament scholar, Luke T. Johnson, describes the joyful experience of early Christians as one of the "certain states in which they found themselves," and then goes on to put this into the context of a "power with which they had been touched" which "came from God." Luke T. Johnson, *The Writings of the New Testament: An Interpretation* (Philadelphia: Fortress Press, 1986), pp. 94-95.

[20] See Annas, *Morality of Happiness,* chapter 19, "Theophrastus and the Stoics: Forcing the Issue."

[21] William Barclay, *The Gospel of Matthew,* Revised Edition (Philadelphia: The Westminster Press, 1975) Vol. I, p. 89.

[22] Matthew 5:4

[23] Augustine: "On Free Will," in *Augustine: Earlier Writings,* trans. and ed., John H.S. Burleigh (Philadelphia: The Westminster Press, 1953), p. 150.

In stronger language, but to the same point, Jacques Ellul wrote:

> The validity of happiness, including that which might come from the fulfillment of needs and passions or the use of earthly things, rests solely on the recognition that it comes from God and is given by God. All happiness in which man does not recognize that it is God's work and stands in relation to him is rejected and is under condemnation.

Jacques Ellul, *The Ethics of Freedom,* trans. & ed., Geoffrey W. Bromiley (Grand Rapids: Eerdmans, 1976) p. 260.

[24] St. Augustine, "The Trinity," in *Augustine: Later Works,* 95. See also Aquinas: "to desire happiness is nothing else than to desire that one's will be satisfied" (*Summa Theologica,* trans. Fathers of the English Dominican Province (London: Burns Oates & Washburn, Ltd., third ed. 1941), I, II, Q. 5, A.8.

[25] Augustine's definition of joy is in fact indistinguishable from his definition of happiness. See the previous footnote for his definition of happiness. On joy, he wrote: "For what is desire or joy but an act of will in agreement with what we wish for. . . . We use the term desire when this agreement takes the form of the pursuit of what we wish for, while joy describes our *satisfaction* in the attainment" St. Augustine, *City of God*, trans., Henry Bettenson, ed., David Knowles (Baltimore: Penguin Books, 1972), p. 556. Emphasis added.

In our day, Peter Kreeft says that the difference between happiness and joy is that happiness comes from ourselves, while joy comes from God: "Pleasure and sense experience come from the world; happiness and knowledge come from ourselves (though many try in vain to find them in the world); joy and wisdom come from God (though many try in vain to find them in themselves or in the world.)."Peter Kreeft, *Heaven*, p. 129

It seems to me that this fails to recognize the important biblical truth that "every good and perfect gift comes from above" – including happiness. When the heart is aware that its desires have been granted by God, its pleasure in that fact becomes a joyful pleasure. To put it another way, when we rejoice in the God-given gratification of our desires, then happiness becomes at least one dimension of our joy.

[26] Karl Barth calls joy "a gratefully perceived and an enjoyed fulfilment." Karl Barth, *Church Dogmatics*, eds., Geoffrey W. Bromiley, T. F. Torrance (Edinburgh: T. & T. Clark, 1968), Vol. III, Part 4, p. 381.

[27] Psalm 37:4, NASB.

[28] As Aquinas put it, "Joy itself is the consummation of happiness." Aquinas, *Summa*, I, II, Q.3,A.4. An analogy may be helpful: as a finger is a member of the body; so happiness is a species of joy. As a finger finds its fulfillment in its relation to the hand and the rest of the body, so happiness is fulfilled in relation to the many other dimensions of joy. A finger is "meant" for a hand, and the rest of one's body; happiness is "meant" for joy in its fullest sense.

Augustine wrote:

> Is it, perchance, that as one joys in this, and another in that, so do all men agree in their wish for happiness, as they would agree, were they asked, in wishing to have joy – and this joy they call the happy life? Although, then, one pursues joy in this way, and another in that, all have one goal, which they strive to attain, namely, to have joy.

Basic Writings of Saint Augustine, ed., Whitney J. Oates, (Grand Rapids, MI: Baker Book House, 1948, reprint. 1980), Vol. 1, p. 163.

[29] Psalm 145:16, NRSV

[30] C.S. Lewis, *God in the Dock: Essays on Theology and Ethics* (Grand Rapids, MI: William B. Eerdmans Publishing Co.1970, pp. 58-59.

This may be the most significant reason behind Christians insisting that happiness and joy cannot be the same thing. It often happens that we learn of someone who has made a morally questionable decision in life (such as leaving a husband or wife for another), and it is justified with the commentary, "At least he's happy." Or "She has a right to be happy." Or we say, "Whatever makes you happy."

[31] See Hebrews 11:25, ESV.

[32] The Greek words for grace and joy are closely related. *Charis* (grace) and *chara* (joy) are related to the root, *char*, which centers on the idea of well-being. In classical Greek *charis* (grace) refers to that which brings well-being, while *chara* (joy) refers the experience of this well-being. See "Grace, Spiritual Gifts" in *The New International Dictionary of New Testament Theology,* ed., Colin Brown (Grand Rapids: Zondervan, 1976) Vol. II, p. 115.

[33] This is true, even if only in the case of the elect, as in the Calvinist tradition. Reformed theologian J.I. Packer doesn't go quite this far, but nevertheless speaks of common grace "serving the interests of special grace." *Transforming Our World*, ed., James Montgomery Boice (Portland: Multnomah Press, 1988), p. 82.

This fits well with the theological structure of Romans 2:4, where Paul says that the kindness of God is meant to lead to repentance. This verse and the next are relevant to our discussion: "Or do you presume upon the riches of his kindness and forbearance and patience? Do you not know that God's kindness is meant to lead you to repentance? But by your hard and impenitent heart you are storing up wrath for yourself on the day of wrath when God's righteous judgment will be revealed."

The happiness of those who are not yet "in Christ," I would say, is an experience granted from the riches of "God's kindness and forbearance and patience." When it is recognized and received for what it truly is – a token of divine kindness – it points people to repentance and salvation. Received ungratefully and impenitently, it becomes a basis for judgment.

[35] Acts 14:8ff.

[36] See Acts 14:21-23 and 16:1-2.

[37] Matthew 6:5

[38] C.S. Lewis, *The Problem of Pain* (New York: Macmillan, 1962), p. 115.

[39] Ibid., p. 93. I am not saying that the people I refer to as "pagans" are "bad men" in Lewis' terms. They live as strangers to God. The true intent of happiness lies here: "What we would here and now call our "happiness" is not the end God chiefly has in view: but when we are such as He can love without impediment, we shall in fact be happy." Ibid., p. 48.

[40] Kreeft, *Heaven*, p. 135.

Chapter 3: Joy and Our Emotions

[1] Our thoughts and emotions are both part of what the Bible refers to as our *heart.*

[2] Justin Oakley describes the experience of joy (without its theological dimensions) as feeling "a certain 'lightness', 'buoyancy', or energy permeating the mind, and affecting the way we see the world, the thoughts and desires we have, and the manner in which we act." Justin Oakley, *Morality and the Emotions*, (London and New York: Routledge, 1992), p. 10.

Dallas Willard describes it as "a pervasive *sense* – not just a thought – of well-being: of overall and ultimate well-being. Its primary feeling component is delight in an encompassing good well-secured." Dallas Willard, *Renovation of the Heart: Putting on the Character of Christ* (Colorado Springs, CO: NavPress, 2002), pp. 132-133. Emphasis original.

[3] St. Augustine, "Confessions," in *The Basic Writings of Saint Augustine,* ed., Whitney J. Oates (Grand Rapids: Baker Book House, 1948, repr. 1980), p. 180. I have contemporized the King James pronouns and verb endings.

[4] Robert Roberts writes, "'Joy' is less the name of a Christian emotion than a name for a characteristic of many of the Christian emotions. Love, hope, peace, and gratitude are all joyful emotions, and I suspect that when one has said enough about these others, there will be nothing left to say about joy." Robert C. Roberts, *Spirituality and Human Emotion,* (Grand Rapids, MI: William B. Eerdmans Publishing Co.,
1982), p. 74.

Roberts has similar things to say about love and humility. About love he writes," [Love] is neither a distinct and particular emotion nor, indeed, a distinct virtue." Rather, he says that *love* is a kind of "summary term." Roberts, "Emotions among the Virtues of the Christian Life," *Journal of Religious Ethics*, 20, 1 (Spring 1992), p. 43. And about humility he writes, "humility does not name an emotion [but] a complex emotional disposition." *Ibid.*, p. 60.

Dallas Willard writes:

> Of course it is impossible to separate love, joy, peace, faith (confidence), and hope from one another in practice. They lose their true nature when separated. Try imagining love without joy and peace, joy without love and peace, or peace without love and joy, or any combination of them without faith and hope. You will see, upon making a slight effort, that love, joy, and so on without the others just wouldn't be themselves.

Willard, *Renovation*, pp. 135-136.

[5] For instance, Richard Niebuhr wrote, "Despair and dreading do not banish rejoicing, nor does gladness extinguish fearing. They are not contradictories; they are opposites and hence do not root each other out." Richard R. Niebuhr, *Experimental Religion (*New York: Harper and Row, 1972), p. 104.

[6] Augustine knew something of this singular experience of joy and sorrow when he wrote, "When in a joyful mind I remember an earlier sadness, my mind hath joy, and my memory sadness." Ibid., p. 114.

[7] Allen Verhey explores the contrast between a dirge and a lament: "The pattern of a dirge moves from past glories to present misery. Lament reverses that pattern, moving from tragedy to confidence in God's good future. While a lament is entirely realistic about sorrow and suffering, it looks to God, and in looking to God finds hope and knows joy even in its

sorrow." Allen Verhey, *Remembering Jesus: Christian Community, Scripture, and the Moral Life* (Grand Rapids, William B. Eerdmans Publishing Co., 2002), pp. 148-151.

8 St. John Climacus, seventh century author of the work, *The Ladder o Divine Ascent*, coined the word *charmolypi*: "mourning joy," or "joy-making sorrow," or "sweet sorrow." See Frederica Mathewes-Green, *The Illumined Heart: The Ancient Christian Path of Transformation*, (Brewster, MA: 2001), p. 43.

9 Matthew 28:8

10 Psalm 2:11. Translators seem to have a difficult time with this emotional tandem. The RSV and NRSV drop the verb "rejoice" entirely. The NASB retains the translation "rejoice with trembling," but softens "fear" to "reverence." The NIV changes "rejoice" to "celebrate." The NEB attaches "with trembling" not to the command to rejoice, but to the following exhortation to pay homage to God.

The ESV ("Serve the LORD with fear, and rejoice with trembling.") follows Luther's translation: "*Dienet dem Herrn mit Furcht und freuet euch mit Bittern!*" See also *Table Talk* #38 and #148: "In the second Psalm he says: Serve the Lord with fear, and rejoice with trembling." *The Table Talk of Martin Luther*, ed., Thomas S. Kepler (Grand Rapids: Baker Book House, 1952, Reprint. 1979), p. 26.

Luther explains:

> So David wrote a psalm, 'Serve the Lord with fear, and exult with trembling" [Ps. 2:11]. Let somebody bring this into harmony for me: exult and fear! My son Hans can do it in relation to me, but I can't do it in relation to God. When I'm writing or doing something else, my Hans sings a little tune for me. If he becomes too noisy and I rebuke him a little for it, he continues to sing but does it more privately and with a certain awe and uneasiness. This is what God wishes: that we be always cheerful, but with reverence.

Luther's Works, American Edition, ed., trans., Theodore G. Tappert, General Ed., Helmut T. Lehman (Philadelphia: Fortress Press, 1967), Vol. 54, p. 21.

11 Edwards, "On Religious Affections," *The Works of Jonathan Edwards,* Perry Miller, Gen. ed., (New Haven: Yale University Press, 1959), Vol. 2, p. 366.

12 A. W. Tozer, *Knowledge of the Holy* (New York: Harper & Row, 1961), p. 112. I have changed the King James verb endings to a contemporary form.

See also Psalm 47:1-2.

13 C.S. Lewis, *Letters to Malcolm: Chiefly on Prayer* (New York: Harcourt, Brace & World, Inc.: 1964), p. 91.

14 Quoted in Niebuhr, *Experimental Religion,* p. 100.

15 This will probably sound familiar if you enjoy singing Van Dyke's hymn, *Joyful, Joyful, We Adore Thee.* The first verse begins with the words, "Joyful, joyful, we adore Thee, God of glory, Lord of love. Hearts unfold like flowers before Thee, praising Thee their sun above."

[16] See, e.g., Psalm 104:15.

[17] See Galatians 5:22. See also Isaiah 55:12; Romans 15:13.

[18] Nicholas Wolterstorff, *Art in Action: Toward a Christian Aesthetic* (Grand Rapids, MI: William B. Eerdmans Publishing Co., 1980), p. 79. P. Daniel Maguire says that the biblical concept of shalom, or peace, "for the Hebrews was the fulfillment of our capacity for rejoicing." Daniel C. Maguire, *The Moral Core of Judaism and Christianity: Reclaiming the Revolution* (Minneapolis: Fortress Press, 1993), p. 236.

[19] Edwards, "Religious Affections," pp. 249-250.

[20] 1 Thessalonians 5:16-18

[21] Lewis B. Smedes, *Mere Morality: What God Expects from Ordinary People* (Grand Rapids, MI: William B. Eerdmans Publishing Co., 1983), p. 109.

Or as Karl Barth put it, "Joy is really the simplest form of gratitude." Karl Barth, *Church Dogmatics*, eds., Geoffrey W. Bromiley, T. F. Torrance (New York: Charles Scribner's Sons, 1957), Vol. III, Part 4, p. 376.

[22] Proverbs 10:28

[23] Romans 15:13

[24] As Barth put it, "Most joy is anticipatory." [24] Karl Barth, *Church Dogmatics*, p. 377.

[25] Romans 12:12, NIV

[26] Proverbs 31:25

[27] John 16:33, KJV

[28] PT

[29] NIV, RSV, NEB

[30] NASB

[31] NASB. The Greek words are *tharreo* and *tharseo*, meaning, respectively, "to be confident, courageous," and "be cheerful, be courageous." William F. Arndt & F. Wilbur Gingrich, *A Greek-English Lexicon of the New Testament* (The University of Chicago Press, 1957), p. 352.

[32] Psalm 94:19, NRSV

[33] Nehemiah 8:10

[34] Philippians 4:13

[35] Proverbs 17:22, ESV

[36] Willard, *Renovation*, p. 133.

[37] Peter Kreeft, *Heaven: The Heart's Deepest Longing* (San Francisco: Ignatius Press, Expanded Edition, 1980), p. 129.

[38] Quoted in William A. Kramer, *Happiness Can Be Yours* (St. Louis: Concordia Publishing House, 1952), p. 96.

[39] See Psalm 30:11, ESV.

[40] See Ecclesiastes 3:4.

[41] See Job 21:11, ESV, and Luke 7:32, ESV

[42] See Exodus 15:20.

[43] See Psalm 149:3, and 150:4, ESV.

[44] See Luke 15:25.

[45] See Jeremiah 31:4, 13, ESV, and Isaiah 65:17-19, ESV.

[46] NIV

[47] Arndt & Gingrich, *Greek-English Lexicon,* p. 763.

[48] See Luke 1:44.

[49] See Luke 6:23. Emphasis added.

[50] "Christ's Joy and Ours," in *Spurgeon's Expository Encyclopedia* (Grand Rapids: Baker Book House, Reprint. 1978), Vol. 10, p. 36.

[51] John Charles Ryle, *Practical Religion* (Cambridge, England: James Clarke & Co., Ltd., 1970), p. 150. Emphasis original.

[52] Ibid.

[53] See Psalm 2:4.

[54] See Genesis 17:17 and 18:12, ESV.

[55] See Job 41:29.

[56] See Ecclesiastes 2:2.

[57] See Genesis 18:12.

[58] See Genesis 21:6.

[59] See Richard G. Cote, *Holy Mirth: A Theology of Laughter* (Stoughton, MA: The Alpine Press, 1986).

[60] Spurgeon, *Expository Encyclopedia,* p. 10.

[61] Exodus 19:4. See also Isaiah 40:31, ESV.

[62] 1 Peter 1:8, KJV

[63] *The New International Dictionary of New Testament Theology*, Gen. ed., Colin Brown (Grand Rapids: Zondervan, 1976) Vol. II, p. 353.

[64] See Psalm 100:1.

[65] Luke 19:40

[66] Joy is often quiet. Spurgeon was mistaken, however, in making it virtually normative for joy:

> People really full of joy do not usually talk much. A person, who is carrying a glass that is full to the brim, does not go dancing along like one who has nothing to carry. He is very quiet and steady, for he does not want to spill the contents of the glass. So, the man who has the joy of the Lord filling his soul is often quiet.

Spurgeon, *Expository Encyclopedia,* p. 40.

Clark Pinnock notes, with irony, "In our culture it is OK to shout in praise of a home-run hitter at a baseball game, but not acceptable to make a joyful noise to the Lord in church." Clark H. Pinnock, *Flame of Love: A Theology of the Holy Spirit* (Downers Grove: InterVarsity Press, 1996), p. 169.

[67] Blaise Pascal, *Greater Shorter Works of Pascal,* trans. Emile Cailliet and John C. Blankenagel (Westport, Connecticut: Greenwood Press, Publishers, 1948, reprint. 1974), p. 117. I have changed the King James pronouns and verb endings to their contemporary forms.

[68] 2 Samuel 6:5, NIV.

[69] 2 Samuel 6:14. An ephod was a hip-length, sleeveless pullover.

[70] 2 Samuel 6:21-22, NIV.

[71] Luke 24:38-40

[72] Luke 24:41

[73] See Matthew 28:8.

[74] See 2 Corinthians 2:14.

[75] C.S. Lewis, *Surprised,* p. 17.

[76] Hebrews 6:5

[77] For two recent works that explore this haunting desire, see Mark Buchanan, *Things Unseen (Living in Light of Forever)* (Sisters, Oregon: Multnomah, 2002) and John Eldridge, *The Journey of Desire: Searching for the Life We've Only Dreamed Of* (Nashville: Thomas Nelson Publishers, 2000).

[78] "I have given them thy word; and the world has hated them because they are not of the world, even as I am not of the world." (John 17:14)

[79] Hebrews 11:16

[80] Hebrews 12:22

[81] See Psalm 16:11, ESV.

[82] Lesslie Newbigen, *Journey into Joy* (Grand Rapids, MI: William B. Eerdmans Publishing Co., 1972), p. 116.

[83] See Philippians 4:4 and 1 Thessalonians 5:16.

Dallas Willard describes what life is like for those who are "well on their way" in the renovation of their hearts: "Finally, here, life in the path of rightness becomes easy and joyous." Dallas Willard, *Renovation of the Heart: Putting on the Character of Christ* (Colorado Springs, CO: NavPress, 2002), p. 227. This is very much what I have in mind when I speak of dispositional joy.

CHAPTER 4: THE JOY OF THE LORD

[1] A. W. Tozer, *Knowledge of the Holy*, (New York: Harper & Row, 1961), p. 9.

[2] John Calvin, *Institutes of the Christian Religion*, trans. Henry Beveridge (Grand Rapids, MI: William B.Eerdmans Publishing Co., eighth printing, 1979), Vol. I, p. 38, "It is evident that man never attains to a true self-knowledge until he has previously contemplated the face of God, and come down after such contemplation to look into himself."

[3] See Acts 17:28, ESV.

[4] Psalm 144:15

[5] For a rich, thorough study of divine joy, see John Piper, *The Pleasures of God: Meditations On God's Delight In Being God* (Portland: Multnomah Press, 1991).

[6] This was a significant theme in the theology of Karl Barth:

> [God's glory] is God Himself in the truth and capacity and act in which He makes himself known as God.

God's glory is the indwelling joy of His divine being which as such shines out from Him, which overflows in its richness, which in its super-abundance is not satisfied with itself but communicates itself.

God's glory is His overflowing self-communicating joy. By its very nature it is that which gives joy.

But we cannot overlook the fact that God is glorious in such a way that He radiates joy.

Karl Barth, *Church Dogmatics*, eds., Geoffrey W. Bromiley, T. F. Torrance (New York: Charles Scribner's Sons, 1957), Vol. II, pp. 641, 647, 653, 655.

7 C.S. Lewis, *Mere Christianity* (New York: Simon & Schuster. Touchstone Edition, 1996), p. 153.

8 Augustine wrote, of God, "Thou art an everlasting joy to Thyself!" St. Augustine, "Confessions," in *The Basic Writings of Saint Augustine,* ed., Whitney J. Oates (Grand Rapids: Baker Book House, 1948, repr. 1980), p. 114. According to Aquinas, God "possesses joy in Himself and all things else for His delight." And, "God is happiness by His Essence: for He is happy not by acquisition or participation of something else, but by His Essence." Aquinas, *Summa Theologica,* trans. Fathers of the English Dominican Province (London: Burns Oates & Washburn, Ltd., third ed. 1941), I, Q. 26, A. 1., and I, II, Q. 3., A. 1.

9 See 1 John 4:8, ESV.

10 Jonathan Edwards wrote:

> The divine virtue, or the virtue of the divine mind, must consist primarily in love to himself, or in the mutual love and friendship which subsists eternally and necessarily between the several persons in the Godhead, or that infinitely strong propensity there is in these divine persons one to another. . . . God's goodness and love to created beings is derived from, and subordinate to his love to himself.

Jonathan Edwards, *The Nature of True Virtue* (Ann Arbor: University of Michigan Press, 1960), p. 23.

11 This moves in the direction of what theologians call a "social Trinity." By this I mean that Father, Son, and Holy Spirit are distinct persons within the unity of the divine nature. By persons I mean that the Father, Son, and Holy Spirit are distinct "centers of consciousness," and by that I mean that they have such properties as self-awareness, knowledge, will, and action. For a clear statement and defense of a social Trinity model see Cornelius Plantinga, Jr., "Social Trinity and Tritheism" in Ronald J. Feenstra and Cornelius Plantinga, Jr., eds., *Trinity Incarnation and Atonement: Philosophical & Theological Essays* (Notre Dame, Indiana: University of Notre Dame Press, 1989).

See also Millard J. Erickson, *God in Three Persons: A Contemporary Interpretation of the Trinity* (Grand Rapids: Baker Book House, 1995), pp. 221ff., Clark Pinnock, *The Bond of Love: A Theology of the Holy Spirit* (Downers Grove, Illinois: InterVarsity Press, 1996 pp. 20-48, and Colin E. Gunton, *The Promise of Trinitiarian Theology* (Edinburgh: T&T Clark, 1991).

[12] Lewis Smedes, "Theology and the Playful Life," in *God and the Good: Essays in Honor of Henry Stob*, eds., Clifton Orlebeke and Lewis Smedes (Grand Rapids, MI: William B. Eerdmans Publishing Co., 1975), pp. 55-56. Emphasis added.

[13] See John 17:5, ESV.

[14] See John 17:2, ESV.

Three centuries later Athanasius wrote in echo that "the Father has love and good pleasure toward His Son who is His own by nature," just as "the Son has love and good pleasure toward the Father." If this were not so, he argued, then the relationship between the persons of the Trinity would be governed by coercion or necessity – either of which would hold disastrous implications for Christian theology. Cited in *The Triune God: A Historical Study of the Doctrine of the Trinity*, Edmund J. Fortman, S.J. (Philadelphia: The Westminster Press, 1972), p. 73.

[15] John 1:1-4. This may well be an early Christian reflection on the personification of wisdom in Proverbs 8. Some believe that the background of this passage is Hellenistic Greek thought, employed by the evangelist in an effort to make Christ intelligible to people with that philosophical orientation. There may be some truth in this, but its nearer background is Hebrew. N.T. Wright puts it this way: "However much the spreading branches of Johannine theology might hang over the wall, offering fruit to the pagan world around, the roots of the tree are firmly embedded in Jewish soil." Marcus J. Borg and N.T. Wright, *The Meaning of Jesus: Two Visions* (San Francisco: Harper San Francisco, 1999), p. 161.

[16] See Isaiah 42:1, ESV and Matthew 3:17, ESV.

[17] See the following: Psalm 40:8, ESV; John 4:345:30; 6:38, ESV.

[18] The Latin terms used by the church to describe the Holy Spirit in the life of the Trinity were *viniculum amoris* –literally "bond of love."

[19] See Galatians 5:22-23, ESV.

[20] This is not to say that he finds joy in all that happens in a fallen world. Clearly he does not. His pleasure is in who he is and in what he does. This is true even in his response to the ugliness of sin in the world. He takes no pleasure in sin, or in the death of the wicked, (Ezekiel 18:23), but he is just in his judgment (Genesis 18:25; Ezekiel 18:25-29), and he delights in his justice (Jeremiah 9:24). Despite the sin of his creatures, and the moral necessity of his judgment, joy is the first and last word in all that God does.

Barth was right:

> The reaction of God against sin, the meaning even of His holiness, even of His judgment, the meaning which is not extinguished but fulfilled even in damnation and hell, is that God is glorious, and that His glory does not allow itself to be diminished, to be disturbed in its gladness and the expression of that gladness, to be checked in the overflowing of its fulness.

Karl Barth, *Church Dogmatics*, p. 648.

[21] See, for example: Ephesians 5:8-10, ESV.

We often use the word "please" in our prayers to add a sense of urgency to our request to God. It can even become an expression of begging God to do something. The relationship between "please" and "pleasure" escapes us. But what if that was our starting point? What if our requests followed this pattern in Psalm 51:18?

> "Do good to Zion *in your good pleasure*;
> build up the walls of Jerusalem." (ESV)
>
> "*May it please you* to prosper Zion,
> to build up the walls of Jerusalem." (NIV)

Seeking the pleasure of God should be preeminent in the way we live and the way we pray because God delights in all that he does, including his answer to our prayers.

[22] See, e.g., the article "Neoplatonism," by Philip Merlan in *The Encyclopedia of Philosophy*, ed., Paul Edwards (New York: Macmillan Publishing Co., 1967), Vols. 5-6, pp. 473-476.

[23] For a good collection of essays on process theology by evangelical thinkers, see Ronald H. Nash, ed., *Process Theology* (Grand Rapids, MI: Baker Book House 1987).

[24] Acts 17:25

[25] Ibid.

[26] Acts 17:28

[27] Henry Stob put it this way:

> God, we learn from the apostle John, is *agape*, or self-giving love, and while this love is centrally displayed in God's redeeming work through Christ, it is by no means absent from creation. In a sense, indeed, it is there exhibited in its purest form. If to love is to impart, and to impart without regard to any foundation in the beloved, then the giving of existence (and essence) to a creature who before was not at all, is the most basic sort of giving or loving that there possibly can be.

Henry Stob, *Ethical Reflections* (Grand Rapids, MI: William B. Eerdmans Publishing Co., 1978), pp. 52-53.

[28] Josef Pieper wrote, "All love has joy as its natural fruit." Josef Pieper, *About Love* (Chicago: Franciscan Herald Press, 1974), p. 71. David Gill speaks of joy as "love's delight." See David W. Gill, *Becoming Good: Building Moral Character* (Downers Grove, Illinois: InterVarsity Press, 2000), p. 54.

[29] Peter Kreeft, *Heaven: The Heart's Deepest Longing* (San Francisco: Ignatius Press, 1989), p. 144. As Louis Smedes put it, God created "for the divine fun of it!" Louis Smedes,"Theology and the Playful Life," in *God and the Good: Essays in Honor of Henry Sto*p. 56.

[30] "The First Epistle of Clement to the Corinthians" in *The Apostolic Fathers,* trans. Kirsopp Lake (Cambridge, Mass.: Harvard University Press, 1912), Vol. I, pp. 63, 65.

[31] The Hebrew word is *tov.* See, *A Hebrew and English Lexicon of the Old Testament,* eds., Francis Brown, S.R. Driver, and Charles A. Briggs (Oxford: Clarendon Press, Reprint. 1953), pp. 373-375.

[32] See Ephesians 2: 10, ESV.

[33] See Deuteronomy 30:9, ESV and Jeremiah 32:40-42, ESV.

[34] See Psalm 35:27, ESV.

[35] See Psalm 18:19, ESV.

[36] See Proverbs 15:8.

[37] See Psalm 69:30-31, ESV.

[38] See Psalm 147:10-11, ESV.

[39] See Philippians 4:18, ESV.

[40] See Colossians 3:20, ESV.

[41] See Philippians 2:13, ESV, and Hebrews 13:21, ESV.

[42] See Luke 12:32, ESV.

[43] It is also attributed to God in 1:11 of this epistle: "in accordance with the glorious gospel of the *blessed* God with which I have been entrusted."

[44] *Theological Dictionary of the New Testament,* ed., G. Kittel, trans., G.W. Bromiley (Grand Rapids, MI: William B. Eerdmans Publishing Co., 1964-1976), Vol. IV, 362. Aristotle, for instance, used it as a synonym for his more frequently used term *eudaimonia.* See Aristotle, *The Nicomachean Ethics,* trans. J.A.K. Thompson (Penguin Books, 2004), p. 76.

[45] Aquinas, *Summa,* I, II Q.5, A.8.

[46] Aquinas, (Ibid., I, Q. 26, A. 1, 4), although indirectly, linked the happiness of God with his sovereignty:

> Beatitude belongs to God in a very special manner. For nothing else is understood to be meant by the term beatitude than the perfect good of an intellectual nature; which is capable of knowing that it has a sufficiency of the good which it possesses, to which it is competent that good or ill may befall, and which can control its own actions.
>
> He possesses joy in Himself and all things else for His delight; instead of riches He has that complete self-sufficiency, which is promised in riches; in place of power, He has omnipotence; for dignities, the government of all things.

Though I see things nuanced differently, for a good discussion of the happiness and sovereignty of God, see John Piper, *Desiring God* (Portland, Oregon: Multnomah, 1986), Chapter 1.

[47] To see that this connection between the happiness of God and the sovereignty of God is a fruitful one, we should note that in 1Timothy 6:15 Paul attributes blessedness, or happiness, to God and then immediately thinks of his sovereignty: "the blessed and only Sovereign, the King of kings and Lord of lords." Phillips translates this phrase, "God, who is the blessed controller of all things, the king over all kings and the master of all masters." The New English Bible renders it this way: "God who in eternal felicity alone holds sway. He is the King of kings and Lord of lords."

[48] Psalm 97:1

[49] Coming to grips with a joyful God will involve making theological adjustments for some. We owe a good deal to our heritage of classical theism. While it has helped to clarify some of our concepts about God, it has, unfortunately, obscured others. Most of us have been taught, for instance, that much of the Bible's language about God is not to be taken literally. That is, it figuratively applies to attributes of God that properly and literally belong to humans. The hand of God and the face of God are examples of this, and no one of orthodox faith disputes this truth. But does language about the emotions of God also fall into this category? Under the influence of classical concepts such as immutability (the idea that God never changes) and impassibility (the idea that God cannot suffer, or be affected by anything outside himself), there are many Christians who would say that they are. To attribute different emotional states to God would seem to imply change, or mutability. And if the emotions of God are responses to his creatures (that is to say, that he is affected by them), then that would seem to imply passibility. Neither, however, can be true of the Supreme Being on this view.

While the notions of the immutability and impassibility of God contain important truths, when they are placed into categories foreign to the Bible (and native to Greek philosophy), they take us further away from, not closer to, the living God. We must first of all get past the idea of an apathetic God: a God without emotions. Emotions are not a part of finitude, but of personhood. A God who loves and hates, and is pleased and displeased, and is happy and sorrowful is not a finite God, but simply a personal God. Emotions are characteristic of all persons and personal relationships. We experience them on a finite level; God, infinitely. They are imperfect in us, and perfect in God. They are embodied experiences for us, and incorporeal for God. Linda Zagzebski argues that “even if God has no sensory states, it would not follow that he has no emotions.” This is so because even in human experience not all emotions are passions, with sensory states. Some emotions are affections, and affections can be either sensory or “intellective.” Among the latter are love and joy. Linda Zagzebski, “The Virtues of God and the Foundation of Ethics,” in Kelley James Clark, ed., *Readings in the Philosophy of Religion* (Canada: Broadview Press, 2000), p. 84.

Second, we must adjust our view of the immutability of God. His essential or necessary attributes do not and cannot change. That which makes him God is forever the same. But that doesn't mean that he is a static being. Far from that! I'm not sure that I can even conceive of a deity whose life is an absolute *stasis*, and who also relates and responds to an ever-changing world. I feel quite confident in saying that the Bible does not present such a God to us. The God who is forever the same responds as well as initiates, and is sovereignly free to change the ways he responds (See, for instance, Jeremiah 18:1-11.). He is a dynamic

Personality who grieves when we sin, is angered by evil, and rejoices when his creatures seek his will. He responds here in judgment, and there in blessing – and all without being anything other than he ever has been or ever will be.

Third, we must take the Incarnation seriously. Christ is the supreme revelation of God. As J.I. Packer has put it, "God is Jesus-like." J.I. Packer, *I Want To Be A Christian* (Tyndale House Publishers: Wheaton, IL, 1977), p. 172. The Christ whom we meet in the pages of the Gospels is far from emotionless. He weeps. He is grieved. He is angered. He experiences the pleasures of joy. These things cannot, then, be alien to the life of God, or be thought of as inconsistent with who he is. We must either be open to emotions in the life of God or stop saying that Christ "reflects the glory of God and bears the very stamp of his nature" (Hebrews 1:3). We cannot have it both ways.

These "adjustments" are not optional for joy. A God who is incapable of real joy and happiness cannot be the Ground and Source of our own. We must, for the sake of joy, move away from philosophical categories and concepts foreign to the Bible, and return to the theism native to God's revelation of himself in Scripture, and, supremely, in Christ.

50 John Piper writes, "The heart of God is large and complex. He is able to be grieved over the pain of his creatures, while at the same time ordaining that this very pain and death take place for a higher and greater purpose that brings him more joy than if he had run the world in another way." John Piper, *A Godward Life* (Sisters, Oregon: Multnomah Press, 1997), p. 269. See also Piper, *Pleasures of God*, pp. 63-69.

51 See Lamentations 3:33.

52 See Ezekiel 18:23, 32, ESV.

53 See Romans 6:23, ESV.

54 See Jeremiah 9:24, ESV.

55 It was commonplace to refer to it as our "final end" – which applies to one's life as a whole. See, for example, Aristotle's comments:

> Human good turns out to be the activity of the soul in accordance with virtue, and if there is more than one virtue, in accordance with the best and most complete.
>
> But we must add 'in a complete life.' For one swallow does not make a summer, nor does one day; and so too one day, or a short time, does not make a man blessed and happy.

Aristotle, *Nicomachean Ethics*, p. 76.

56 While I agree that "classical" theism has sometimes moved the church further away from the God of the Bible than closer to him, I do not agree with contemporary "free-will" theists and "openness theologians" who say that a God for whom there is novelty and surprise is somehow greater than a God who knows all things (or, more importantly, that such a view is more biblical than one which acknowledges God's knowledge of all future events). For that sub-biblical view, see e.g., Clark H. Pinnock. ed., *The Grace of God, the Will of Man: A Case for Arminianism* (Grand Rapids, Michigan: Zondervan, 1989), Clark H. Pinnock, et al, *The*

Openness of God (Downers Grove, Illinois: InterVarsity Press, 1994), Clark H. Pinnock, *Most Moved Mover: A Theology of God's Openness* (Grand Rapids, MI: Baker Academic, 2001), David Basinger, *The Case for Freewill Theism* (Downers Grove, Illinois: InterVarsity Press, 1996) and Gregory A. Boyd, *God of the Possible* (Grand Rapids: Baker Book House, 2000).

57 In the words of the 14th century writer, William Langland, "All the wickedness in the world that man might work or think is no more to the mercy of God than a live coal in the sea." And in his mercy, he finds great delight. Quoted in Madeleine L'Engle, *An Acceptable Time* (New York: Crosswicks, Ltd., 1989), pp. 330-331.

58 "But we cannot overlook the fact that God is glorious in such a way that He radiates joy." Karl Barth, *Church Dogmatics*, p. 655.

59 C.S. Lewis, *Mere Christianity*, p. 153.

60 See Psalm 36:8, ESV.

CHAPTER 5: JOY INCARNATE

1 Isaiah 53:3

2 See Isaiah 53:4-5, ESV.

3 See Hebrews 12:2, ESV.

4 *Pascal's Pensées*, trans. W.F. Trotter (New York: E.P. Dutton & Co., Inc.,1958), p. 228.

5 We begin with what theologians call "Christology from above," or thinking about Jesus first in terms of what the New Testament says about his deity, Sonship in the Trinity, and Incarnation.

6 See J.B. Phillips, *Your God is Too Small* (London: Epworth Press, 1953), pp. 56 ff., where Phillips talks about what a "focused" God would look like in our humanity, and how this fits what we see in Jesus of Nazareth.

7 See Job 38:4-7, ESV.

Ancient theologians used the term *perichoresis* (literally, "a round dance") to describe the Trinity as a community of being. The Three dwell together as One. They share a mutual indwelling. Each shares in the life of the Others.

8 From Charles Wesley, "Love Divine, All Loves Excelling" in the *Hymnal for Worship and Celebration*, (Waco, Texas: Word Music, 1986), Hymn 92.

9 John 8:56

10 Luke 1:42, 44

[11] Luke 1:46-47

[12] See Luke 3:1-3; 4:1-2, ESV.

[13] Jürgen Moltmann writes, "John lived the life of an ascetic in expectation of judgment. Jesus' life is a festive life, in joy over the dawn of God's Kingdom." Jürgen Moltmann, *The Trinity and the Kingdom: The Doctrine of God, trans., Margaret Kohl (San Francisco: Harper & Row, 1981), p.* 69.

[14] See Matthew 11:19, ESV.

[15] Mark 2:19

[16] See Matthew 4:2, ESV.

[17] See: Matthew 6:16-18, ESV.

[18] Rudolph Schnackenburg, quoted in Daniel, C. Maguire, *The Moral Core of Judaism and Christianity: Reclaiming the Revolution* (Minneapolis: Fortress Press, 1993), pp. 232-233.

[19] See, for example, Acts 10:37-39, ESV.

[20] Luke 7:34

[21] See Luke 5:27-32; 7:34; 15:1-2, ESV.

[22] See his article, "Who Is Jesus? An Introduction to Jesus Studies" in *Jesus under Fire: Modern Scholarship Reinvents the Historical Jesus,*" eds. Michael J. Wilkins and J.P. Moreland (Grand Rapids: Zondervan, 1995, footnote pp. 37, 71.

[23] See Matthew 18:1-6; 19:13-15, ESV.

[24] See Luke 9:51-55, ESV.

[25] The literal meaning of "Boanerges" in Mark 3:17. See William F. Arndt & F. Wilbur Gingrich, *A Greek-English Lexicon of the New Testament* (The University of Chicago Press, 1957), p. 143.

[26] David Elton Trueblood, *The Humor of Christ* (New York: Harper & Row, 1964), pp. 63-64.

[27] Ibid., pp. 127ff.

[28] See Matthew 5:10-12, ESV, and John 16:33, ESV.

[29] Wilbur Smith wrote:

> When we come to the public ministry of the last days of our Lord we are face to face with a most astonishing fact, namely that it was in the last twenty-four hours of Jesus' life on earth, that He spoke more frequently both of peace and joy than He did in all the rest of His three years of preaching and teaching combined, as far

> as the records inform us. It was on this last night that Jesus Himself was betrayed by Judas, He was denied by Peter, He was hated by the world, He was rejected by His own brethren, He was mistreated by the soldiers, He was about to suffer every indignity physical and mental. He knew within twenty-four hours He would be nailed to a cross, He was Himself in such agony that He shed as it were drops of blood and cried out that His own soul was exceeding sorrowful even unto death. And yet it was in this very twenty-four hour period, which in many ways may be called the darkest night in human history, that Jesus spoke exclusively of *His own joy.*

Wilbur M. Smith, *Therefore, Stand: Christian Apologetics* (Grand Rapids: Baker Book House, 1945), p. 470.

30 John 12:27

31 Jonathan Edwards, "On Religious Affections," *The Works of Jonathan Edwards,* Perry Miller, Gen. ed. (New Haven: Yale University Press, 1959), Vol. 2, p. 111.

32 John 13:21, NRSV

33 John 13:31-32

34 John 14:1

35 John 16:33

36 John 17:1, 4-5, ESV

37 John 17:13, NRSV

38 Matthew 26:37-38; Mark 14:33-34

39 Luke 23:43, Codex Bezae. Bruce M. Metzger, *A Textual Commentary on the Greek New Testament* (London, New York: United Bible Societies, 1971), p. 181.

40 Hebrews 12:1-2

41 John 15:10-11. A grammarian would tell us that the plural demonstrative pronoun "these things" must refer back to the word" commandments": the commandments of the Father, which Jesus kept, and the commandments of Jesus, which the disciples were to keep. He did not identify any commandment in particular, as if joy were limited in its scope to any one moral prescription. Imparting joy was the purpose of all his moral teaching.

42 NRSV

43 See Matthew 11:29-30, ESV, and John 10:10, ESV.

44 *Martin Luther, Selections From His Writings*, ed., John Dillenberger (Garden City, New York: 1961), p. 15.

Jürgen Moltmann wrote, "For Jesus, the gospel of the kingdom is a messianic message of joy, not an apocalyptic threat to the world." Moltmann, *Trinity and the Kingdom*, p. 69.

[45] See Luke 2:10, ESV.

[46] Matthew 13:44

[47] Mark 1:15

[48] See Luke 15:3-7, ESV.

[49] See Luke 15:8-10, ESV.

[50] Luke 15:11-32

[51] See Luke 15:18, 21, ESV.

[52] Luke 15:17

[53] Luke 15:32, NASB.

[54] See Matthew 13:44, ESV.

[55] The Heidelberg Catechism captures this dimension of joy at the outset of spiritual life. "What is the birth of the new self?" it asks, and then answers, "Complete joy in God through Christ and a strong desire to live according to the will of God in all good works." "The Heidelberg Confession," in *The Book of Confessions* (United States: The General Assembly of the United Presbyterian Church in the United States of America, 1967). Q. 90.

[56] E.g., Matthew 24:51; 25:30.

[57] See Matthew 25:21, 23, ESV.

[58] See Matthew 22:1-10, ESV; Luke 14:15-24, ESV; Revelation 19:6-9, ESV.

[59] It appears some thirty times in the Gospels on the lips of Jesus (with some repetition between Matthew and Luke), and once again in one of his sayings recalled in Acts 20:35.

[60] Some scholars see it, however, merely as a statement of divine approval, with little or nothing to do with human happiness. Thus, when Jesus said, "Blessed are the poor in spirit" he was referring not to a state of happiness belonging to the spiritually poor, but simply to God's approval of this sort of humility. It was Jesus' way of saying, "This is a good thing. God approves of it, and so should you." For instance, Robert Gundry writes, "'Blessed' means 'to be congratulated' in a deeply religious sense and with more emphasis on divine approval than on human happiness." Robert H. Gundry, *Matthew, A Commentary on His Literary and Theological Art* (Grand Rapids, MI: William B. Eerdmans Publishing Co., 1982), p. 68.

The approbation of God is certainly important to the beatitudes taught by Jesus. Can we really imagine God granting happiness in a disapproval of our lives? Of course not. But I can't see how it follows that Jesus meant nothing more by his words than congratulations for possessing certain spiritual traits.

[61] Archibald M. Hunter, *A Pattern for Life* (Philadelphia, The Westminster Press, Revised Edition, 1965), 34. The great New Testament scholar, A.T. Robertson, lamented the translation of the word *makarios* with the English word "blessed" rather than "happy." See Archibald Thomas Robertson, *Word Pictures in the New Testament* (Grand Rapids, MI: Baker Book House, 1930), Vol. I, pp. 38-39.

[62] They are part of what we know as the "Sermon on the Mount" in Matthew 5-7, and the "Sermon on the Plain" in Luke 6.

[63] For beatitudes in other settings, see: Matthew 11:6; 13:16; 16:17; 24:46; Luke 10:23; 11:28; 12:38, 43; 14:14-15; John 13:17; 20:39. See also Acts 20:25.

[64] See Matthew 5:3, ESV.

[65] See Matthew 5:5, ESV.

[66] See Matthew 5:6, ESV.

[67] See Matthew 5:7, ESV.

[68] See Luke 14:12-14, ESV, and Acts 20:35, ESV.

[69] See Matthew 5:10-12, ESV.

[70] See Matthew 11:6, ESV.

[71] See John 13:17, ESV.

[72] Kreeft, *Heaven*, p. 159.

Chapter 6: The Joyful Spirit

[1] The Latin term for *Trinity*, coined by the second century North African theologian, Tertullian.

[2] John Calvin, *Institutes of the Christian Religion*, trans. Henry Beveridge (Grand Rapids, MI: William B. Eerdmans Publishing Co., eighth printing, 1979), Vol. I, p. 127.

[3] C.S. Lewis, *Mere Christianity* (Macmillan: New York, 1958, Reprint. 1978), p. 142.

[4] Ibid. Lewis goes on, more profoundly, to put the Trinity into our experience of prayer.

[5] Dorothy L. Sayers, *The Mind of the Maker* (San Francisco: Harper & Row, 1941, Reprint. 1979), p. xiii.

[6] Ibid., pp. 37-38.

[7] Augustine, "The Trinity," in *Basic Writings of Saint Augustine*, ed., Whitney J. Oates (Grand Rapids: Baker Book House, 1948, reprint. 1980), Vol. II, pp. 787-788:

> But what is love or charity, which divine Scripture so greatly praises and proclaims, except the love of good? But love is *of* some one that loves, and *with* love something *is* loved. Behold, then, there are three things: he that loves, and that which is loved, and love. What, then, is love, except a certain life which couples or seeks to couple together some two things, namely, him that loves, and that which is loved? And this is so even in outward and carnal loves. But that we may drink in something more pure and clear, let us tread down the flesh and ascend to the mind. What does the mind love in a friend except the mind? There, then, are also three things: he that loves, and that which is loved, and love. It remains to ascend also from hence, and to seek those things which are above, as far as is given to man. But here for a little while let our purpose rest, not that it may think itself to have found already what it seeks; but just as usually the place has first to be found where anything is to be sought, while the thing itself is not yet found, but we have found already where to look for it; so let it suffice to have said thus much, that we may have, as it were, the hinge of some starting-point, whence to weave the rest of our discourse.

[8] Cyril C. Richardson, "The Enigma of the Trinity," in *A Companion to the Study of St. Augustine*, ed., Roy W. Battenhouse, (Baker Book House: Grand Rapids, Reprint. 1979), p. 248.

Jürgen Moltmann wrote, "If God is love he is at once the lover, the beloved and the love itself." Jürgen Moltmann, *The Trinity and the Kingdom, trans. Margaret Kohl* (San Francisco: Harper and Row, 1981), p. 57. C.S. Lewis developed this theme in the chapter, "The Good Infection," in *Mere Christianity*.

[9] See 1 John 4:8.

[10] Brian Hebblethwaite has written in this connection, "They (the early followers of Christ) also came to realize that the very notion of a God who is Love requires us to think in terms of an internally differentiated and relational deity." "Jesus, God Incarnate," in *The Truth of God Incarnate,* ed., Michael Green (Grand Rapids, MI: William B. Eerdmans Publishing Co, 1977), p. 102.

Asserting the contrary, Archbishop William Temple wrote, "We are not . . . called upon to handle riddles such as, How can God be Love if there is no object for His love? For there is the whole Universe for such object." Quoted in *The Living God: Readings is Christian Theology*, ed., Millard J. Erickson (Grand Rapids: Baker Book House, 1973, Reprint. 1975), p. 430.

There is a serious problem with this, however. The universe would fulfill the need for an object of divine love only if it were eternal. It would have to be co-extensive with the love of God. If God is love (i.e., if love describes his eternal, unchanging essence), if love requires an object, and if the universe is that object, then this would have to be the case. If the universe had a beginning, however, as the Bible teaches and modern science has confirmed, then the object of God's primordial love must be something other than the universe. The nature of love and the temporal finitude of the cosmos point us, as Hebblethwaite contends, in the direction of "an internally differentiated and relational deity."

Richard Swinburne makes a similar case in his essay, "Could There Be More Than One God?" in *Faith and Philosophy* 5 (July 1988), pp. 225-241. See also "The Trinity" in his work *The Christian God* (Oxford: Clarendon Press, 1994), pp. 170ff.

11 The analogy of love moves us in the direction of a social model of the Trinity. The Father, Son, and Holy Spirit are a Community of love. However, we must move beyond the Augustine's notion of the Spirit as the bond of love between the Father and the Son. As a distinct Person in the Trinity, the Spirit is a Lover and Beloved in his own right. In my view this best fits the witness of the Scriptures.

12 See 1 John 4:8.

13 See Matthew 3:17; 17:5.

14 See Romans 5:5 and 15:30.

15 Clark Pinnock, *The Bond of Love: A Theology of the Holy Spirit* (Downers Grove, Illinois: InterVarsity Press, 1996), p. 15. Emphasis added.

16 See Psalm 16:11, ESV; Hebrews 1:8-9, ESV.

17 See Mark 1:9-11, ESV.

18 See Luke 10:21-22.

19 Augustine, "The Trinity," p. 770. There (Ibid.) he also wrote:

> The Father and the Son have willed that we enter into communion among ourselves and with them through That which is common to them, and to bind us into one by this Gift which the two possess together, that is by the Holy Spirit, God and gift of God. It is in him in fact, that we are reconciled with the Divinity and take our delight in it.

See also:

> The human will is divinely assisted to do the right in such manner that, besides man's creation with the endowment of freedom to choose, and besides the teaching by which he is instructed how he ought to live, he receives the Holy Spirit, whereby there arises in his soul the delight in and the love of God, the supreme and changeless Good.

Augustine, "The Spirit and the Letter" in *Augustine: Later Works,* trans. and ed., John Burnaby (Philadelphia: The Westminster Press, 1955), p. 197.

20 Philip Melancthon, *Melancthon on Christian Doctrine: Loci Communes 1555*, trans., and ed., Clyde L Manschreck (Grand Rapids: Baker Book House, 1982 ed.), pp. 13, 16-17.

21 Quoted in Erickson, *The Living God*, p. 429.

[22] Jonathan Edwards, "Treatise on Grace," in *Treatise on Grace and Other Posthumously Published Writings*, ed., Paul Helm (Cambridge: James Clarke and Co., 1971), p. 63. Emphasis added.

Barth also discusses the relationship between the triunity and the joy of God:

> As the triunity – and by this we mean in the strictest and most proper sense, God Himself – is the basis of the power and dignity of the divine being, and therefore, also of His self-declaration, His glory, so this triune being and life (in the strict and proper sense, God Himself) is the basis of what makes this power and dignity enlightening, persuasive and convincing. For this is the particular function of this form. *It is radiant, and what it radiates is joy. It attracts and therefore it conquers. It is, therefore, beautiful. But it is this, as we must affirm, because it reflects the triune being of God.* It does not do this materially, so that a triad is to be found in it. It does it formally, which is the only question that can now concern us. It does this to the extent that in it there is repeated and revealed the unity and distinction of the divine being particular to it as the being of the triune God. To this extent the triunity of God is the secret of His beauty. If we deny this, we at once have a God without radiance and without joy (and without humour!); a God without beauty (emphasis added).

Karl Barth, *Church Dogmatics*, eds., Geoffrey W. Bromiley, T. F. Torrance (New York: Charles Scribner's Sons, 1957), Vol. II, p. 661.

[23] See Psalm 139:7, ESV.

[24] See Genesis 1:2; Job 33:4; Psalm 104:30, ESV.

[25] See Ezekiel 11:19-20; 36:24-27.

[26] See Matthew 3:11 and Acts 2:3ff.

[27] See Joel 2:28-29.

[28] See John 7:37-39.

[29] See John 3:8; Acts 1:8.

[30] See Luke 24:49.

[31] See John 14:16-18; 14:25-26, and 2 Corinthians 3:17-18.

[32] See Acts 13:52.

[33] See 1 Thessalonians 1:6.

[34] See Romans 14:17.

[35] See 1 Peter 4:13-14, ESV.

[36] In an early Christian document we find this exhortation to joy:

Clothe yourself in gladness, that always has grace with God and is welcome to him – and revel in it. For every glad man does what is good, and thinks what is good. *The Holy Spirit is a glad spirit* . . . yes, they shall all live to God, who put away sadness from themselves and clothe themselves in all gladness.

T.R. Glover, *The Conflict of Religions in the Early Roman Empire* (Washington D.C.: Canon Press, Reprint. 1974), p. 166. Emphasis added. I have changed the King James pronouns to a contemporary idiom.

37 Literally the meaning of *eudaemonism*, the chief term for that pleasure. *Eudaemonism* developed a secondary meaning when used by philosophers. Its focus shifted from the supernatural agency behind flourishing in life, to the quality of flourishing in life itself. Nevertheless, it would have been understood in its primary sense by many.

A similar development took place with the Latin word *genius*, an equivalent term for the Greek *daimon*. Originally a *genius* was a guiding spirit or tutelary deity. By the time of Augustus, a secondary meaning emerged, shifting focus from the presence of a deity in the life of an accomplished individual to that of 'inspiration, talent.'" *Oxford Latin Dictionary* (Oxford: Clarendon Press, 1982, 1985 reprinting), p. 759.

38 Glover, *Conflict of Religions*, pp. 90-100. When Paul preached in the city of Athens, some in his audience concluded, "He seems to be a preacher of foreign divinities" because "he preached Jesus and the resurrection." (Acts 17:18.) The word "divinities" in the Greek is *daimonia.*

39 Quoted in Glover, *Conflict of Religions*, p. 101.

40 John Calvin, *Institutes*, pp. 6-49.

41 C. S. Lewis, *Mere Christianity*, p. 54.

42 In the words of historian E.R. Dodds, the new religion "wielded both a bigger stick and a juicier carrot." E.R. Dodds, *Pagan & Christian in an Age of Anxiety* (New York: W.W. Norton & Company, Inc., Reprint. 1970), p. 135.

Chapter 7: The Joyful Heart

1 This is known as a *deontological* approach to ethics, from two Greek words, *deon*, or duty, and *logos*, the study of. Doing one's duty should be one's chief ethical concern.

2 Deuteronomy 5:29, NIV. The English Standard Version renders it this way: "Oh that they had such a heart as this always, to fear me and to keep all my commandments." And take note: The fear of the Lord precedes obedience. A posture of reverence and awe before God motivates and inspires obedience. It is a matter of the heart, not another rule or regulation that we add to a list.

Joy bridges deontological and *aretaic* approaches to Christian ethics. Deontological ethics focus on commands and our duty to obey them, while *aretaic* ethics focus on who we are as moral agents and the acquisition of moral excellence. Although it includes obedience, an important dimension of joy is the enduring character of our hearts as we embrace and live out divine commands.

[3] Kant's famous dictum, "Ought implies can."

> For despite the fall, the injunction that we ought to become better men resounds unabatedly in our souls; hence this must be within our power. . . .
>
> But if a man is corrupt in the very ground of his maxims, how can he possibly bring about this revolution of his own powers and of himself become a good man? Yet duty bids us do this, and duty demands nothing of us which we cannot do.

See Immanuel Kant, *Religion Within the Boundaries of Reason Alone*, trans. Theodore M. Greene and Hoyt H. Hudson (New York: Harper Torchbooks, 1960), pp. 40, 43.

[4] The apostle Paul put it this way: "Do not be deceived: God is not mocked, for whatever one sows, that will he also reap." (Galatians 6:7)

[5] For instance, in his parable of the sower, Jesus contrasts three heart conditions, and how they determine one's receptivity to the word of the Kingdom. Of the last he says, "But the seed on good soil stands for those with *a noble and good heart*, who hear the word, retain it, and by persevering produce a crop." (Luke 8:15, NIV)

[6] Matthew 7:17-18. The New Testament uses agricultural metaphors to illumine our moral life. Picture a field, and a farmer planting seed and later harvesting. In every moment we are both reaping (from our past) and sowing (for our future). Or picture an orchard. Healthy trees bear good fruit; unhealthy trees bear bad fruit. All of this is very different from a moral code, and a set of rules to which we are duty-bound!

[7] See Acts 5:1-10.

[8] See Matthew 6:5.

[9] See James 4:3.

[10] See Matthew 6:2.

[11] See Philippians 1:15-18.

[12] See Titus 1:11.

[13] See Matthew 5:27-28.

[14] See Matthew 5:21-22.

[15] Isaiah 29:13; cf. Mark 7:7-8

[16] In the words of King David, "Behold, you desire truth in the inward being; you teach me wisdom in the secret heart." (Psalm 51:6)

[17] This is a distinguishing factor in Christian virtue ethics. There is a God who sees, evaluates, and is personally involved in what happens in our hearts.

[18] See Hebrews 4:13.

[19] 1 Samuel 16:7, NRSV

[20] See Romans 8:27.

[21] See Psalm 139:2, 4, ESV.

[22] Proverbs 4:23, NIV

[23] Justin Oakley comments:

> It is not surprising that Kant made such claims, since his view seems to be based on a simple sensation model of emotions as non-cognitive phenomena over which we have little if any control. Kant regarded emotions (other than respect for the moral law) as belonging to a causally determined empirical world of sense, and, as such, amenable to natural scientific description and explanation.

Justin Oakley, *Morality and the Emotions* (London and New York: Routledge, 1992), p. 94.

[24] Ibid., pp. 6ff.

[25] This love begins with the affirmation, "It is *good* that you exist; how wonderful that you are!" Josef Pieper, *About Love* (Chicago: Franciscan Herald Press, 1974), p. 27.

[26] Fear and anger can be reflective and deliberative, however. The more I think about a perceived wrong, the angrier I can get. The more I think about a looming crisis, the more fearful I may become. But this simply underscores my point, that our emotions – whether they emerge quickly, or "simmer" over a period of time – are part of, or at least overlap with, our thought life, and this makes them morally significant.

[27] This is the foundational premise of cognitive therapy. Daniel Goleman makes a distinction between a "first impulse" in an emotional situation, and a slower emotional reaction in which "there is a more extended appraisal; our thoughts – cognition – play the key role in determining what emotions will be roused." Daniel Goleman, *Emotional Intelligence* (New York: Bantam Books, 1995), p. 293. See also pp. 13ff. Not in the same way, perhaps, but cognition plays a key role even in our "first impulses."

Robert Roberts is right: "Human life, even when it is far from intellectual, is fundamentally a life of the mind." This includes our emotions. Robert C. Roberts, *Spirituality and Human Emotion*, (Grand Rapids: Williams B. Eerdmans Publishing Co., 1982), p. 26

[28] This is the significance of what Goleman calls "emotional intelligence," managing our emotions in healthy ways. See his chapter, "Schooling the Emotions." Ibid., pp. 261 ff.

[29] Jonathan Edwards, "On Religious Affections" in *The Works of Jonathan Edwards,* Perry Miller, Gen. ed., (New Haven: Yale University Press, 1959), Vol. 2, p. 100.

[30] Ibid., p. 101.

[31] James E. Gilman, *Fidelity of the Heart: an Ethic of Christian Virtue* (Oxford: Oxford University Press, 2001), p. 20. Louis P. Pojman refers to healthy emotions as "enabling virtues." *Ethics: Discovering Right and Wrong* (Belmont, CA: Wadsworth Publishing House, 1995), p. 175. In his discussion of spiritual formation, Dallas Willard writes: "Unfortunately, the fact that feelings and thoughts are largely a matter of choice is not widely understood – especially as it concerns feelings. We speak of feelings as 'passions,' and that is a word that implies passivity. But we are in fact very active in inviting, allowing, and handling our 'passions.'" Dallas Willard, *Renovation of the Heart: Putting on the Character of Christ* (Colorado Springs, CO: NavPress, 2002), p. 34.

[32] Linda Zagzebski writes that "the primary bearers of moral properties are emotions." See Linda Zagzebski, "The Virtues of God and the Foundations of Ethics," in Kelley James Clark, ed., *Readings in the Philosophy of Religion* (Canada: Broadview Press, 2000), p. 80.

[33] Courage is an emotion. Shaped by values (what is important to us) and volition (moral resolve), it is an affective state of consciousness that moves us to act in certain ways, even when those actions may put us at risk.

[34] Pojman gives this example of courage as an enabling virtue. Pojman, *Ethics*, p. 175.

[35] Edward John Carnell, *Christian Commitment: An Apologetic* (Grand Rapids, Michigan: Baker Book House, 1957), pp. 160-161.

[36] Ibid., p. 161. Paul Tournier sees it the same way: "I would not care for it at all if my wife's love for me were disinterested. I want her love for me to give her a personal – and so not a disinterested – joy." Paul Tournier, *The Adventure of Living* (New York: Harper & Row, 1976), p. 65.

[37] For more on this, re-read the section on the sorrow of God in Chapter 4, "The Joy of the Lord."

[38] See Psalm 11:5.

[39] See Malachi 2:16.

[40] See Isaiah 1:14.

[41] See Amos 6:8.

[42] See Proverbs 12:22.

[43] See Hosea 6:6.

[44] See Isaiah 61:8.

[45] See Jeremiah 9:24.

[46] See Psalm 1:2.

[47] See Psalm 119:47, ESV.

[48] See Isaiah 11:3.

[49] See Micah 6:8.

[50] See 1 Corinthians 13:6.

[51] See Titus 1:8.

[52] See Titus 2:14.

[53] Roberts, *Spirituality and Human Emotion,* p. 1.

[54] According to Justin Oakley, Aristotle's view of virtue includes "having the right emotions in the right way towards the appropriate objects and to the right degree." Justin Oakley, *Morality*, p. 2. Rosalind Hursthouse writes, "The emotions are morally significant. . . . The virtues . . . are all dispositions not only to act, but to feel emotions as reactions as well as impulses to action. (Aristotle says again and again that the virtues are concerned with actions and feelings.") Rosalind Hursthouse, *On Virtue Ethics* (Oxford: Oxford University Press, 1999), p. 108.

[55] This approach to moral philosophy is known as *aretaic* or virtue ethics. Unlike deontological ethics, with its focus on the intrinsic rightness or wrongness of an action, or consequentialism, which focuses on the outcome of actions, virtue ethics places its primary emphasis on moral agents and their character traits. In my own view, a complete accounting of the moral life includes virtue, commands, and outcomes, in that order. With respect to moral guidance, virtues provide a general wisdom (what a virtuous person would do, e.g., Jesus); commands inform virtues and give guidance when virtue might allow multiple courses of action; outcomes provide "tie-breakers," i.e., all other things being equal (with respect to virtue and duty), one ought to seek the best outcome possible.

[56] See Deuteronomy 6:5 and 30:2.

[57] He wrote, "In the same way just acts give pleasure to a lover of justice, and virtuous conduct generally to the lover of virtue." Aristotle, *The Nicomachean Ethics,* trans. J.A.K. Thompson (Penguin Books, 1976), p. 79.

[58] Immanuel Kant, *Fundamental Principles of the Metaphysics of Morals,* trans., Thomas K. Abbott (New York: The Liberal Arts Press, 1949), pp. 15-16.

[59] Augustine, "The Spirit and the Letter" in *Augustine: Later Works,* ed., John Burnaby (Philadelphia: The Westminster Press, 1955), p. 197.

[60] Jonathan Edwards, "On Religious Affections," p. 97.

[61] C.S. Lewis wrote, "If there lurks in most modern minds the notion that to desire our own good and earnestly to hope for the enjoyment of it is a bad thing, I submit that this notion has crept in from Kant and the Stoics and is no part of the Christian faith." C.S. Lewis, "The Weight of Glory" in *The Weight of Glory and Other Addresses* (Grand Rapids: Eerdmans Publishing Co., 1949, reprint. 1974), p. 1.

[62] Roberts, *Human Emotion,* p. 49.

[63] C.S. Lewis, *The Problem of Pain* (New York: Macmillan, 1962), p. 98.

[64] Matthew 6:10, NRSV

[65] Martin Luther, "Preface to Romans," in *Martin Luther: Selections From His Writings,* ed., John Dillenberger (Garden City, NY: Doubleday & Company, Inc., 1961), p. 31.

[66] Ibid., p. 28.

[67] Matthew 13:44, NRSV.

[68] King David wrote, "Restore to me the joy of your salvation, and sustain me with a willing spirit" (Psalm 51:12, NRSV). The parallel between the two phrases teaches us that the joy of salvation and a willing spirit in our life before God go hand in hand. The greater our joy, the greater our willingness to obey God. The greater our willingness to obey, the greater our joy. If we find ourselves saying "maybe," "not yet," or even "no" to God, or we find ourselves holding his will at arm's length or even pushing him away, the remedy is to ask him, as David did, to restore the joy of our salvation. It is in that joy that our spirits become willing to do whatever God asks; and in that willingness our joy is increased.

[69] See 1 Samuel 13:14 and Acts 13:22.

[70] Luther wrote:

> Although I am an unworthy and condemned man, my God has given me in Christ all the riches of righteousness and salvation without any merit on my part, out of pure, free mercy, so that from now on I need nothing except faith which believes that this is true. Why should I not therefore freely, joyfully, with all my heart, and with an eager will do all things which I know are pleasing and acceptable to such a Father who has overwhelmed me with his inestimable riches?

Luther, "Freedom of a Christian," p. 75.

Lewis Smedes has written, "What God expects of ordinary people is obedience born of gratitude; what God gives ordinary people is forgiveness born of grace. Once forgiven, we hear his commands, not as a burden, but as an invitation to enjoy our humanity, and in our joy to glorify our Creator." Lewis B. Smedes, *Mere Morality: What God Expects from Ordinary People* (Grand Rapids, MI: William B. Eerdmans Publishing Co., 1983), p. 243.

[71] Psalm 100:2

[72] Isaiah 64:5. Donald Bloesch writes, "The evangelical Christian does not believe that one can merit salvation by good works but that good works will flow spontaneously out of a joyful heart." Donald G. Bloesch, *Freedom for Obedience: Evangelical Ethics in Contemporary Times* (San Francisco: Harper and Row, 1987), p. 32.

[73] See Matthew 11:30.

[74] See 2 Corinthians 9:7.

Jonathan Edwards wrote, "A cheerful practice of our duty, or doing the will of God, is the proper evidence of a truly *holy joy.*" Edwards "On Religious Affections," p. 449.

75 For a recent treatment of character transformation, see Dallas Willard, *Renovation of the Heart: Putting On the Character of Christ* (Colorado Springs: NavPress, 2002).

76 Aristotle, *The Nicomachean Ethics,* Book 10, Sections 4-5.

77 From the movie, *Chariots of Fire,* Warner Brothers and the Ladd Company, 1981. Emphasis added.

78 In the memorable phrase, "*Pleasure is the measure of our treasure.*" Quoted in Sam Storm, *Pleasures Evermore: The Life-Changing Power of Enjoying God* (Colorado Springs, CO: NavPress, 2000), p. 39. Emphasis original.

79 Luther wrote, "Now he who is obedient . . . knows that he pleases God, and receives joy . . . as a reward." Martin Luther, from "The Large Catechism," quoted in *Christian Ethics: Sources of the Living Tradition*, eds., Waldo Beach, H. Richard Niebuhr (New York: John Wiley & Sons, Second Edition, 1973), p. 252.

80 C.S. Lewis wrote:

> We are afraid that heaven is a bribe and that if we make it our goal we shall no longer be interested. It is not so. Heaven offers nothing a mercenary soul can desire. It is safe to tell the pure in heart that they shall see God, for only the pure in heart want to. There are rewards that do not sully motives. A man's love for a woman is not mercenary because he wants to marry her, nor his love for poetry mercenary because he wants to read it, nor his love for exercise less disinterested because he wants to run and leap and walk. Love by its very nature seeks to enjoy its object.

Lewis, *Problem of Pain*, p. 145.

81 ESV. Emphasis added.

82 John 15:10-11

83 Matthew 25:21, 23

CHAPTER 8: JOY AND THE THEOLOGICAL VIRTUES

1 Psalm 40:8, NRSV. This is the opposite of "cherishing iniquity" in our hearts. (See Psalm 66:18.)

2 David Gill reminds us, "The content of a good character is the content of God's character. Goodness is godliness (literally, 'God-like-ness')." David W. Gill, *Becoming Good: Building Moral Character* (Downers Grove, Illinois: InterVarsity Press, 2000), p. 74.

[3] In him, we see "Divine life operating under human conditions." C.S. Lewis, *The Four Loves* (New York: Harcourt, Brace, Jovanovich, 1960), p. 17.

[4] See Matthew 3:17; 17:5; John 8:29; 2 Peter 1:17.

[5] See Romans 8:29; Galatians 4:19.

[6] See Ephesians 4:13.

Spiritual formation, as Dallas Willard puts it, is "the Spirit-driven process of forming the inner world of the human self in such a way that it becomes like the inner being of Christ himself." Its goal, he says, "is focused entirely on Jesus." Dallas Willard, *Renovation of the Heart: Putting on the Character of Christ* (Colorado Springs, CO: NavPress, 2002), p. 22.

[7] Philippians 2:12

[8] Matthew 6:10, NRSV

[9] James E. Gilman, *Fidelity of Heart: An Ethic of Christian Virtue* (Oxford: Oxford University Press, 2001), p. 54.

[10] It is important to say that the joy we experience now in part is the *same* joy that we will one day experience in full. Jonathan Edwards wrote, "The love and joy of the saints on earth is the beginning and dawning of the light, life, and blessedness of heaven, and is like their love and joy there; or rather, the same in nature, though not the same in degree and circumstance." Jonathan Edwards, "On Religious Affections" in *The Works of Jonathan Edwards,* Perry Miller, Gen. ed., (New Haven: Yale University Press, 1959), Vol. 2, p. 241.

[11] See 1 Corinthians 13:13.

Aquinas says that they are *theological* virtues both because: "Their object is God, inasmuch as they direct us aright to God: secondly, because they are infused in by God alone: thirdly, because these virtues are not made known to us, save by Divine Revelation, contained in Holy Writ." Thomas Aquinas, *Summa Theologica,* trans. Fathers of the English Dominican Province (London: Burns Oates & Washburn, Ltd., third ed. 1941), I-II, Q 62. A. i.

[12] Stanley Hauerwas calls it the "presupposition of all the virtues." Stanley Hauerwas, *The Peaceable Kingdom: A Primer in Christian Ethics* (Notre Dame: University of Notre Dame Press, 1983), p. 147.

[13] Which is another way of saying that joy has a *sine quo non* relationship to the virtues. It is necessary and essential. Without it, virtue does not exist.

[14] Romans 15:13

[15] Philippians 1:25

Luther wrote, "Behold, from faith thus flow forth love and joy in the Lord." "Freedom of a Christian," in *Martin Luther: Selections From His Writings*, ed., John Dillenberger (Garden City, NY: Doubleday & Company, Inc., 1961), p. 75.

[16] Josef Pieper, *About Love,* trans., Richard and Clara Winston (Chicago: Franciscan Herald Press, 1974), p. 73.

Jonathan Wilson defines faith as the "means by which persons come to know the person of Jesus Christ and by which we are transformed in our knowing. Faith is not something that marks only one aspect of our humanity. It transforms our whole way of being and our whole way of living. Faith becomes the habit by which we live and know." Jonathan R. Wilson, *Gospel Virtues: Practicing Faith, Hope and Love in Uncertain Times* (Downers Grove, Illinois: InterVarsity Press, 1998), p. 51.

Robert Roberts writes, "The gospel message provides people with a distinctive way of construing the world; the maker of the universe is your personal loving Father and has redeemed you from sin and death." Robert C. Roberts, *Spirituality and Human Emotion* (Grand Rapids, MI: William P Eerdmans Publishing Co., 1982), p. 16.

[17] The fact that joy is perspectival does not make it merely subjective. That we can and do experience joy is evidence that the perspective is true! It fits the world that we live in.

[18] Faith is one of the "foundational conditions" for joy. Dallas Willard, *Renovation of the Heart: Putting on the Character of Christ* (Colorado Springs, CO: NavPress, 2002), p. 141.

[19] James 2:19

[20] Edwards, "Religious Affections," p. 272.

For a good contemporary discussion of "head" knowledge and "heart" knowledge, see Bruce Demarest, *Satisfy Your Soul* (Colorado Springs: NavPress, 1999), especially chapter 4: "Knowing God . . . as Intimates."

[21] A noetic structure is the "sum total of everything that (a) person believes." Ronald H. Nash, *Faith and Reason: Searching for a Rational Faith* (Grand Rapids: Zondervan Publishing House, 1988), p. 21. See also Alvin Plantinga, "Reason and Belief in God" in *Faith and Rationality*, eds., Alvin Plantiga and Nicholas Wolterstorff (Notre Dame, Indiana: University of Notre Dame Press, 1983), pp. 48-63.

[22] See Nicholas Wolterstorff, *Reason within the Bounds of Religion* (Grand Rapids: Eerdmans Publishing Co., 1976), pp. 63-66.

[23] When spouses stop trusting each other, it represents a change in their control beliefs. The same is true in our relationship with God. It is here that we see trust and commitment as essential components of faith. To the extent that I actually trust God and commit my life to him, to that extent my beliefs about God play a controlling role in my vision of life. If my trust and commitment weaken, my beliefs about him – even if they are still orthodox – lose their power to influence the many other beliefs that I live by.

[24] Of Paul's view of the Christian mind, Herman Ridderbos wrote:

> It is not so much a matter of thinking in an intellectual sense, but of the new moral and religious consciousness, of the new insight into who God is and what his will is according to his revelation in Christ, and of permitting oneself to be determined thereby in the manifestation and circumstances of . . . life.

Herman Ridderbos, *Paul: An Outline of His Theology*, trans. John Richard De Witt (Grand Rapids, MI: William B. Eerdmans Publishing Co., 1975), p. 228.

[25] This is illustrated in Paul's words on God's providential care, "We know that in everything God works for good with those who love him, who are called according to his purpose" (Romans 8:28). The actualizing of this" good" in the circumstances and events of our lives ("all things") engages:

> our minds ("we know"),
> our affections ("love him"), and
> the government of our lives ("are called according to his purpose").

[26] See Hebrews 11:1.

[27] Romans 15:13

[28] Joy is the "interior of hope." David W. Gill, *Becoming Good: Building Moral Character* (Downers Grove, Illinois: InterVarsity Press, 2000), p. 199.

[29] Romans 12:12, NEB

[30] Karl Barth wrote, "Most joy is anticipatory." Karl Barth, *Church Dogmatics*, eds., Geoffrey W. Bromiley, T. F. Torrance (Edinburgh: T.&T. Clark, 1968), Vol. III, Part 4, p. 377.

[31] Romans 14:17

[32] Psalm 42:7

[33] Augustine wrote:

> And as we do not yet possess a present, but look to a future salvation, so it is with our happiness, and this "with patience;" for we are encompassed with evils, which we ought patiently to endure, until we come to the ineffable enjoyment of unmixed good; for there shall no longer be anything to endure. Salvation, such as it shall be in the world to come, shall be our final happiness.

Augustine, *The City of God* in *Basic Writings of Saint Augustine*, ed., Whitney J. Oates, (Grand Rapids, MI: Baker Book House, 1948, reprint.1980), Vol. 2, p. 478.

[34] See 1 Corinthians 13:13; Matthew 22:36-40)

[35] Gilman, *Fidelity of Heart*, p. 43.

[36] See 1 John 4:11. Stanley Hauerwas writes, "For Israel, therefore, to love God meant to learn to love as God loved and loves." Stanley Hauerwas, *The Peaceable Kingdom: A Primer in Christian Ethics* (Notre Dame, Indiana: University of Notre Dame Press, 1983), p. 78.

[37] C.S. Lewis, *The Four Loves* (New York: Harcourt, Brace, Jovanovich, 1960), p. 33.

[38] Ibid., p. 13.

[39] See Exodus 20:3 and Jeremiah 2:11-13.

[40] Psalm 16:4

[41] Acts 17:25

[42] See Isaiah 62:3-5 and Zephaniah 3:17.

[43] For instance, see Hosea 6:6.

[44] See Proverbs 15:8.

[45] See Psalm 69:30-31.

[46] See Psalm 147:11.

[47] See Colossians 3:20.

[48] See Philippians 4:18.

[49] See 2 Thessalonians 2:8.

[50] John MacQuarrie writes, "As a relationship develops there is less awareness of giving and receiving as separate acts – gradually the giving and receiving are recognized only as part of the single act of sharing." From the article, "Blessedness" in *The Dictionary of Christian Ethics* (Philadelphia: The Westminster Press, 1967), p. 33.

[51] Jonathan Edwards wrote, "Love to God causes a man to delight in the thoughts of him, in his presence; to desire . . . the enjoyment of him; *and so it is with a man's love to his friend*" (emphasis added). "Religious Affections," p. 208.

[52] Philippians 4:1, ESV

[53] Josef Pieper, *About Love* (Chicago: Franciscan Herald Press, 1974), p. 27.

[54] Augustine wrote, "Man . . . is a rational soul with a mortal and earthly body in its service. Therefore he who loves his neighbor does good partly to the man's body, and partly to his soul." Augustine, *The Morals of the Catholic Church* in *Basic Writings of Saint Augustine*, ed., Whitney J. Oates, (Grand Rapids, MI: Baker Book House, 1948, reprint.1980), Vol. 1, p. 343.

[55] 2 Corinthians 1:24

[56] Augustine, *Morals*, 343. Jonathan Edwards said much the same thing when he saw the exercise of true virtue as a benevolence to others, seeking their good – which, he says, consists of the knowledge of "God's glory and beauty," the soul's "union with God, conformity to him and love to him, and joy in him." Jonathan Edwards, *The Nature of True Virtue* (Ann Arbor, MI: The University of Michigan Press, 1960), p. 25.

[57] This, and not threats of hell, should frame the Church's evangelism – not for pragmatic reasons (though it is likely to give us better results), but because it is true to the configuration of life in God's design.

[58] "A benevolent propensity of heart is exercised not only in seeking to promote the happiness of the Being towards whom it is exercised but also in *rejoicing in* his happiness." Jonathan Edwards, *True Virtue*, p. 16. The philosopher, Leibniz, said, "To love means to rejoice in the happiness of another." Quoted in Pieper, *About Love*, pp. 77-78.

[59] Pieper, *About Love*, p. 76.

[60] Ibid., p. 74.

[61] See Galatians 5:22-23.

[62] To quote Pieper again, "All love has joy as its natural fruit." Ibid., p. 71.

[63] Wilson, *Gospel Virtues*, p. 19. Donald Bloesch thinks that we should speak:

> . . . more of graces than of virtues. Virtues indicate the unfolding of human potentialities, whereas graces are the manifestations of the work of the Holy Spirit within us. It is not the fulfillment of human powers but the transformation of the human heart that is the emphasis in an authentically evangelical ethics.

Donald G. Bloesch, *Freedom for Obedience: Evangelical Ethics for Contemporary Times* (San Francisco: Harper & Row, 1987), p. 81.

[64] Quoted in Romanus Cessario, O.P., *The Moral Virtues and Theological Ethics Notre Dame, Indiana: University of Notre Dame Press, 1991*), p. 15.

[65] Aquinas wrote:

> Man is perfected by virtue, for those actions whereby he is directed to happiness ... Now man's happiness is twofold ... One is proportionate to human nature, a happiness, to wit, which man can obtain by means of his natural principles. The other is a happiness surpassing man's nature, and which man can obtain by the power of God alone.

Aquinas, *Summa*, I-II, Q. 62. A. i.

[66] Philippians 2:12-13

[67] See Romans 11:36.

[68] "When the theological virtues animate the life of the believer, the moral energies of the human person, including the fundamental resolve to live a virtuous life, originate and find their sustaining power in the triune God." *The Moral Virtues and Theological Ethics*, Romanus Cessario, O.P. Notre Dame, Indiana: University of Notre Dame Press, 1991, p. 95.

[69] Augustine wrote:

> The human will is divinely assisted to do the right in such manner that, besides man's creation with the endowment of freedom to choose, and besides the teaching by which he is instructed how he ought to live, he receives the Holy Spirit, whereby there arises in his soul the delight in and the love of God, the supreme and changeless good.

Augustine, "The Spirit and the Letter" in *Augustine: Later Works,* trans. and ed., John Burnaby (Philadelphia: The Westminster Press, 1955), p. 197.

Jonathan Edwards wrote, "The Spirit of God is given to the true saints to dwell in them, as his proper lasting abode; and to influence their hearts, as a principle of new nature, or as a divine supernatural spring of life and action." Jonathan Edwards, "On Religious Affections," p. 200.

[70] Recall the words of Augustine from an earlier chapter:

> The human will is divinely assisted to do the right in such manner that, besides man's creation with the endowment of freedom to choose, and besides the teaching by which he is instructed how he ought to live, he receives the Holy Spirit, whereby there arises in his soul the delight in and the love of God, the supreme and changeless Good.

Augustine, "The Spirit and the Letter" in *Augustine: Later Works,* trans. and ed., John Burnaby (Philadelphia: The Westminster Press, 1955), p. 197.

Chapter 9: Joy and the Good Life

[1] To elevate it to the status of our *reason* for obeying God would actually demote it to an expression of self-love, which is a form of idolatry before God.

[2] For Christian perspectives on intelligent design and the anthropic principle in the development of life on our planet, see, e.g., Michael J. Behe, *Darwin's Black Box: The Biochemical Challenge to Evolution* (New York: Free Press, 1996, 2006); William Lane Craig, "The Teleological Argument and the Anthropic Principle," *in The Logic of Rational Theism*, ed. William Lane Craig and M. McLeod (Lewiston, N.Y: Edwin Mellen, 1990), pp. 127-153; William A. Dembski, *The Design Inference: Eliminating Chance through Small Probabilities* (Cambridge: Cambridge University Press, 1998); J.P. Moreland, ed., *The Creation Hypothesis: Scientific Evidence for an Intelligent Designer* (Downers Grove, Ill.: InterVarsity Press, 1994); Hugh Ross, *The Fingerprint of God* (New Kensington, PA: Whitaker House, 1989).

[3] Just as knowledge is made possible by a physically ordered universe, joy is made possible by a morally ordered universe.

[4] Louis B. Smedes, *Mere Morality: What God Expects from Ordinary People* (Grand Rapids, MI: William B. Eerdmans Publishing Co, 1983), p. 15.

5 Arthur Holmes, *Contours of a World View* (Grand Rapids, MI: William B. Eerdmans Publishing Co., 1983), p. 64

6 To use the primary Greek word, *eudaemonia.*

7 See Chapter 2 for more on this view.

8 Rosalind Hursthouse offers a neo-Aristotelian view when she writes, "a virtue is a character trait a human being needs for *eudaimonia*, to flourish or live well." Rosalind Hursthouse, *On Virtue Ethics* (Oxford: Oxford University Press, 1999), p. 29.

9 In ancient Hebrew parlance, the word "way" is a metaphor for life, and the verb *halak*, literally to go or to walk, was used to describe the process of living. See, for instance, entry #2143 in *New International Dictionary of Old Testament Theology and Exegesis*, gen. ed., Willem A. VanGemeren (Grand Rapids, MI: Zondervan Publishing House, 1997), Vol. 1, pp. 1032-1033.

10 Jürgen Moltmann writes, "Man is to give glory to the true God and rejoice in God's and his own existence, for this by itself is meaningful enough. Joy is the meaning of human life, joy in thanksgiving and thanksgiving as joy." Jürgen Moltmann, *Theology and Joy* (London: SCM Press, LTD, 1973), p. 42.

11 St. Augustine, "The Trinity," in *Augustine: Later Works*, trans. & ed., John Burnaby (Philadelphia: The Westminster Press, 1955), p. 95.

12 Augustine, "The Confessions," in *Saint Augustine: The Basic Writings of Saint Augustine*, ed., Whitney J. Oates (Grand Rapids, MI: Baker Book House, 1948, reprint. 1980), Vol. 1, p. 163.

13 Augustine, "The Morals of the Catholic Church," in *Saint Augustine: The Basic Writings of Saint Augustine*, ed., Whitney J. Oates (Grand Rapids, MI: Baker Book House, 1948, reprint. 1980), Vol. 1, p. 328.

14 Augustine, "Confessions," p. 162. I have changed the King James pronouns to a contemporary form.

15 Augustine, "Morals," p. 328. I have changed the King James idioms to a contemporary form.

16 Thomas Aquinas, *Summa Theologica,* trans. Fathers of the English Dominican Province (London: Burns Oates & Washburn, Ltd., 1946), I-II, Q 62. A. 1.

17 Ibid., I, II, Q. 3. A.1.

18 Ibid., I, II, Q. 2. A. 8.

19 Ibid., I, II, Q.3, A.4.

20 This vision of life, taught by Augustine, Aquinas and the Westminster Divines, centers around a set of common convictions: 1) that being precedes doing, that what we do flows from who we are; 2) that our emotions play an important role in our life as moral agents; 3) that joy is central to a life of virtue, indicating the heart's pleasure in God's design for life,

and a harmonious ordering of our inner life, our decisions and our ways of living in the world; and, more than that, 4) that joy – the enjoyment of God, his will, his works and his ways – is the *telos* of human existence.

[21] Joseph Kotva writes: "The virtues are instruments or means to the human good, but they are never simply means. The virtues are constituent elements and essential components of the human good. . . . The virtues and their coinciding activity largely constitute the *telos*." Joseph J. Kotva, Jr., *The Christian Case for Virtue Ethics*, (Washington D.C.: Georgetown University Press, 1996), p. 20.

[22] Augustine, "Morals," p. 321.

[23] Ibid.

[24] Ibid.

[25] Augustine, *City of God*, Vol. 2, p. 110.

[26] Aquinas, *Summa*, I, II, Q. 3. A. 4.

[27] On this statement in the Catechism Peter Van Inwagen has written:

> Human beings have not been made merely to mouth words of praise or to be passively awash in a pleasant sensation of the presence of God. They have been made to be intimately aware of God and capable of freely acting on this awareness; having seen God, they may either glorify and enjoy what they have seen – the glorification and the enjoyment are separate only by the intellect in an act of severe abstraction – or they may reject what they have seen and attempt to order their own lives and to create their own objects of enjoyment.

Peter Van Inwagen, "Non Est Hick" in *The Rationality of Belief & the Plurality of Faith*, Thomas D. Senor, ed., (Ithaca and London: Cornell University Press, 1995), p. 220.

[28] Bernard Ramm calls glory "both a modality of the self-revelation of God, and an attribute of God." Bernard Ramm, *Them He Glorified* (Grand Rapids, MI: William B. Eerdmans Publishing Co., 1963), p. 10. Karl Barth wrote: "[God's glory] is God Himself in the truth and capacity and act in which He makes himself known as God." Karl Barth, *Church Dogmatics*, eds., Geoffrey W. Bromiley, T. F. Torrance (New York: Charles Scribner's Sons, 1957), Vol. II, p. 64.

[29] See Psalm 24:7.

[30] See Acts 7:2.

[31] See Ephesians 1:17.

[32] See 2 Peter 1:17.

[33] The Westminster Shorter Catechism tells us that there are two dimensions of our chief end – glorifying God and enjoying him. We do not have two chief ends, but one with two facets (As John Piper observes in his work, *Desiring God: Meditations of a Christian Hedonist*

[Portland, Oregon: Multnomah Press, 1986], p. 13. As C.S. Lewis saw it, "Fully to enjoy is to glorify. In commanding us to glorify Him, God is inviting us to enjoy Him." C.S. Lewis, *Reflections on the Psalms* [New York: Harcourt Brace Jovanovich, 1958], p. 97.)

Glorifying God and enjoying him are united in our life before him, if Karl Barth is right, because glory and joy are united in God himself:

> God's glory is the indwelling joy of His divine being which as such shines out from Him, which overflows in its richness, which in its super-abundance is not satisfied with itself but communicates itself.
>
> God's glory is His overflowing self-communicating joy. By its very nature it is that which gives joy.
>
> But we cannot overlook the fact that God is glorious in such a way that He radiates joy.

Barth, *Church Dogmatics*, Vol. II, pp. 647, 653, 655.

34 Francis Brown, S.R. Driver, C.A. Briggs, *Hebrew and English Lexicon of the Old Testament* (Oxford: Clarendon Press, 1907, reprint. 1978), pp. 457-459.

35 See Genesis 31:1; Psalm 49:16-17.

36 Revelation 4:11, NRSV

37 2 Corinthians 3:18

38 Deuteronomy 11:26-28

39 Old Testament scholars refer to this pattern of obedience/blessing and disobedience/curse as "Deuteronomic theology."

40 See Deuteronomy 4:40; 5:16, 29; 6:3, 18; 8:16; 12:25, 28; 19:13; 22:7; 2 Kings 25:24; Proverbs 24:25; Jeremiah 38:20; 42:6.

41 Wisdom books include Job, Proverbs, Ecclesiastes, and, for some, the Song of Solomon. There are also wisdom Psalms (e.g., 1, 10, 12, 15, 19, 32, 34, 36, 37, 49, 50, 52, 53, 73, 78, 82, 91, 92, 94, 111, 112, 119, 127, 128, and 139) In the New Testament, the beatitudes of Jesus and the Epistle of James reflect the Wisdom tradition.

42 R.N. Gordon summarizes the ultimate motive behind the book of Proverbs as, "*Life*, when *life* is understood as a full, satisfying, integrated and enjoyable existence." Quoted in Walter C. Kaiser, Jr., *The Old Testament Documents: Are They Reliable and Relevant?* (Downers Grove, IL: InterVarsity Press, 2001), p. 156.

43 Cornelius Plantinga, Jr., *Not the Way It's Supposed to Be: A Breviary of Sin*, (Grand Rapids, MI: William B. Eerdmans Publishing Company, 1995), p.10.

44 See Matthew 4:4.

[45] See, for example Matthew 5:17; Luke 24:25-27; John 5:39.

[46] See John 15:11; 17:13.

[47] See John 10:10.

[48] See Matthew 11:28-30.

[49] In Greek the word for "blessed" is *makarios*, one of the leading terms for happiness in the first century world. In turn, *makarios* translates the Hebrew word *asher*, or blessed in the wisdom literature (e.g., Psalm 1:1).

[50] 2 Corinthians 1:20

[51] See 1 Peter 1:8, NASB.

[52] See Romans 14:17.

Chapter 10: Joy and the Pursuit of Pleasure

[1] See, e.g., John Piper's, *Desiring God: Meditations of a Christian Hedonist* (Portland, OR: Multnomah Press, 1986). See also John Piper, *The Dangerous Duty of Delight* (Sisters, OR: Multnomah Publishers, Inc., 2001).

A few years after the publication of Piper's first book on Christian hedonism, a proposal was advanced by Howard Redmond, published as part of the American University Studies series, with the title, *Christian Hedonism.* See Howard A. Reymond, *Christian Hedonism* (New York: P. Lang, 1990).

[2] See, e.g., the article "Cyrenaics" by A.A. Long in *Encyclopedia of Ethics*, eds. Lawrence C. Becker and Charlotte B. Becker (New York and London: Routledge, 2nd ed., 2001), Vol. 1, pp. 370-372.

[3] Luke 12:19

[4] 2 Timothy 3:4

[5] Philippians 3:19

[6] Ironically, Epicurus would have shunned much of what is described as *Epicurean* in our day, i.e., titillating, indulging, and sating one's senses. See, e.g., the articles, "Epicurus" and "Epicureanism and the Epicurean School" by P.H. DeLacy in *The Encyclopedia of Philosophy* (New York: Macmillan Publishing Co., and the Free Press, 1967), Vols. 3-4, pp. 2-5.

[7] See Rem B. Edwards, *Pleasures and Pains: A Theory of Qualitative Hedonism* (Ithaca, NY: Cornell University Press, 1979).

[8] What follows is not an exposition and critique of John Piper's *Christian hedonism.* Although the moniker is deliciously thought-provoking, it is probably a misnomer for his work. Piper himself says, "I put little stock in whether anybody calls this vision of God and life

'Christian hedonism.' That is a term that will pass away like a vapor." John Piper, *Future Grace: The Purifying Power of the Promises of God* (Colorado Springs: Multnomah Books, 2012), p. 400. In this chapter, I try to take hedonism seriously as an ethical system and see if it can be made compatible with a Christian pursuit of joy.

9 Rem B. Edwards, *Pleasures and Pains*, p. 19.

10 The highest good must be an intrinsic good. If it were a means to anything else, the end to which it is a means would be higher.

11 God is *the* highest good. As we saw in the last chapter, however, there are both objective and subjective dimensions to this. God is *the* highest good; the enjoyment of God, or joy, is *our* highest good.

12 The notion of soul-sorrow as an existential problem was central to the thought of Edward John Carnell. See his *An Introduction to Christian Apologetics: A Philosophic Defense of the Trinitarian-Theistic Faith* (reprinted, Eugene, OR: Wipf & Stock Publishers, 2007)

13 See Psalm 16:11, ESV.

14 To use language honored by centuries of spiritual experience, we can think of joy as the *beatific vision* of God. The opposite term, the *miserific vision* of God, is a painful experience. In C.S. Lewis' *Perelandra*, Ransom says:

> As there is one face above all worlds merely to see which is irrevocable joy, so at the bottom of all worlds that face is waiting whose sight alone is the misery from which none who beholds it can recover. And though there seemed to be, and indeed were, a thousand roads by which a man could walk through the world, there was not a single one which did not lead sooner or later either to the Beatific or the Miserific Vision.

C.S. Lewis, *Perelandra* (New York: Scribner, reprinted, 1996) p. 96.

15 The fact that *unjoy* doesn't exist in our dictionaries, and seems so awkward, should probably tip us off that this isn't going to end well in our thought experiment.

16 Quoted in Waldo Beach and H. Richard Niebuhr, eds., *Christian Ethics: Sources of the Living Tradition* (New York: John Wiley & Sons) sec. ed., 1973), p. 310.

17 From *hedone,* the classical Greek word for pleasure.

18 McGill, V.J., *The Idea of Happiness* (New York: F.A. Praeger, 1967), p. 291.

19 See Isaiah 59:1-2and 1 John 1:6.

20 See, e.g., John Dillenberger, *God Hidden and Revealed: The Interpretation of Luther's Deus Absconditus and Its Significance for Religious Thought* (Philadelphia: Muhlenberg Press, 1953). In the Scriptures, see, for example, Job 13:24; Psalm 10:1; 44:24.

[21] See, e.g., "The Christian Ethic" by Thomas J. Bigham and Albert T. Mollegen in *A Companion to the Study of St. Augustine*, ed., Roy W. Battenhouse (Grand Rapids, MI: Baker Book House, 1955, reprint. 1979), pp. 371ff.

[22] See Exodus 20:3.

[23] Jonathan Edwards, "On Religious Affections," *The Works of Jonathan Edwards,* Perry Miller, Gen. ed., (New Haven: Yale University Press, 1959), Vol. 2, pp. 251-252.

[24] Here is the quote, in its larger context:

> Tyndale, as regards the natural condition of humanity, holds that by nature we can do no good works without respect of some profit either in this world or in the world to come. . . . That the profit should be located in another world means, as Tyndale clearly sees, no difference. Theological hedonism is still hedonism. Whether the man is seeking heaven or a hundred pounds, he can still but seek himself, of freedom in the true sense—of spontaneity or disinterestedness—nature knows nothing. And yet by a terrible paradox, such disinterestedness is precisely what the moral law demands.

C.S. Lewis, *English Literature in the Sixteenth Century: Excluding Drama*, (Oxford: Clarendon Press, 1954), p. 188.

[25] Edwards wrote:

> The grace of God may appear lovely two ways; either as *bonum utile*, a *profitable good* to me, what greatly serves my interest, and so suits my self-love; or as *bonum formosum*, a *beautiful good* in itself, and part of the moral and spiritual excellency of the divine nature. In this latter respect it is that true saints have their hearts affected, and love captivated, by the free grace of God.

Edwards in *The Works of Jonathan Edwards*, pp. 262-263.

[26] Bernard of Clairvaux saw this paradox clearly:

> All true love is without calculation and nevertheless is instantly given its reward, in fact it can receive its reward only when it is without calculation. . . . Whoever seeks as the reward of his love only the joy of love will receive the joy of love. But whoever seeks anything else in love except love will lose both love and the joy of love at the same time.

Quoted in Josef Pieper, *About Love* (Chicago: Franciscan Herald Press, 1974), p. 90.

[27] Can we think of ourselves as Christian hedonists in a weaker sense? According to Dr. Edwards, whose paradigm for hedonism we have been using for comparison, a weaker version of hedonism might acknowledge that pleasure is an intrinsic good, but not the only intrinsic good, or that there are other considerations, in addition to the pursuit of pleasure and the avoidance of pain, which factor significantly into the equation of a good life. Edwards declines to call this hedonism at all. He refers to it as "pluralism," which he includes in the category of a non-hedonistic approach to life (*Pleasures and Pains*, p. 19). It loses its cohesiveness as a moral guide. It requires too many qualifications to make it work. We would

encounter the same difficulties in trying to patch together a weaker form of Christian hedonism.

28 Clark Pinnock writes, "The Christian way is not hedonism in the ordinary sense, of course. It does not make a god out of sensual pleasure. But it does involve enjoying God and his gifts, pleasure deeper than all others." Clark H. Pinnock, *Reason Enough: A Case for the Christian Faith* (Downers Grove: InterVarsity Press, 1980), p. 54.

29 See Mark 2:21-22.

30 This will be the focus of the next chapter.

31 From the Greek word *chara*, which is usually translated *joy*.

32 Jacques Ellul's comment about happiness fits well with the pursuit of pleasure, even if it is the pleasure of joy:

> I believe that biblically there is a constant contradiction between the pursuit of happiness and obedience to the will of God. I add at once that this does not mean that happiness is forbidden the Christian. As Jesus puts it, happiness is given as an extra. It is given and not won nor passionately sought. It is an extra and hence it is not the essential and decisive thing but a secondary supplement. What I have in view in this context, then, is not actual happiness but the pursuit of it, the claiming of it, the passion for it, and the value attributed to it. It is the fact of finding the whole meaning of life in it, of sacrificing everything for it, and of justifying everything by it.

Jacques Ellul, *The Ethics of Freedom*, trans. & ed., Geoffrey W. Bromiley (Grand Rapids: Eerdmans, 1976), p. 258.

33 James Gustafson refers to the "believer's epistemological privilege" – which means, in less technical terms, that we have "inside information" from God on how he has designed the universe and our lives to operate. Quoted in Lewis B. Smedes, *Mere Moralilty: What God Expects from Ordinary People* (Grand Rapids, MI: William B. Eerdmans Publishing Co., 1983), p. 52.

34 For an introduction to, and critique of, utilitarianism, see e.g., Louis P. Pojman, *Ethics: Discovering Right and Wrong* (Belmont, CA: Wadsworth Publishing Co., 1995), pp. 105-132, and the article "Utilitarianism" by J.J.C. Smart in *The Encyclopedia of Philosophy*, Vols. 7-8, pp. 206-212.

35 John 8:29

36 This is really just a paraphrase of the Westminster Catechism's definition of our chief end as glorifying God and enjoying him forever.

37 Jonathan Edwards wrote, ""A benevolent propensity of heart is exercised not only in seeking to promote the happiness of the Being towards whom it is exercised but also in *rejoicing in* his happiness." Jonathan Edwards, *The Nature of True Virtue* (Ann Arbor, MI: The University of Michigan Press, 1960), p.16. The philosopher, Leibniz, said, "To love means to rejoice in the happiness of another." Quoted in Pieper, *About Love*, pp. 77-78.

[38] Karl Barth, *Church Dogmatics*, eds., Geoffrey W. Bromiley, T. F. Torrance (Edinburgh: T.&T. Clark, 1968), Vol. III, Part 4, p. 379.

[39] Augustine, "The Morals of the Catholic Church," in *Saint Augustine: The Basic Writings of Saint Augustine*, ed., Whitney J. Oates (Grand Rapids, MI: Baker Book House, 1948, reprint. 1980), Vol. 1, p. 343.

There is great wisdom in seeing joy as an acronym for *J*esus, *O*thers, *Y*ourself. I am unsure of its source.

[40] See 2 Timothy 3:2.

[41] See Matt Jensen, *The Gravity of Sin: Augustine, Luther and Barth on 'Homo Incurvatus In Se'* (London: T&T Clark, 2006).

[42] Matthew 22:39. We are not commanded to love ourselves. It is assumed that we do, demonstrated daily by the fact that we feed and clothe ourselves, and do a great many other things that serve our own interests. The command to love others as we love ourselves can only be good if loving ourselves is a good thing.

[43] See Ephesians 5:28-29.

[44] See Genesis 1:31.

[45] Jürgen Moltmann writes:

> Man is to give glory to the true God and rejoice in *God's and his own existence.*
>
> The glorification of God lies in the demonstrative joy of existence. In that case man in his uninhibited fondness for this finite life and by his affirmation of mortal beauty shares the infinite pleasure of the creator.

Jürgen Moltmann, *Theology and Joy* (London: SCM Press, LTD, 1973), pp. 42, 44.

[46] Augustine, "Morals," p. 342.

[47] As Paul Ramsey put it:

> Promise of reward may be the condition of action, the ground or the promise of strength, but reward is never the action's goal. Reward is always added to the nature of the act, not a direct result of it such as might become part of the agent's own prudential calculation. If he were calculating the nature of his act would change, it would not be the kind of action for which reward is promised.

Paul Ramsey, *Basic Christian Ethics* (Chicago: The University of Chicago Press, 1950, Paperback ed., 1980), p. 133.

[48] "No, you should not pursue your joy . . . you should pursue God. . . . If we focus our attention on our own subjective experience of joy, we will certainly be frustrated and God will not be honored." The first part of the quote is a "helpful objection" to his view of

Christian hedonism, and the second part is his response. See John Piper, *Desiring God*, p. 215.

[49] This is true even when we think of joy as our pleasure in virtue. God is both the rewarder of this pleasure and the reward (since joy is the God of joy giving himself to us.)

[50] Linda Zagzebski writes:

> Emotions are affective states with intentional objects. In an emotional state one feels a distinctive way *about* something, the intentional object. . . . Emotions are individuated in part by their intentional object. So when I speak of an individual emotion, I do not mean fear or love, but love *of* something of a certain kind, or féar *that* something is the case.

Linda Zagzebski, "The Virtues of God and the Foundations of Ethics" in Kelly James Clark, ed., *Readings in the Philosophy of Religion* (Canada: Broadview Press, 2000), p. 80.

The Jewish philosopher, Abraham Heschel, was right: "Joy itself attaches not to the subject but to the object." Abraham Joshua Heschel, *God in Search of Man* (New York: Farrar, Straus & Giroux: 1955), p. 386.

[51] Piper, *Desiring God*, p. 216.

Peter Van Inwagen has written:

> Human beings have not been made merely to mouth words of praise or to be passively awash in a pleasant sensation of the presence of God. They have been made to be intimately aware of God and capable of freely acting on this awareness; having seen God, they may either glorify and enjoy what they have seen – the glorification and the enjoyment are separate only by the intellect in an act of severe abstraction – or they may reject what they have seen and attempt to order their own lives and to create their own objects of enjoyment.

Peter Van Inwagen, "Non Est Hick" in *The Rationality of Belief & the Plurality of Faith*, Thomas D. Senor, ed., (Ithaca and London: Cornell University Press, 1995), p. 220.

Chapter 11: Joy as an Imperative

[1] All passages cited here are from the NIV.

[2] For instance, Anthony Thiselton disputes Barth's treatment of the phrase "rejoice in the Lord" as a command which we can obey or disobey. After noting that the Greek verb can be used simply as a form of greeting, he continues:

> Secondly, even if we insist, after examining the historical and literary setting . . . that . . . (it) still means '"rejoice", the fact that it occurs in the imperative is no guarantee that it must be understood as a "command". If I cry "Help!" in the imperative, or "Lord, save me", this is a plea; if someone tells me "enjoy yourself",

but in the end I spend a miserable afternoon, this need not be "disobedience to a command."

Anthony C. Thiselton, "Semantics and New Testament Interpretation," in *New Testament Interpretation: Essays on Principles and Methods*, I. Howard Marshall, ed. (Grand Rapids: William B. Eerdmans Publishing Company, 1977), pp. 77-78.

I understand that we must often look beneath surface grammar to see how language actually functions. I contend here, however, that what influences an interpreter to deny the significance of the surface grammar of a command to rejoice is a misunderstanding of human emotion and its relation to beliefs, values, and volition.

3 Martin Luther, *Luther's Works: Table Talk,* vol. 54, ed., Theodore G. Tappert and Hulmut T. Lehmann; trans. Theodore G. Tappert (Philadelphia: Fortress Press, 1967), p. 96.

4 Karl Barth, *Church Dogmatics*, eds., Geoffrey W. Bromiley, T. F. Torrance (Edinburgh: T.&T. Clark, 1968), Vol. III, Part 4, p. 376.

5 Henri J.M. Nouwen, *Here and Now: Living in the Spirit* (New York, NY: Crossroad Publishing Company, 1994), p. 29.

6 C.S. Lewis, *The Problem of Pain* (New York: Macmillan, 1962), p. 67. See also his letter to Sheldon Vanauken, in which he writes, "There is great good in bearing sorrow patiently: I don't know that there is any virtue in sorrow as such. It is a Christian duty, as you know, for everyone to be as happy as he can." Sheldon Vanauken, *A Severe Mercy* (New York: Harper and Row, 1977), p. 189.

7 C.S. Lewis, *Letters to Malcolm: Chiefly on Prayer* (New York: Harcourt, Brace & World, Inc.: 1964), p. 93.

8 Richard Foster calls this the "principle of indirection" in spiritual formation. Richard J. Foster, with Kathryn A. Helmers, *Life with God: Reading the Bible for Spiritual Transformation* (New York, NY: HarperCollins, 2008), pp. 15-16.

9 Dallas Willard makes a distinction between feelings (the actual sensations that we experience in the grip of an emotion) and their underlying conditions. We have little or no control, for instance, over feelings of peacefulness, but we can make pursue the condition of peace. He writes, "So, as far as our planning for spiritual formation is concerned, we must choose and act with regard to the condition, good or bad, and allow the feelings to take care of themselves, as they certainly will." Dallas Willard, *Renovation of the Heart: Putting on the Character of Christ* (Colorado Springs, CO: NavPress, 2002), p. 123.

10 Karl Barth, *Church Dogmatics*, p. 374-375.

11 The Greek word, transliterated into English, is *homologeo.*

12 Jonathan Edwards, "On Religious Affections" in *The Works of Jonathan Edwards,* Perry Miller, Gen. ed., (New Haven: Yale University Press, 1959), Vol. 2, p. 99.

13 Mark 9:24

[14] See Galatians 5:22-23.

[15] The natural "fruit" of the Spirit (Galatians 5) must be balanced with the freedom and surprising nature of the Spirit's work (John 3). We are speaking of general patterns here.

[16] Literally the meaning of the Greek. The Greek word is *sbennumi*, which means literally *to extinguish or put out.* See William F. Arndt and F. Wilbur Gingrich, *A Greek-English Lexicon of the New Testament and Other Early Christian Literature* (Chicago: The University of Chicago Press, 1957), pp. 752-753.

[17] See 1 Thessalonians 5:16-22, ESV.

[18] See Ephesians 4:30.

[19] See 1 Corinthians 6:19.

[20] This is the theological heart of Romans 8:28, "We know that in everything God works for good with those who love him, who are called according to his purpose."

[21] Genesis 50:20

[22] Bitterness emerges when we focus on blame. We blame others and may even blame God. The way forward begins when we make a distinction between the blameworthy acts of others and the possible good that God desires to bring from them. Our focus shifts from those who have wronged us to God in his goodness, wisdom and power – even when we cannot yet see their practical outcome. Bitterness is conquered when, with Joseph, we can then revisit the wrongs that others have done to us and see them as an instrument in the hands of God to bring about good.

[23] See Philippians 4:6-7.

[24] *St. Thomas Aquinas: Philosophical Texts*, ed. and trans. Thomas Gilby (Durham, North Carolina: The Labyrinth Press, 1982), p. 275.

[25] C.S. Lewis, *The Screwtape Letters* (New York: Macmillan, reprinted in 1982), pp. 41-42.

[26] See Hebrews 11:24-26.

[27] Augustine wrote that the happy life is "not 'living as you will,' but the satisfaction of all wants when nothing is wanted wrongly." St. Augustine, "The Trinity," in *Augustine: Later Works*, trans. & ed., John Burnaby (Philadelphia: The Westminster Press, 1955), p. 95.

[28] John Eldredge writes:

> I suppose the architects of Madison Avenue are for the most part motivated merely by success. It's their job to sell. But behind the whole mimetic madness is an even more brilliant schemer. The evil one has basically two ploys. If he cannot get us to kill our hearts and bury our desire, then he is delighted to seduce our desire into a trap. Once we give over our desire for life to any object other than God, we become ensnared.

John Eldredge, *The Journey of Desire: Searching for the Life We've Only Dreamed Of* (Nashville: Thomas Nelson Publishers, 2000), pp. 83-84.

29 See Deuteronomy 8:11-19.

30 C.S. Lewis "The Weight of Glory" in *The Weight of Glory and Other Addresses* (Grand Rapids, MI: William B. Eerdmans Publishing Co., sixth printing 1975), p. 2.

31 Pascal, *Pascal's Pensées*, trans. W.F. Trotter (New York: E.P. Dutton & Co., Inc., 1958), p. 113.

32 See Matthew 24:36-44.

33 Karl Barth, *Church Dogmatics*, p. 377.

34 This was one of Jesus' quarrels with the Pharisees.

35 Ephesians 6:10.

36 See Nehemiah 8:10.

37 See, for example 1 Chronicles 16:27; Psalm 16:11 and 21:6, ESV.

38 Dallas Willard, *The Divine Conspiracy: Rediscovering Our Hidden Life in God* (Harper Collins Publishers: San Francisco, 1998), p. 61.

39 See Psalm 139:7-12, ESV.

40 1 Corinthians 10:31

41 Thomas Howard, *Splendor in the Ordinary* (Wheaton, IL: Tyndale House Publishers, Inc., 1976), p. 21.

42 C.S. Lewis, *Reflections on the Psalms* (New York: Harcourt, Brace and Company, 1958), pp. 94-95.

43 A.W. Tozer wrote: "There are very few unqualified things in our lives, but I believe that the reverential fear of God mixed with love and fascination and astonishment and admiration and devotion is the most enjoyable state and the most purifying emotion the human soul can know." A.W. Tozer, *What Ever Happened to Worship*? Ed., Gerald B. Smith (Camp Hill, PA: Christian Publications, 1985), pp. 30-31.

Leon Morris put it this way in describing lovers of God in the Bible:

> Those who truly love God have in all ages delighted in worshipping him, and the Psalms show that from very early days worshippers loved everything associated with the activity of honoring God. So we find references to love for God's house (Ps. 26:8); for Jerusalem, where the house of God was (Ps. 122:6); for God's name (Ps. 5:11; 69:36; 119; 132; and for his salvation (Ps. 40:16; 70:4).

This shared joy in worship includes not only our singing and our praying, but the two sacraments, or sacred ordinances, of baptism and the Lord's Supper, which were such an important part of the worship of the early church.

Leon Morris, *Testaments of Love: A Study of Love in the Bible* (Grand Rapids, MI: William B. Eerdmans Publishing Co., 1981), p. 49.

Ralph Martin, sees this clearly in the worship of the New Testament Church. On the sacraments, he writes:

> We learn that the observance of the Gospel ordinances is no human invention, but is rather our response to the divine command. Such obedience, however, is no irksome duty and unpleasant task to be performed because it is imposed upon us by a tyrannical authority. Quite the contrary. Human obedience is an occasion of glad acceptance of God's will.

Ralph P. Martin, *Worship in the Early Church* (Grand Rapids: Eerdmans, 1964, reprint. 1975), p. 87.

On baptism, he writes:

> The blessings of the new age which baptism makes real – forgiveness, entry into the Church, the fellowship of believers and that conquering new-born joy which is denoted by the word "exultation" . . . and "boldness of speech" . . . were offered by the Apostolic preaching as men "heard the word" and "believed." (Ibid., p.100.)

He draws these conclusions about the celebration of the Lord's Supper in the early church:

> The symbol of a cup had long been part of the Old Testament vocabulary to express man's relationship to God. Under the Divine blessing, his life is a happy one, with a cup filled with joy. . . fulfilment of this hope is announced in the upper room.
>
> The term '"eucharistic'" relates to the note of thankfulness and joy which must Have sounded in the early Christian convocations.
>
> Past, present, and future are thus gathered up in one sacred and joyful festival of the Lord's Table in the Apostolic practice and teaching. (Ibid., pp. 117, 134, 128.)

44 Edwards, "Religious Affections," p. 274.

45 Paul put it this way in his letter to the church in Corinth (1 Corinthians 5:8): "Let us, therefore, celebrate the festival, not with the old leaven, the leaven of malice and evil, but with the unleavened bread of sincerity and truth." William Morrice translates it this way, "Live true and sincere lives in a continual festival of joy." He then comments:

> The Greek word used here is *heortazein* (to keep festival), and it is found only here in the New Testament. The festival spoken of is not the Jewish Passover nor even the Christian Eucharist. The reference is to the whole Christian life. . . . Paul realized that one essential condition for Christian joy was ethical purity, the supreme motive for which lay in the sacrifice of Jesus Christ for sins. Thus, relying

upon Christ's finished work of reconciliation and redemption, *the Christian ought to aim at moral purity and sincerity and to make his whole life a festal celebration.*

William G. Morrice, *Joy in the New Testament* (Grand Rapids: Eerdmans Publishing Co.,1984, 117. Emphasis added.

[46] C.S. Lewis, *Mere Christianity* (New York: Macmillan, 1952, reprinted by HarperCollins), p. 93.

[47] Or in what is known as a hortatory subjunctive plural: "let us rejoice." See, e.g., Revelation 19:7.

[48] Søren Kierkegaard, *Either/Or*, trans. David F. Swenson, Lillian Marvin Swenson (Princeton: Princeton University Press, 1959, paperback ed., 1971) Vol. I, p. 167.

[49] As quoted in Jürgen Moltmann, *Theology and Joy* (London: SCM Press, LTD, 1973), p. 80. Elsewhere Augustine wrote: "For when many rejoice together, the joy of each one is the fuller, in that they are incited and inflamed by one another." Augustine, "The Confessions," in *Saint Augustine: The Basic Writings of Saint Augustine*, ed., Whitney J. Oates (Grand Rapids, MI: Baker Book House, 1948, reprint. 1980), Vol. 1, p. 115.

[50] See also Luke 15:9 and 1 Corinthians 13:6.

[51] Acts 2:46. New Testament scholar, Leon Morris, comments:

> Love is to be valued because of the sheer joy it brings. A fellowship of love is a wonderful thing. A warmth and devotion not easily discernible in a larger group will become apparent in a small group united by a common bond. Everyone who has experienced God's love in Christ will have known something of the value of the fellowship of love that exists among the redeemed and will have responded to it. It is one of God's good gifts, one that was particularly gratifying for the small group of New Testament Christians.

Leon Morris, *Testaments of Love: A Study of Love in the Bible* (Grand Rapids, MI: William B. Eerdmans Publishing Co., 1981), p. 209.

[52] For a classic work on this, see Stanley Hauerwas, *A Community of Character* (South Bend, Ind.: University of Notre Dame Press, 1981. For more recent works, see, for example, David W. Gill, *Becoming Good: Building Moral Character* (Downers Grove, IL: InterVarsity Press, 2000), and especially the chapter, "The Reality of Our Communities." See also James E. Gilman, *Fidelity of Heart: An Ethic of Christian Virtue* (Oxford: Oxford University Press, 2001). See also Philip D. Kenneson, *Life on the Vine: Cultivating the Fruit of the Spirit in Christian Community* (Downers Grove, IL: InterVarsity Press, 1999).

[53] 1 Timothy 6:17

[54] In the words of Martin Luther: "Our loving Lord God will that we eat, drink, and be merry. . . He will not that we complain, as if he had not given sufficient, or that he could not maintain our poor carcasses; he asks only that we acknowledge him for our God, and thank him for his gifts. Luther, *Table Talk*, p. 67. Emphasis added.

[55] 1 Timothy 4:4

CHAPTER 12: JOY AND THE WORLD'S TRAVAIL

[1] The observation of C.S. Lewis is significant here:

> If you read history you will find that the Christians that did most for the present world were those who thought most of the next. The apostles themselves, who set out on foot to convert the Roman Empire, the great men who built up the Middle Ages, the English evangelicals who abolished the slave trade, all left their mark on earth, precisely because their minds were occupied with heaven. It is since Christians have largely ceased to think of the other world that they have become so ineffective in this one. Aim at heaven and you will get earth "thrown in." Aim at earth and you will get neither.

C.S. Lewis, *Mere Christianity* (New York: Simon & Schuster, 1996), p. 119.

Earthly-minded Christians in our day merely reflect the world. Christopher Lasch put it this way:

> After the political turmoil of the sixties, Americans have retreated to purely personal preoccupations. Having no hope of improving their lives in any of the ways that matter, people have convinced themselves that what matters is psychic self-improvement: getting in touch with their feelings, eating health food, taking lessons in ballet or belly-dancing, immersing themselves in the wisdom of the East, jogging, learning how to "relate," overcoming the "fear of pleasure."
>
> The contemporary climate is therapeutic, not religious. People today hunger not for personal satisfaction, let alone for the restoration of an earlier age, but for the feeling, the momentary illusion, of personal well-being, health and psychic security.

Christopher Lasch, *The Culture of Narcissism* (New York: Norton, 1978), pp. 4, 7.

[2] Paul Tournier described the problem this way:

> What I am concerned about are the large numbers of people who are victims of a tragic misunderstanding. They take no further interest in worldly matters because their interest has – quite properly – been awakened in regard to the spiritual verities, as if the latter could exist in themselves in the abstract, outside of their incarnation in the world.

Paul Tournier, *The Adventure of Living* (New York: Harper & Row, 1976), p. 202.

[3] See Ephesians 1:11.

[4] See Daniel 4: 17, 25, 32.

[5] See Matthew 10:29.

6 Karl Barth said that joy "should not be limited by the suffering of life, because even life's suffering (or what we regard as such) comes from God, the very One who summons us to rejoice." Karl Barth, *Church Dogmatics*, eds., Geoffrey W. Bromiley, T. F. Torrance (Edinburgh: T.&T. Clark, 1968), Vol. III, Part 4, p. 383. This is so, whether you take this in the strong sense of God's causal activity, or you see suffering related permissively to the will of God. Either way, God takes ultimate responsibility.

7 Quoted in see William Morrice, *Joy in the New Testament* (Grand Rapids, Michigan: Eerdmans, 1984), p. 107.

8 Matthew 5:11-12a

9 Acts 5:41

10 Colossians 1:24

11 James 1:2, ESV

12 1 Peter 4:13

13 If we ask, "Why?" when we experience or see suffering, no answer may be given. But if we ask the far more fruitful question, "To what end?" the Scriptures give us much more to work with.

14 Romans 12:15

15 Jürgen Moltmann wrote, "Only those who are capable of joy can feel pain at their own and other people's suffering. A man who can laugh can also weep. "Jürgen Moltmann, Theology and Joy (London: SCM Press, LTD, 1973), p. 52. Similarly, Barth wrote "It is a matter of the proof of our joy in the fact that our capacity for enjoyment shows itself to be also a capacity for suffering." *Church Dogmatics*, Vol. III, Part 4, p. 384.

16 Robert C. Roberts, *Spirituality and Human Emotion*, (Grand Rapids: William B. Eerdmans Publishing Co., 1982), p. 25.

17 James Gilman calls sorrow and joy the "empathic virtues" of love. See James E. Gilman, *Fidelity of Heart: An Ethic of Christian Virtue* (Oxford: Oxford University Press, 2001), pp. 53ff.

18 See Jeremiah 9:24.

19 See Micah 6:8.

20 See Matthew 5:4.

21 See 2 Corinthians 6:10.

22 See John 16:20.

23 See Revelation 21:4.

[24] Of course, I don't know that this will be the case. But it could be suggested in this prophetic picture of the new heavens and the new earth: "And the city has no need of sun or moon to shine on it, for the glory of God gives it light, and its lamp is the Lamb. By its light will the nations walk, and the kings of the earth will bring their glory into it, and its gates will never be shut by day—and there will be no night there." (Revelation 21:23-25)

[25] We are speaking here of the eschatological kingdom, which is both present and future to us. The Old Testament also speaks of God's kingdom, which refers to God's reign over human history during the era of messianic promise. See, e.g., John Bright, *The Kingdom of God: The Biblical Concept and Its Meaning for the Church* (Nashville: Abingdon, 1953), pp. 17-186. See also Bruce K. Waltke, *Old Testament Theology: The Making of the Kingdom* (Grand Rapids, MI: Zondervan).

[26] Matthew 6:10, ESV

[27] Romans 14:17

[28] Note the present tense: "The kingdom of God *is* . . . ." The verb in English is not supplied by the translators, as it sometimes is. In this instance it is there in the original.

[29] Charles Hodge, *Commentary on the Epistle to the Romans* (Grand Rapids, MI: William B. Eerdmans Publishing Co., Rev. ed., 1886, reprint. 1980), p. 424.

[30] Romans 14:18, literal translation.

[31] See the preceding verses, Romans 14:13-17.

[32] C.E.B. Cranfield, *A Critical and Exegetical Commentary on The Epistle to the Romans* (Edinburgh: T&T Clark Limited, 1979, reprint. 1981), Vol. 2, p. 718.

[33] C.K. Barrett, *A Commentary on the Epistle to the Romans* (New York: Harper & Row Publishers, 1957), p. 265.

If we let Paul speak for himself, and speak his mind fully, he sees righteousness both as a judicial standing before God, and as action that seeks the well-being of others before God. The first is his doctrine of justification ("righteousness by faith") and is especially in view in chapters 3-5 of his letter to the Romans. The second is a "righteousness leading to sanctification" (e.g., Romans 6:13, 16, 18, 19), and includes the many practical exhortations that seek the good of others in Romans 12-14.

[34] See the following:

> For I have chosen him, that he may command his children and his household after him to keep the way of the LORD by *doing righteousness* and justice, so that the Lord may bring to Abraham what he has promised him." (Genesis 18:19)
>
> Blessed are they who observe justice, who *do righteousness* at all times! (Psalm 106:3)

> To *do righteousness* and justice is more acceptable to the LORD than sacrifice. (Proverbs 21:3)
>
> Thus says the LORD: "Keep justice, and *do righteousness*, for soon my salvation will come, and my righteousness be revealed. (Isaiah 56:1)
>
> Thus says the LORD: *Do justice and righteousness*, and deliver from the hand of the oppressor him who has been robbed. (Jeremiah 22:3)

35 Contextually, Paul is concerned with those who "put a stumbling block or hindrance in the way of a brother" (14:13). If righteousness is action taken to help others flourish before God, then acting in ways that cause others to fall is a direct contradiction to this. The positive commitment to righteousness in this sense is found, for instance, in 14:19 – "Let us then pursue what makes for peace and for mutual up building." and in 15:2 – "Let each of us please his neighbor for his good, to edify him."

36 Psalm 97:2

37 From the beginning of the human project, God exercises dominion in developing the world through human agents. This is true of the "cultural mandate" given in creation, and it is true in our era of the Kingdom.

38 NIV. You can see from these passages that the biblical concepts of righteousness and justice overlap. Biblical justice is not the same as the classical Greek understanding of this moral quality. In its Aristotelian sense, justice is calculating and disinterested. It is giving a person his due. From a biblical perspective the just person is not merely one who acts justly because it is required of him; he desires justice, loves justice, and delights in justice. It is not disinterested or detached, but passionately involved. It is not giving a person his due on the basis of merit, but acting in ways that will promote human flourishing as an expression of love.

39 Daniel C. Maguire, *The Moral Core of Judaism and Christianity: Reclaiming the Revolution* (Minneapolis: Fortress Press, 1993), p. 279.

40 Joy is both a centrifugal and a centripetal spiritual force: It reaches out and draws others in. Joy is hospitable: always seeking company and inviting and bringing others home to share its boon. Our own joy is enhanced, enriched, and enlarged as we give ourselves to its largess. James Gilman puts this into the context of our concern for the poor, "The community's joy lies in the privilege of sharing with the poor the same gracious kindness it receives from God, so that in the end both donor and recipient rejoice together." Gilman, *Fidelity of the Heart*, p. 61.

41 Though they are related, and outwardly may appear to be the same, it is important to say here that kingdom righteousness is not an equivalent term for social justice. Donald Bloesch writes:

> Both humanitarian works of mercy and works of social reform are at best approximations of kingdom righteousness. If the church identified itself with the cause of social justice, this might indeed make people more receptive to the kingdom message. Social justice is a partial fulfillment of the law of God; the

eschatological kingdom is the perfect fulfillment of the teachings of the law. Social justice is related to the law of God; the righteousness of the kingdom is related to the gospel. Social justice is conducive to human happiness; Christian obedience brings blessedness – contagious, radiant joy.

Donald G. Bloesch, *Freedom for Obedience: Evangelical Ethics in Contemporary Times* (San Francisco: Harper and Row, 1987), p. 84.

42 See Philippians 4:6-7.

43 See Romans 14:19.

44 Romans 12:18

45 Maguire, *Moral Core*, p. 236.

46 Nicholas Wolterstorff, *Art in Action: Toward a Christian Aesthetic* (Grand Rapids: Eerdmans, 1980), p. 79.

47 Donald G. Bloesch, *Freedom for Obedience: Evangelical Ethics in Contemporary Times* (San Francisco: Harper and Row, 1987), p. 90.

48 For a discussion of the kingdom of God as both indicative and imperative for the Christian life, see George Eldon Ladd, *A Theology of the New Testament* (Grand Rapids, MI: William B. Eerdmans Publishing Co., 1974), pp. 524-525.

49 Emil Brunner wrote, "A Christian is a person who not only hopes for the Kingdom of God, but one who, because he hopes for it, also does something in this world already, which he who has not this hope does not do." Emil Brunner, *The Divine Imperative,* trans. Olive Wyon, (The Westminster Press: Philadelphia, 1947), p. 128.

50 James Gilman puts this into the context of our concern for the poor, "The community's joy lies in the privilege of sharing with the poor the same gracious kindness it receives from God, so that in the end both donor and recipient rejoice together." Gilman, *Fidelity of Heart*, p. 61.

51 "Indeed, joy is a primary emotional force without which love's project of sorrowing with the poor, is unlikely to be accomplished." Ibid., p. 60.

52 David Gill writes, "Our hunger for righteousness and our peacemaking have too often been accompanied by the long, sad face, the angry denunciation, and a holier-than-thou, sanctimonious spirituality. The Bible doesn't know this grumpy righteousness: 'Rejoice in the LORD, O you righteous.'" David W. Gill, *Becoming Good: Building Moral Character* (Downers Grove, Illinois: InterVarsity Press, 2000), p. 200.

53 The Greek word translated "cheerfully" is *hilaros*, from which we get the word *hilarious*.

54 It is the Greek word *hilaros* again.

55 Malcolm Muggeridge, *Something Beautiful for God*; *Mother Teresa of Calcutta* (New York, Harper and Row, Publishers, 1971, p. 52.

[56] Ibid., p. 49. In his recorded interview with her, Muggeridge comments, "Spending a few days with you, I have been immensely struck by the joyfulness of these Sisters who do what an outsider might think to be an almost impossibly difficult and painful task." Her response:

> That's the spirit of our society, that total surrender, loving trust and cheerfulness. We must be able to radiate the joy of Christ, express it in our actions. If our actions are just useful actions that give no joy to the people, our poor people would never be able to rise up to the call which we want them to hear, the call to come closer to God. We want to make them feel that they are loved. If we went to them with a sad face, we would only make them much more depressed.

Ibid., p. 98.

Another wrote of Mother Teresa:

> More and more every day I realized the importance of Mother Teresa's insistence that the Missionaries of Charity renounce gloominess along with everything else of the world. She requires that the Sisters be persons of cheerful disposition in their work with people who lead deprived lives. "A joyful Sister," she says, "is like the sunshine of God's love."
>
> "Joy," affirms the guideline of the Society, "is a net of love by which we catch souls. A Sister filled with joy preaches without preaching. Joy is a need and a power for us even physically, for it makes us always ready to go about doing good. The joy of the Lord is our strength."
>
> When one of the Sisters, wearing a mournful expression on her face, was getting ready to visit the poor, Mother Teresa said, "Don't go. Go back to bed. We cannot meet the poor with sad faces."

Eileen Egan and Kathleen Egan, OSB, *Suffering Into Joy: What Mother Teresa Teaches About True Joy* (Ann Arbor, MI: Servant Publications, 1994), pp. 45-46.

[57] See Matthew 5:16.

Made in the USA
Columbia, SC
14 December 2020

28181431R00152